PREPARING QUALITY EDUCATORS FOR ENGLISH LANGUAGE LEARNERS

Research, Policies, and Practices

PREPARING QUALITY EDUCATORS FOR ENGLISH LANGUAGE LEARNERS

Research, Policies, and Practices

Edited by

Kip Téllez
University of California, Santa Cruz

Hersh C. Waxman
University of Houston

LAWRENCE ERLBAUM ASSOCIATES, PUBLISHERS
2006 Mahwah, New Jersey London

Lawrence Erlbaum Associates, Inc., Publishers
10 Industrial Avenue
Mahwah, New Jersey 07430
www.erlbaum.com

Cover design by Kathryn Houghtaling Lacey

Library of Congress Cataloging-in-Publication Data

Preparing quality educators for English language learners : research, policies, and practices / [edited by] Kip Téllez, Hersh C. Waxman.
p. cm.
Includes bibliographical references and index.
ISBN 0-8058-5437-1 (cloth : alk. paper)
ISBN 0-8058-5438-X (pbk. : alk. paper)
1. English teachers—Training of—United States. 2. English language—Study and teaching—United States. 3. Teacher effectiveness—United States. 4. Education and state—United States. I. Téllez, Kip. II. Waxman, Hersholt C.

LB1715.P725 2005
428′.0071—dc22 2005040136
CIP

Books published by Lawrence Erlbaum Associates are printed on acid-free paper, and their bindings are chosen for strength and durability.

Printed in the United States of America
10 9 8 7 6 5 4 3 2 1

Contents

Foreword

Donna Christian
Center for Applied Linguistics

As Gandara and Maxwell-Jolly (chap. 5, this volume) point out, teacher quality is clearly linked to student achievement. The reauthorization of the Elementary and Secondary Education Act of 2001, *No Child Left Behind*, brings attention to the need for highly qualified teachers for all students in its requirements. If we want all students to reach their academic potential, we must provide them with such highly qualified teachers. Among the student population, English language learners (ELLs) are increasingly represented in our schools. However, many teachers have not received preparation to help ELLs achieve their best. These observations are easy to make, but hard to address. The chapters in this volume take good steps in sorting out the issues and charting some means of addressing them.

Because of the diverse backgrounds and needs of ELLs, educators need specialized preparation to work effectively with them. It is increasingly clear that all teachers with ELLs in their classes need to know about second language development, cross-cultural issues, and methods to teach both language and academic content. However, most classroom teachers, counselors, and administrators receive no special training in these areas. In the latest figures available (1997 from NCES), we see that only 2.5% of teachers in the United States who instruct ELLs have an academic degree in ESL or bilingual education; only 30% of the teachers with these students in their classes have received any training at all in teaching them. Although the numbers may have changed somewhat between then and now, I think everyone's experience would confirm that the basic principle remains true today.

We do not have an adequate supply of teachers with preparation as specialists in language and culture (English as a second language and bilingual teachers). Moreover, demographic information about the student population continues to point to increasing numbers of students from non-English language backgrounds, meaning that more and more teachers have such students in their classrooms. Thus, all teacher candidates really need to know strategies for teaching linguistically and culturally diverse students, but teacher education by and large does not provide this preparation. Snow and Wong Fillmore (2002) argued, for example, that *all* teachers need specific knowledge about language in order to work effectively with students from diverse language backgrounds, including basic understanding of the processes of language and literacy development, second language learning, and academic language growth.

Policymakers and educators who want to improve the quality of teachers for ELLs must overcome the common belief that ELLs need only to learn English, and once they do that, they are effectively the same as all the other students. Lack of English proficiency is the "problem" and once the problem is "fixed," that's the end of the story. As a result, some schools and policymakers place their sole focus on English proficiency, often without taking into account the connections between language development and academic learning. It is, of course, extremely important for all students to develop high levels of proficiency in English. Well-prepared English language teachers are essential, and all teachers should be prepared to support English language development. We know that language learning takes a long time and many linguistic and cultural issues remain to be addressed to promote academic progress long after basic levels of English language proficiency have been achieved.

In order to achieve teacher quality in our educational system, we must prepare educators with the "knowledge, skills, and dispositions" to work effectively with ELLs (González & Darling-Hammond, 1997). Achieving this goal calls for improved preparation programs for teachers and administrators, and appropriate, coherent professional development for practicing educators. All teachers must be prepared to foster language development and sheltered content instruction to create the best possible environment for ELLs. They must understand the full range of factors that may put diverse students at risk and notice and appreciate the diverse strengths the students bring with them. It is also extremely important to provide qualified bilingual teachers and adult bilingual models, as well as English language teachers.

The chapters in this volume seek to respond to the issues raised by the quest for teacher quality for English language learner populations. Among the many questions to be explored are:

- What kind of teacher is best suited to teach English learners? Does having the same ethnic or language background make someone more highly qualified? How can we best develop and use the talents of members of language minority communities in the teaching profession?
- How can we recruit and keep highly qualified teachers, especially those from language minority communities? Are there incentives we can and should provide? Are there ways we can reduce the disincentives that exist?
- How do specialists (bilingual and ESL teachers) differ from other classroom teachers in their preparation needs?
- What should the content of pre-service and in-service professional development be? How can we ensure that all teachers know what they need to know about language?
- Is this just a matter of quality of *teachers* or should we be concerned with all school staff (administrators, counselors, etc.)?
- What pathways can we identify (traditional and alternative) that can lead to the creation of highly qualified teachers?

None of these issues can be tackled in isolation. The authors refer to the broader system into which teacher quality fits: the lack of policy about programs, the poor working conditions for teachers in schools with large populations of ELLs, an accountability system that doesn't work for ELLs, school leaders with little knowledge of language instruction, and so on. However, a focus on teacher quality promotes changes to this system beyond those focused on teachers. This volume challenges us not only to think, but to act, and the authors provide us with some excellent pathways to follow.

REFERENCES

Gonzalez, J., & Darling-Hammond, L. (1997). *New concepts for new challenges, Professional development for teachers of immigrant youth.* McHenry, IL: Delta Systems Co., Inc. and Center for Applied Linguistics.

Snow, C., & Wong Fillmore, L. (2002). What teachers need to know about language. In C. Adger, C. Snow, & D. Christian (Eds.), *What teachers need to know about language.* McHenry, IL: Delta Systems, Co., Inc. and Center for Applied Linguistics.

Chapter 1

Preparing Quality Teachers for English Language Learners: An Overview of the Critical Issues

Kip Téllez
University of California, Santa Cruz

Hersh C. Waxman
University of Houston

Recent political imperatives have pushed the issue of teacher quality to the top of the reform agenda in U.S. education (e.g., Cochran-Smith & Fries, 2001; Darling-Hammond & Youngs, 2002). Although the recent attention on teacher quality may give us the illusion that it is a new topic, questions about the preparation, recruitment, and retention of good teachers have been an ongoing concern (Urban, 1990). Nor is the topic limited to interest in the United States. Teacher quality has been and remains an international issue (Hopkins & Stern, 1996).

However, the interest in teacher quality has yet to yield research or policy studies examining specifically the quality of teacher preparation for English language learners (ELL). Indeed, up until the 1980s, the preparation of teachers for ELL was largely ignored in the teacher professional development literature. Even the advent of bilingual education in the late 1960s failed to foment much specific training in language instruction. Bilingual teachers were, by and large, simply told to teach their students in Spanish with little regard for the inevitable transition to English. Many programs devoted their curriculum to improving the Spanish skills of their future bilingual teachers. Similarly, English language development (ELD) teachers were simply told to speak as much English as possible to their ELL students and made to believe that "they'll catch on." This lack of attention to specific pedagogy for language learners has no doubt curtailed the academic growth of ELL students.

The issue of teacher quality for ELL was quickly underscored, however, when García (1990) made clear the pitiful state of teacher quality for ELL. Citing the results taken from several national reports, he concluded, "Such data continue to suggest that linguistic minority education programs are staffed by professionals not directly trained for such programs who might be acquiring their expertise on the job" (p. 719).

More recently, teacher education researchers have discovered that a great many ELD teachers, unprepared for conditions working with a culturally and linguistically diverse student population, fail to acquire much expertise "on the job" (Britzman, 1991). Instead, they grope for quick-fix strategies, often becoming stressed at their lack of success. Such teachers can "burn out" quickly, leaving the profession or, worse, remain in teaching but without the motivation to provide a quality education or the requisite skills.

Garcia's report and other factors (e.g., the sheer growth in the ELL population) motivated teacher educators and policymakers to initiate improvements in the quality of ELD instruction, and the decade of the 1990s saw a host of new policies and programs for the preparation of ELD teachers. Many universities began specialized preparation for ELL students, although some needed state legislation to initiate such improvements. Even in states with relatively few ELL (e.g., Iowa), educators saw the need to provide special language teaching preparation. During the 1990s, such states were exporting the vast majority of their teachers to "growth" states (e.g., Texas, Arizona), where many of the new teaching positions were in bilingual or ELD classrooms. Consequently, teacher education programs with almost no local need for language educators developed a strong focus on ELL.

In addition, school districts nationwide now routinely provide in-service professional development for ELD teachers. Districts may develop their own in-service programs or they may rely upon the expertise of the many organizations providing such information. Although it is impossible to know how many professional development opportunities are offered to ELD teachers, it is clear that ELD instruction has become a growing professional development opportunity since the 1990s.

In spite of additional ELD coursework and field experiences with ELL required of newly licensed teachers, as well as the many opportunities for in-service teachers to learn more about language teaching, Lewis et al. (1999) found that most teachers who taught ELL and other culturally diverse students did not feel they were well prepared to meet their students' needs. Other reports corroborate this finding, suggesting that the current preparation for all ELD teachers is inadequate (Alexander, Heaviside, & Farris, 1999). Furthermore, the data documenting the academic underperformance by ELL (NCES, 1998) provide additional evidence that teacher quality for ELL is in need of a major reappraisal.

Who or what is to blame for the inadequate quality of teachers for ELL? We can certainly point to the general shortcomings in teacher education (both preservice and in-service) with regard to students outside the "mainstream." For instance, the quality of teachers for ELL students may be no better or worse than the quality of teachers who work with gifted children or those who have special instructional needs. Teachers have always been troubled by their lack of knowledge in dealing with students who represent special needs groups (McLesky & Waldon, 2002).

The continued low achievement among ELL and the prospect for continued growth in this population in U.S. schools, as well as the data reporting the lack of preparation for ELD teachers, suggests to us the immediate need for an appraisal of teacher quality for ELL. This chapter examines the research and policy constraints and opportunities that have contributed to the general lack of quality among ELD teachers. We begin by framing teacher quality around several important policy "levers." We follow this discussion by examining the structural factors central to teacher quality. As part of this effort, we briefly explore the role teacher education has played in the development of ELD teachers, moving next to recently developed standards for ELD teachers, and on to legislative and policy issues in licensing teachers for ELL. Finally, we move from the structural to the pedagogical, discussing the knowledge base in ELD instruction, considering—and speculating—on the specific kinds of knowledge ELD teachers need to provide high-quality instruction.

GENERAL STUDIES OF TEACHER QUALITY

In spite of the recent attention, teacher quality remains a construct with few agreed-upon characteristics. So, to begin our discussion of teacher quality issues for ELL, we propose that the four areas of opportunity and policy "levers" for teacher quality set forth by Reinhardt (2001) reflect well the issues and policies concerning teacher quality for ELL. For our review, we pay close attention to the Recruitment/Selection and In-service areas. Although we recognize the importance of initial teacher preparation, the primary interest of the book is the development and growth of practicing teachers, where teacher quality is most likely to affect student performance. The breadth and depth of the following sections reflect this emphasis.

PRESERVICE TEACHER EDUCATION

Recent research findings (Goldhaber & Brewer, 2000) and policy reports (Abell Foundation, 2001) have called into question the value of preservice teacher education. Of course, critiques of teacher education are not new;

TABLE 1.1
Areas of Opportunity and Policy Levers to Affect Teacher Quality

Areas of Opportunity to Influence Teacher Quality	*Policy Levers to Affect Teacher Quality*
Preservice	• Scholarships, loans, and loan forgiveness as incentives to enter teaching • Licensure/certification requirements • Accreditation of teacher preparation programs • Models of exemplary practices and programs
Recruitment & Selection	• Effective communication with applicants • Alternative approaches to entering teaching • Teacher mobility policies
In-Service	• Professional learning • Induction programs to help new teachers • Compensation to encourage gaining new skills • Re-certification requirements to support high quality professional learning
Retention	• Working conditions • Compensation

they appeared soon after the initiation of formal teacher preparation itself. In this chapter, we do not review the general attacks on teacher education. Instead, we explore the effects of teacher education on the quality of teachers for ELL.

Although none of the new attacks on preservice teacher education has specifically named preparation of teachers for ELL as a weakness, teacher educators themselves have been some of the most vocal critics of ELD teacher preparation. Tedick and Walker (1994) maintain that second language teacher education has failed in the following five areas. First, they argue, we have undervalued the interdependence between first and second languages and cultures; that is, prospective teachers are told that acquiring English subsumes all other language skills and that the acquisition of English should proceed more rapidly than the research suggests it can. Furthermore, teachers have not understood the importance of validating home culture and language for the development of additional language and culture understanding. Second, they argue that second language teacher education is too often fragmented. In most programs, bilingual, ELD, and foreign language teachers are separated for courses in language teaching principles and methods. This leads to an unhealthy dichotomy in which foreign language teaching is considered high-status teaching while bilingual and ELD teachers and their students are thought of as compensatory. Third, Tedick and Walker maintain that many teacher educators consider language as a content area, much like mathematics or science. This misunderstanding suggests that teachers simply must know the language to teach it. In addition, when language becomes object we believe that second language teaching is teaching *about* language rather than teaching *with* language. Teacher education courses that emphasize only the linguistic features of a language (e.g., phonology, syntax) fail to imbue students with a communicative understanding of the language, that teaching language is nothing more than form, facts, and rules. Fourth, second language education has become paralyzed by its focus on effective teaching methods. Many of the textbooks used in second language teacher education amount only to a laundry list of strategies. The contexts in which such strategies may be effective is not addressed, and beginning teachers are left with teaching tools but no knowledge of when or where to use them. Finally, they maintain that the disconnect between language and culture has led to teachers who teach language without any consideration of home or target culture, or the ways in which these two may relate.

Several general critiques of language teacher education have emerged in recent years. For instance, Milk, Mercado, and Sapiens (1992) suggested that future ELD teachers have knowledge of the kinds of programs and other instructional services for ELL; an understanding of the principles of second language acquisition; how to use parents as an instructional resource in the classroom; and the ability to deliver an instructional program that provides many opportunities for listening, speaking, reading, and writing, preferably integrated into an instructional theme.

In one of the most scathing judgments of language teacher education, Ada (1986) endorsed new ELD/bilingual teachers' sharp criticism of their teacher education programs. In particular, she is sympathetic to the view that teacher educators failed to practice what they taught, expressed forcefully by one of the teachers in her study, "They preached to us to teach creatively, but we were never allowed any creativity. They encouraged us to be good communicators, but the classes they taught were deadly" (p. 393). From Ada's perspective, preservice ELD and bilingual teachers are not provided with the proper knowledge and experiences to best serve ELL students, and teacher educators are to blame. Ada concludes by suggesting that bilingual teachers have been marginalized like the students they serve and advocates for an approach to teacher education that validates students' lived experiences as linguistic and cultural outsiders. From this validation, Ada argues, will emerge a solidarity that bilingual teachers can use to transform their position from passivity to active leadership. In spite of her admonishments, Ada is not entirely clear on how to achieve such solidarity.

Preservice teacher preparation is undergoing nothing short of a major reappraisal (Tom, 1997). Researchers and policy analysts from both inside and outside the profession are calling into question the field's ability to enhance the quality of ELD teachers. And while preservice teacher education is unlikely to disappear entirely, educators and policymakers are considering alternatives to traditional style programs. Many such reformers, armed with the belief that teachers learn best when they are teaching their own class(es), are focusing their attention on in-service teacher development, the topic of the next section.

IN-SERVICE TEACHER EDUCATION

Given the troubling data on the underachievement of ELL, we might expect to find research documenting the federal and state in-service programs designed to raise teacher quality for ELL. But in our review of the literature, we could find no such research. Reviews of general in-service teacher preparation programs are somewhat common. For instance, Darling-Hammond and McLaughlin (1995) described features of successful in-service professional development. Their research suggests that the "one-shot" in-service programs are unlikely to alter teaching practice. Instead, they argue that teacher knowledge growth should build on what we know about human learning. Therefore, the most effective professional growth opportunities are those whose topics emerge from teacher interests, require a long-term commitment from all parties, and engage in clear measurement and evaluation of goals and teaching targets (Knight & Wiseman, chap. 4, this volume).

Professional growth for ELD teachers remains troubled by the general challenges of in-service teacher development (e.g., one-shot in-services, few connections to specific teaching contexts). Successful professional development programs require both additional time and resources many schools cannot afford. And we suspect that the vast majority of professional growth efforts are not as well received (see Penner, 1999, for a review of in-service programs).

The professional development of ELD teachers must be addressed in order to improve the education of ELL (Jiménez & Barrera, 2000). As Jackson and Davis (2000) put it, "teachers cannot come to expect more of their students until they come to expect more of their own capacity to teach them, and until they have the opportunity to witness their power to elicit dramatically better work from those groups of students who are today failing" (p. 14). Much more emphasis must be placed in providing high-quality professional learning experiences and opportunities for teachers serving ELL. While some professional development programs create a collaborative culture for the teachers, they are rarely enough to help teachers overcome some of the state, district, and school policies that limited their capacity for helping ELL in their classroom. For instance, high-stakes testing creates a sense of powerlessness and alienation which results in a weak sense of teacher self-efficacy and self-belief. When teachers have a strong sense of their own efficacy, they can make a real difference in the lives of their students (Ashton & Webb, 1986). On the other hand, when teachers lack hope, optimism, and self-belief, schools and classrooms will "become barren wastelands of boredom and routine" (Hargreaves & Fullan, 1998, p. 1).

Schools need to provide continuous, quality professional learning experiences for all teachers. These learning experiences need to help teachers become optimistic, hopeful, and empowered so that they believe they can help improve the education of all children. Professional development projects need to be developed, implemented, and tested that focus on "reculturing" or changing the entire school climate so that teachers and administrators create more collaborative, supportive work cultures that enable them to be "out there" in ways that make a difference for all students (Hargreaves & Fullan, 1998).

In-service teacher professional development has some distance to go before it is worthy of the name. However, in-service teacher programs are often without a clear direction. We know that improving teacher quality requires clear goals and objectives, standards that guide the direction of the teacher development, and it is this topic we address next.

STANDARDS FOR ELD TEACHERS

Having reviewed the shortcomings and success in teacher education (both preservice and in-service), it might be tempting to lay the blame for low ELD teacher quality on those who plan and manage teacher development. However, even if we agree that those educators responsible for ELD teacher professional growth have not provided the proper training opportunities, we might justifiably ask, "What specific knowledge should ELD teachers possess?" Even if teacher educators provided ample time and resources for ELD teachers to learn the content they needed to provide quality instruction, would it be enough? In other words, is the knowledge base adequate to provide ELD teachers with the direction they need to conduct their work? If the lack of quality among ELD teachers is owing to a failing of the knowledge base, then perhaps the researchers and policymakers who work in this area have been remiss.

The knowledge base promoted by professional organizations concerned with ELD instruction must undergo considerable scrutiny. We know that each subject-oriented professional association has, at some point, been interested in the teacher knowledge base. For instance, the International Reading Association (IRA) has developed "standards" or recommendations for the reading teacher knowledge base. IRA standards include a focus on valuing and understanding linguistic diversity as it relates to the teaching of reading (http://www.reading.org/advocacy/standards/free_index.html).

The two professional organizations whose focus is squarely placed on the education of ELL students in the United States are the National Association of Bilingual Education (NABE) and the Teachers of English to Speakers of Other Languages (TESOL). Between them, their U.S. membership totals more than 30,000. And while they are both primarily concerned with curriculum and instruction for practicing teachers, they are also devoted to the education of teachers (each has a special interest group for teacher education), and both have developed recommendations for the preparation of teachers for their respective disciplines. The guidelines from NABE (1994) suggest adherence to the general standards recommended by other teacher education organizations (e.g., NCATE) such as the requirement for institutional commitment to the teacher education program and extended supervised field experiences, in addition to standards specific to bilingual education. These specific standards include an understanding of the philosophy, theory, and history of bilingual education in the United States as well as processes of second language acquisition, the integration of language and content instruction, and first language acquisition processes.

TESOL, in conjuction with NCATE, recently developed standards for ELD teacher education (TESOL, 2003). Like those articulated by NABE, the TESOL standards are designed for initial teacher preparation, but we can look to them as guides for quality ELD teaching in the early career and beyond. The TESOL/NCATE program standards divide ELD instruction into five domains.

- *Language.* Teachers must understand language as a system, knowing components of language such as phonology, syntax, semantics, pragmatics, and writing conventions. They should also understand first and second language acquisition.
- *Culture.* Teachers must understand the nature of role of culture in language development and academic achievement. In addition, they must understand the nature of cultural groups and how students' cultural identifications affect language learning.
- *Planning, implementing, and managing instruction.* Teachers must understand how to teach to standards in ELD, as well as use resources effectively in both ELD and content instruction.
- *Assessment.* Teachers must understand how systematic biases in assessment may affect ELL. Further, they must know the proper methods and techniques for assessing student language growth.
- *Professionalism.* Teachers must know the research and history in the field of ELD. In addition, they must act as advocates for both their students and field, working in cooperation with colleagues when appropriate.

Teacher education programs are reviewed in site visits (common to NCATE) and given a rating on each. Thus far, we are not certain how many teacher preparation programs have been reviewed using the new ELD standards. No school system (e.g., a school district) to our knowledge has adopted the standards for use as a policy document.

In addition to both the NABE and TESOL standards, the National Board for Professional Teaching Standards (NBPTS) has developed ELD standards for the purpose of awarding board recognition for exemplary practicing teachers. The NBTS standards for teachers of English as New Language represent a set of ideas similar to those articulated by the other professional organizations, but represent expert knowledge in teaching of ELL. Briefly, the 12 standards are (only those that relate particularly to the ELD knowledge base are explained further): (a) knowledge of students (how development, language and culture affects students' knowledge, skills, interests, aspirations, and values); (b) knowledge of language and language development (expert knowledge of the target language as well as processes by which students learn their native and new languages); (c) knowledge of culture and diversity (how to use culture to structure for successful academic experiences); (d) knowledge of subject matter (a comprehensive command of subject knowledge, as well as how to facilitate student learning); (e) meaningful learning; (f) multiple paths to knowledge; (g) instructional resources; (h) learning environment; (i) assessment; (j) reflective practice; (k) linkages with families; (l) professional leadership.

Like the TESOL standards, it is hard to disagree with the NPBTS criteria. The measurement of the criteria is far more troublesome, especially for the NPBTS assessors, who must distinguish between merely good ELD teachers and those who are truly exemplary. Nevertheless, educators vested in ELD should pay careful attention to the NPBTS process and the relationship between teachers who choose board certification and the achievement of their students.

Interestingly, the major teacher education organizations have been largely absent from the discussion on the preparation of quality teachers for ELL. The two primary teacher education organizations in the United States, the Association of Teacher Educators (ATE) and the American Association for Colleges of Teacher Education (AACTE), have devoted great attention to preparing teachers for culturally diverse students while paying little attention to teachers who will face language diversity. Indeed, AACTE has commissioned no less than six reports or books (e.g., Smith, 1998) on the preparation of teachers for cultural diversity, but not one focused on language diversity. AATCE only recently developed a resolution on the preparation of teachers for language minority students, encouraging the development of "programs that recruit, train, and support teachers of all subjects and grade levels who can meet the needs of second language learners." (http://www.aacte.org/Multicultural/bilingual_resolution.htm)

It is not clear why ATE and AACTE have largely neglected the preparation and professional growth of ELD teachers. One reason may be that the history of these organizations reveals a long and lasting interest in the education of African-American students and the development of teachers who view multicultural education as central to their work. Such a focus is, of course, warranted, given their respective missions, but we believe that both must soon devote more interest in the preparation and growth of ELD teachers.

We cannot be certain that the knowledge bases developed by various professional organizations are sufficient to produce high-quality teachers. However, it seems to us that these organizations have developed thoughtful and warranted goals for ELD teachers. Our concern regarding the knowledge base for developing high-quality ELD teachers is not the standards themselves, but the failure of the various professional groups to prioritize among their standards. We believe that teacher preparation at either the preservice or in-service level could address only a fraction of the standards they promote given the time and resources available for teacher development. Educators have known for many years that the challenge in developing instructional goals is not what knowledge to include but what knowledge can be thoughtfully excluded. Comprehensiveness in developing standards is a worthy goal, but prioritizing goals and considering the instructional space devoted to them is equally important.

LEGISLATIVE AND POLICY ISSUES

The shortcomings of language teacher quality may be owing to teacher educators and the failure of adequate standards or knowledge base, but the revealing data on legislated ELD teacher requirements and other initiatives sheds light on the neglect and misdirection policymakers have shown toward the preparation of teachers for ELD classrooms.

In a recent report, Menken and Antunez (2001) assessed the preparation and certification of teachers working with ELL students. Before surveying those universities and colleges that prepare bilingual teachers (the focus of their study), Menken and Antunez developed a matrix or knowledge set based on existing professional standards and interviews with experts. Their matrix, divided into three broad areas of knowledge, served as the categories for their survey:

- Knowledge of Pedagogy (e.g., native language literacy methods, assessment of English literacy, practicum in bilingual education setting)
- Knowledge of Linguistics (e.g., first language acquisition, structure/grammar of English, contrastive analysis)

- Knowledge of Cultural and Linguistic Diversity (e.g., history of bilingual education, cross-cultural studies, parent involvement)

Based on 417 (out of 1,075 sent) surveys returned by schools, colleges, and departments of education in the United States, they found that only 93 of the institutions even offered the bilingual education credential and only 103 offered a program in ELD for teachers. But the most striking finding is how few states actually required classes for certification on any of the topics suggested by the matrix. Just six states consistently required courses on the areas of expertise; almost all others simply require a "competency" with only vague guidelines for assessing that competency. Still more shocking is the location of those states requiring coursework. Only Maine and Connecticut, whose total "LEP" population amounts to a fractional percentage of the nationwide total, consistently required courses for the ELD certificate. An earlier report by McKnight and Antunez (1999) confirmed states' loose or nonexistent requirements for ELD and bilingual teachers. Of the 50 states, 37 offer ESL (ELD) teacher certification/endorsement, yet only 23 of these have a legal mandate to require ESL certification, leaving room for emergency teaching permits. As for bilingual/dual language certification/endorsement, just 19 states require such endorsement (only 17 of those have legal mandate to require such certification).

It is also important to note that even in the states requiring certification or endorsement, many allow emergency or "exam-only" credentials to teach both ELD and bilingual classrooms. In Texas, for instance, any teacher with a standard elementary certificate can request that bilingual or ESL "endorsement" be added by passing a single paper-and-pencil examination (and an oral test of Spanish in the case of the bilingual endorsement) and teaching in a classroom with at least one ELL student for 1 year. No field supervision is required for the exam-only option. Such a system, not surprisingly, promotes a climate in which teachers quickly receive their initial certificate to begin their careers and then simply take tests to add endorsements. The licensing shortcomings found in the states must certainly shoulder some of the responsibility for poor teacher quality for ELL.

Other possible causes of low teacher quality are the failure to retain expert ELD teachers and inadequate compensation for working with ELL. For instance, are schools and school systems doing enough to retain the strong ELD teachers they employ, or do many ELD teachers leave the profession just as they are becoming highly capable language teachers? Or perhaps the challenges of teaching ELL merits higher pay for teachers. It may also be the case that ELD teachers need resources (e.g., books, technology, instructional assistance) well beyond what the non-ELD teacher receives. When the extra resources needed are scarce, teachers may choose to work with native English-speaking students rather than struggle with under-resourced ELD classes.

The cause of low teacher quality for ELL is likely a complicated interaction of all the previous points. Teacher educators have not provided a strong enough focus on language instruction while state legislators and policymakers have generally failed to require the specialized knowledge needed for quality ELD teaching. The professional associations devoted to language teaching have only recently developed standards for teaching ELD, while the "major" teacher education professional organizations have given scant attention to the preparation of quality ELD teachers. Furthermore, several issues that likely impact the quality of teaching for ELL (e.g., inadequate resources) have not been studied.

If we agree that state policies for the development of ELD professional knowledge has been inadequate, what does the research recommend that may improve teacher quality for ELL? One study suggests that policymakers can increase teacher quality in high-poverty schools by requiring schools to report teachers' credentials, including those who lack the proper license for the subject or students (Galston, 2000). For instance, perhaps a national proposal to report to parents those teachers working with ELL but who lack the required state certification may increase the quality of ELD in such schools. Of course, such a policy may have limited impact in immigrant communities where parents may have few opportunities to choose a different school or teacher who could better serve their ELL child. Additionally, Galston (2000) suggested that federal policymakers revisit the use of teacher aides, on the suspicion that high-poverty schools and, by extension, those with many ELL, rely on aides for instruction in the place of a credentialed teacher. We believe such proposals, although well-intentioned, may not be necessary. The teacher shortage in high-poverty schools is rarely the result of schools *choosing* to hire teachers who lack the required credentials. Rather, the lack of a credentialed teacher in nearly all cases is the result of (a) no new teachers with the proper qualifications applied for a teaching position, or (b) existing teachers who cannot be forced to add credentials or endorsements.

In place of mandating requirements to increase teacher quality, legislators and other policymakers have used the "tool" of additional compensation for teachers who perform well or teach in high-need areas. For instance, in the Houston Independent School District (the nation's fourth largest, and behind only Los Angeles Unified School District in the number of ELL), the school board just approved a new stipend for ESL (ELD) Special Education teachers. Teachers with both the ESL and Special Education credentials will receive an additional $2,000 annually. How such a stipend will affect teacher quality is unknown, primarily because the stipends are linked only to additional certifications and the willingness to work with special needs students.

More common are stipends for ELD teachers in the range of $500 to $1,000. Of course, many districts offer no stipend for ELD teaching, and instead rely upon hiring only new teachers who hold the appropriate ELD license. Such a practice may indeed lower teacher quality because only the beginning teachers are invited to work with ELL. Gándara (chap. 5, this volume) puts incentive pay near the top of the list when considering ways to improve teacher quality for ELL.

At the preservice level, federal efforts to improve teacher quality at low-income schools or in high-need areas include the Perkins, Stafford, and private loan cancellation program. These programs reward preservice teachers who commit to working in certain schools or teaching certain subjects by forgiving loans (up to approximately $20,000) a beginning teacher may have accrued either as an undergraduate or in pursuit of a teaching license. Because states are free to determine which subjects and schools qualify, variation is common. Currently in California, for instance, the following subjects and schools are included in the federal loan forgiveness program: Mathematics (Grades 7–12), Science (Life/Physical; Grades 7–12), Foreign Language, Special Education, Reading Specialist, Low-Income Area School, School Serving Rural Area, State Special School, School with a High Percentage of Emergency Permit Teachers, and Low-Performing School. ELD teaching is not included, nor is bilingual education. Of course, many schools with large ELL populations will be included as a qualifying school under another category (e.g., Low-Income Area School), but it is somewhat of a mystery why beginning teachers working only with ELD students would not qualify. We wonder whether an expansion of the loan forgiveness program to include schools with large proportions of ELL could improve teacher quality.

At the in-service level, the role of additional compensation for ELD teachers has received even less attention. The closest compensation policy we can analyze at this time are the stipends many school districts offer to bilingual teachers. The effects of such stipends on teacher quality are largely unknown. However, from our own experience, we have found that the stipends have typically served not to increase the number or quality of bilingual teachers but, rather, created a competition among school districts for *any* bilingual teacher. It stands to reason that districts that pay more for bilingual teachers will be able to compete more successfully for the highest quality teachers. While the shortage for bilingual teachers is less acute than in the 1990s (owing primarily to the passage of Proposition 227 in California), states that continue bilingual education still face shortages.

In practice, stipends for teaching ELD are rare. In spite of the legislative appeal of additional payment for ELD teachers, general studies of increasing salaries for teachers does not always result in the intended affects. For instance, Ballou and Podgursky (1995) have shown that increasing teacher salaries can have the counterintuitive effect of decreasing teacher quality. Two perverse actions may be at work: (a) Higher salaries may discourage older teachers, whose teaching effectiveness may have diminished, from retiring, and (b) higher salaries may reduce a school system's overall resources, thus eliminating professional development opportunities for all teachers, both beginning and experienced. Whether higher salaries have a differential effect on ELD teachers remains an open question.

We should point out that higher salaries for teachers is a legislative goal we promote, and therefore call into question the results of the Ballou and Podgursky study, particularly because they analyzed data from a short-term salary increase. Raising teacher salaries over the long term would no doubt increase the talent of those choosing a career and encourage those who do teach to spend more time and resources improving their instruction. Increasing salaries over the long term in any profession tends to result in more productive and higher quality workers. It seems unlikely this would be true in every context but teaching.

Ingersoll (1999) suggested that teacher quality, specifically teacher knowledge of the subject they are teaching, is affected dramatically by building-level administrators. Ingersoll argues that principals have great latitude in assigning teachers to out-of-field assignments and thus greatly affecting the quality of teaching. For instance, if a school's administration cannot find a licensed math teacher, they may—and often must—use a teacher who is not licensed for the content area. Mathematics remains the teaching field where teachers are most likely working out-of-field and is coincidentally mentioned as one of the subjects U.S. students find most difficult. Similarly, ELD remains a "shortage" teaching field. Are ELL failing dispropotionalely because their teachers are teaching out-of-field? We have to wait for a definitive answer from the research, but new programs such as those initiated by Reyes (chap. 7, this volume) and Suttmiller and Gonzáles (chap. 8, this volume) offer hope.

Policy-making does not, however, routinely employ the extant knowledge base in systematic ways. In an insightful paper, Hawley (1990) argued that the policies developed for preparing and maintaining quality teachers "are not burdened by their fit with available knowledge or systematically developed theory" (p. 136). One striking, recent example of the lack of fit between policy and education (particularly teacher development and testing theory) emerged from the "bubble" days in the California legislature. The Certificated Staff Performance Incentive Act (Assembly Bill 1114, 2000) was developed to provide cash payments to teachers at low-performing schools where test scores improved (many of these schools enrolled a large proportion of ELL). Fraught with challenges, the payments often went to schools whose scores went high in one year and then down to average the next. Furthermore, teachers at the awarded schools found themselves increasingly reluctant to accept the money, pointing out that their colleagues in other schools were teaching just as well and getting no award. Indeed, the largest teacher association in the state suggested that teachers refuse to accept the money.

Another way policymakers have intended to raise teacher quality is by raising the so-called quality of those who enter the field. The inexpensive and quick way of ensuring quality by raising the "bar" on tests of pedagogy or subject matter holds enormous political potential (Téllez, 2003) but may also limit the teacher pool in ways that work against the achievement of certain groups of students (Memory, Coleman, & Watkins, 2003).

Teacher evaluation programs are common targets for policymakers hoping to raise teacher quality. And we found one study relevant to the teacher quality for ELL. Gallagher (2002) studied the relationship between teacher evaluation scores and student achievement in a school with an ELL majority. Using a teacher evaluation system based on the National Board on Professional Teaching Standards and standardized test scores, Gallagher found a positive and statistically significant correlation between teacher evaluation and student scores in literacy but not in mathematics. This finding is explained by the fact that the study took place in the aftermath of Proposition 227, in which native language instruction was eliminated in nearly all California schools. With the entirely new focus on English instruction, Gallagher speculates that the attention to preparing ELL students for the English standardized test pushed teachers to align their work with state content standards, thus linking teacher evaluation with student scores. We cannot be sure how such a finding might be used to enhance teacher quality, but we share the belief that strong instructional goals and offering teachers the means to achieve them strengthens teacher quality.

Policies developed to raise or reward teacher quality, though often well intentioned, can have unintended consequences. Two common policy practices for raising teacher quality, rewards for improved student test scores and raising the bar for entry to the field, have shown appeal in the policymaking community but less promise in actual practice.

Teacher Verbal Ability and Its Potential Relationship to Quality ELD Instruction

Our review thus far has avoided issues typically raised by the production/function research; we have preferred to explore those issues that yield to the development or growth of teachers. Production/function research, while important in some policy contexts, tends to focus on variables out of the control of school or university systems. In spite of our focus here, we mention one particular finding common to the findings in the production/function literature because it may relate particularly to the quality of ELD teachers; namely, the relationship between teacher verbal ability and student achievement.

Teacher verbal ability (as measured by SAT Verbal scores, for instance) is routinely associated with increased student achievement (see Verstegen & King, 1998, for a review of this research). To our knowledge, no studies to date have associated ELD teacher effectiveness with verbal ability. However, we might assume that for ELD teachers, who are responsible for teaching language, verbal capacity and flexibility may prove to be related to student achievement.

The measurement of verbal ability is, of course, a very controversial topic in psychometric research. Like all measures of ability, verbal ability is designed to assess how well a person can respond to novel uses of language in a testing condition. The test evidence is thought to then indicate the capacity for understanding and using verbal agility in other contexts. Our speculation is that ELD teachers who easily see patterns and relationships among words and sentences, as well as the coherence of text as a whole, may be able to "see" the ways that ELL are using or misusing English. Differences in verbal capacity and flexibility could mean that one teacher could find patterns in the ways ELL are using English, correct or endorse those patterns, while another teacher would be left wondering why the students continued to make the same error repeatedly. Interestingly, secondary students seem to be able to recognize verbal ability and identify it with effective teaching (Brosh, 1996).

Again, we admit that such an assertion is speculative, but the attention paid to the relationship between verbal ability and quality teaching warrants further consideration. This is especially true when, as some recent proposals suggest, it is believed that teacher quality is not a consequence of training but rather a matter of intellectual capacity and life experiences. In particular, those who argue for alternative credentialing favor careful selection over training to ensure teacher quality.

Pedagogical Strategies

The discipline of L2 teaching has produced a long and rich history of methods for teaching language. While some once-common methods of language teaching have now been rendered as ineffective, the discipline has had traditionally been receptive to the use of experimental research to uncover the most effective methods for language teaching in specific contexts for specific students.

In a recent review of effective instructional practices for ELL, Waxman and Téllez (2002) found seven instructional practices associated with high academic achievement for ELL.

1. Collaborative Learning/Community-Building Teaching Practices

2. Multiple Representations Designed for Understanding Target Language
3. Building on Prior Knowledge
4. Instructional Conversation/Protracted Language Events
5. Culturally Responsive Instruction
6. Cognitively-Guided Instruction
7. Technology-Enriched Instruction

We refer readers to the earlier report for a discussion of these practices, as well as suggestions about how teachers can implement them. Unlike some researchers (e.g., Lakdawalla, 2001), we believe that innovations in pedagogy, based on sound research, can greatly improve the quality of ELD teaching.

The essence of our findings in the earlier report suggest that effective teachers of ELL distinguish themselves by their capacity to link academic and conceptual ideas with the everyday reasoning skills students already possess (Duran, Dugan, & Weffer, 1997). Accomplishing such a task, however, requires teachers to pay close attention to the culture of the students. Furthermore, quality ELD teachers must understand how the home culture of the students interacts with the instruction of English. The complexity of this task suggested to us a section addressing the cultural knowledge needed by ELD teachers.

Cultural Knowledge

Teaching ELL almost always implies teaching immigrant children or the children of immigrants. For this reason, ELD teachers must have specialized knowledge of how students' home culture interacts with the formal school curriculum. So it comes as no surprise to find that each of the professional organizations in ELD have developed goals related to teacher knowledge of student culture. But as with the other categories we have discussed, the question is not *whether* such knowledge is important, but rather *how much* knowledge is needed to provide quality instruction. In addition, we must also address the best methods for developing such knowledge in practicing ELD teachers.

Like ELL's native languages, the culture of ELL can vary widely, and in some instances, it may be impossible for ELD teachers to have a complete and coherent knowledge of all the cultures represented by their students. For example, in one year, an ELD teacher might find an Armenian student in the class, whereas the next year a Hmong student may enroll in her place.

We recognize that ELD teachers should know the culture of the ELL in their class deeply enough to develop curriculum relevant to students' lived experiences, but we also are aware of the extraordinary challenge such a mandate implies.

In response to the challenge of creating culturally relevant teaching, teacher educators, policymakers, and school district administrators have created two different, though not exclusive, paths to quality cultural instruction for ELL.

The two fundamental strategies thought to create culturally consistent teaching are (a) recruit teachers who represent the culture of the ELL, or (b) recruit well-prepared and motivated teachers, irrespective of their home culture, and provide professional development opportunities so that they can learn the culture of the students and link it to schooling activities (see Téllez, 2004/2005, for a discussion of the merits of each strategy).

The first strategy is primarily a recruitment effort designed to improve teacher quality (cf. Reinhardt, 2001). One of the more recent challenges in the study of culture in schools—and one that appears to be long lasting—is the relationship between the culture of the teacher and the culture of the students. For many years, this relationship was of little concern to anyone. It was simply assumed that teachers, as representatives of the dominant culture, would impart their cultural values and beliefs to the students, irrespective of how those beliefs may conflict with those of the students. We regarded the culture of the teacher and the students as a single flowing river, making its predictable path to the ocean. But more recently, we have, with good reason, come to question our earlier neglect of this relationship, asking perhaps if the cultural mismatch between the teacher and the students could prevent ELL from achieving to their capabilities.

Teachers who are representatives of the culture of the students have a distinct advantage when creating instruction based on their shared culture. Such an advantage doubles when the teacher and students share a common language. Recruitment may appear to be a simple, straightforward strategy for matching culture to instruction, but several research studies have demonstrated that many university students who represent the language and culture background of ELL often choose other professions (Gordon, 1994; Heninger, 1989). Further, researchers have raised questions about just how obvious it is for teachers of a certain ethnicity to develop curriculum based on their own culture when the school is promoting a different set of ideas (Téllez, 1999), implying that irrespective of the culture of teachers, they still require new pedagogical understandings to create culturally unified instruction. In addition to the challenges already described, we find that in the case of many ELL, their cultural groups are not well represented among those preparing to teach, and a challenging puzzle emerges. For instance, the data reveal that as the number of Mexican-American students increase, the number of Mexican-American teachers is decreasing, both proportionate to the student population and in number (Lewis, 1996). With fewer Mexican-American teachers to connect home culture to schooling for Mexican-American ELL, fewer ELL will be successful in school and less likely to attend postsecondary education, required for a career as a teacher. Thus, the cycle produces fewer Mexican-American teachers.

We can believe no longer that ELD teaching is "merely" language instruction. Teachers must understand how culture and language interact in the development of youth as active participants in a democracy as well as the learning of English.

SUMMARY AND CONCLUDING THOUGHTS

In spite of state mandates and recent "mini" reforms promoting teacher quality, many teachers remain unsure about their capacity to teach ELL. The wholesale improvement of teacher education in the interests of ELL students is, of course, the goal, but the issues are diverse and often complicated. We must keep in mind the complexity of raising teacher quality and not be tempted by simple functionalist views of teaching and learning. We agree with Jere Brophy, one of the leaders in the quality teacher research, who cautions against the misuse of such a view, arguing against rigid guidelines such as "Behavior X correlates with student achievement gain, so teachers should always do Behavior X." A straightforward recommendation derived from the production/function research literature, while alluring to those looking for quick ways to improve student learning, fails to capture the varied contexts of a specific instructional context (Brophy, 1987). We argue that ELD is clearly such a specific context.

But the desire for a quick fix is compelling. The achievement gap between native English-speaking children and ELL must be addressed. Capability in English is becoming a worldwide necessity for professional employment. And while the United States has always been tolerant of those who speak multiple languages, one of those languages must be English. In spite of the importance of English, we share Edwards' (1994) view that the goal of language education is the multi-glossic culture, in which most members use two or more languages for varying purposes. High-quality ELD teachers can balance the need for English with a respect and encouragement for students' native languages. But again, ELL must learn to speak, read, and write English quickly and accurately. Although language educators may disagree on the proper role of students' native languages in ELD (e.g., McCarty, 2003), each of us recognizes that with a strong command of English, our children and youth can all become full participants in U.S. economic, political, and cultural life. High-quality ELD teachers represent our best hope for achieving this goal.

OVERVIEW OF THIS BOOK

One of this nation's greatest educational challenges is improving the education of ELL—students whose first language is not English and are either beginning to learn English or have demonstrated some proficiency in English. Hispanic students constitute the largest group of ELL, but they have the lowest levels of education and the highest dropout rate. Hispanic students' educational aspirations and academic performance in science, mathematics, and reading is significantly lower than White students. In addition, approximately 40% of Hispanic students are one grade or more below expected achievement levels by the eighth grade and only about 50% graduate "on time." These facts and reports are especially problematic, given that Hispanic children primarily reside in urban cities and are immersed in neighborhoods of concentrated poverty where the most serious dropout problems exist. Furthermore, Hispanic ELL students are more than twice as likely to attend a "low-performing" school than White students.

This book brings together a broad range of authors, all of whom are interested in the underperformance of English Language Learners (ELL) in U.S. schools. Their particular interest is in the quality of the preparation and development of educators (both preservice and in-service) who will work with ELL. They recognize that instructional improvements cannot be met via curriculum alone; that educators are the focal point for improving the education of this large and growing population of students. Their recommendations range from radical changes in current state and federal policy to promising new practices in teacher education.

The chapters in this book were all presented as papers at a conference that was convened by the Mid-Atlantic Regional Laboratory for Student Success in Washington, DC, in November of 2003. The conference was designed to facilitate the input of the participants and the participants were chosen to be representative of a variety of fields such as teachers, administrators, and policymakers. Our conclusion chapter summarizes some of the key findings from all the chapters, as well as the conference discussion. Our nation faces very serious challenges in serving ELL and we think this book addresses some of these important concerns and some solutions to these problems. We welcome and encourage further development of the ideas of this chapter and book.

REFERENCES

Abell Foundation. (2001). *Teacher certification reconsidered: Stumbling for quality.* Baltimore, MD: Author.

Ada, A. F. (1986). Creative education for bilingual teachers. *Harvard Educational Review, 56*(4), 386–393.

Alexander, D., Heaviside, S., & Farris, E. (1999). *Status of education reform in public elementary and secondary schools: Teachers' perspectives.* Washington, DC: U.S. Department of Education, National Center for Education Statistics.

Ashton, P., & Webb, R. (1986). *Making a difference: Teacher's sense of efficacy.* New York: Longman.

Ballou, D., & Podgursky, M. (1995). Recruiting smarter teachers. *Journal of Human Resources, 30*(2), 326–338.

Britzman, D. (1991). *Practice makes practice: A critical study of learning to teach.* Albany, NY: State University of New York Press.

Brophy, J. (1987). *Research on teacher effects: Uses and abuses.* East Lansing, MI: The Institute for Research on Teaching.

Brosh, H. (1996). Perceived characteristics of the effective language teacher. *Foreign Language Annals, 29*(2), 121–139.

Cochran-Smith, M., & Fries, M. K. (2001). Sticks, stones, and ideology: The discourse of reform in teacher education *Educational Researcher, 30*(8), 3–15.

Darling-Hammond, L., & McLaughlin, M. (1995). Policies that support professional development in an era of reform. *Phi Delta Kappan, 77,* 597–604.

Darling-Hammond, L., & Youngs, P. (2002). Defining "highly qualified teachers": What does "scientifically-based research" actually tell us? *Educational Researcher, 31*(9), 13–25.

Duran, B. J., Dugan, T., & Weffer, R. E. (1997). Increasing teacher effectiveness with language minority students. *The High School Journal, 80*(4), 238–246.

Edwards, J. (1994). *Multilingualism.* London: Routledge.

Gallagher, H. A. (2002). *The relationship between measures of teacher quality and student achievement: The case of Vaughn Elementary.* Unpublished doctoral dissertation, University of Wisconsin–Madison.

Galston, W. A. (2000). *Federal policies to improve teacher quality for low-income students.* Unpublished doctoral dissertation, University of Maryland.

García, E. (1990). Educating teachers for language minority students. In W. R. Houston (Ed.), *Handbook of research on teacher education* (pp. 712–729). New York: Macmillan.

Goldhaber, D., & Brewer, D. J. (2000). Does teacher certification matter? High school teacher certification status and student achievement. *Educational Evaluation and Policy Analysis, 22*(2), 129–145.

Gordon, J. A. (1994). Why students of color are not entering teaching: Reflections from minority teachers. *Journal of Teacher Education, 45*(5), 346–353.

Hargreaves, A., & Fullan, M. (1998). *What's worth fighting for out there.* New York: Teachers College Press.

Hawley, W. D. (1990). Systematic analysis, public policy-making, and teacher education. In W. R. Houston (Ed.), *Handbook of research in teacher education* (pp. 136–156). New York: Macmillan.

Heninger, M. L. (1989). Recruiting minority teachers: Issues and options. *Journal of Teacher Education, 40*(6), 35–39.

Hopkins, D., & Stern, D. (1996). Quality teachers, quality schools: International perspectives and policy implications. *Teacher and Teacher Education, 12*(5), 501–517.

Ingersoll, R. M. (1999). The problem of underqualified teachers in American secondary schools. *Educational Researcher, 28*(2), 26–37.

Jackson, A. W., & Davis, G. A. (2000). *Turning points 2000: Educating adolescents in the 21st century.* New York: Teachers College Press.

Jiménez, R. T., & Barrera, R. (2000). How will bilingual/ESL programs in literacy change in the next millennium? *Reading Research Quarterly, 35,* 522–523.

Lakdawalla, D. (2001). *The declining quality of teachers* (Working Paper 8263). Cambridge, MA: National Bureau of Economic Research.

Lewis, L., Parsad, B., Carey, N., Bartfai, N., Farris, E., & Smerdon, B. (1999). *Teacher quality: A report on the preparation and qualifications of public school teachers.* Washington, DC: U.S. Department of Education, Office of Educational Research and Improvement, National Center for Education Statistics.

Lewis, M. (1996). *Supply and demand of teachers of color* (Digest 94/8). Washington, DC: ERIC Clearinghouse on Teaching and Teacher Education.

McCarty, T. L. (2003). Revitalising indigenous languages in homogenising times. *Comparative Education, 39*(2), 147–163.

McKnight, A., & Antunez, B. (1999). *State survey of legislative requirements for educating limited English proficient students.* Washington, DC: National Clearinghouse for Bilingual Education.

McLesky, J., & Waldron, N. L. (2002). Professional development and inclusive schools: Reflections on effective practice. *The Teacher Educator, 37*(3), 159–172.

Memory, D. M., Coleman, C. L., & Watkins, S. D. (2003). Possible tradeoffs in raising basic skills cutoff scores for teacher licensure: A study with implications for participation of African Americans in teaching. *Journal of Teacher Education, 54*(3), 217–227.

Menken, K., & Antunez, B. (2001). *An overview of the preparation and certification of teachers working with Limited English Proficient (LEP) students.* Washington, DC: National Clearinghouse for Bilingual Education.

Milk, R., Mercado, D., & Sapiens, A. (1992). *Re-thinking the education of teachers of language minority children: Developing reflective teachers for changing schools.* Washington, DC: National Clearinghouse for Bilingual Education.

National Center for Education Statistics. (1998). *Mini-digest of education statistics 1997.* Washington, DC: U.S. Department of Education.

Penner, J. (1999). *Teacher and principal perceptions of factors influencing teachers' decisions to participate in professional development.* Unpublished doctoral dissertation, The University of Houston.

Reinhardt, R. (2001). *Toward a comprehensive approach to teacher quality.* Aurora, CO: Mid-Continent Educational Research for Education and Learning.

Smith, G. P. (1998). *Common sense about uncommon knowledge: The knowledge bases for diversity.* Washington, DC: American Association of Colleges for Teacher Education.

Tedick, D. J., & Walker, C. L. (1994). Second language teacher education: The problems that plague us. *Modern Language Journal, 78*(3), 300–312.

Téllez, K. (1999). Mexican-American preservice teachers and the intransigency of the elementary school curriculum. *Teaching and Teacher Education, 15*(5), 555–570.

Téllez, K. (2003). Three themes on standards in teacher education: Legislative expediency, the role of external review, and test bias in the assessment of pedagogical knowledge. *Teacher Education Quarterly, 30*(1), 9–18.

Téllez, K. (2004/2005). Preparing teachers for Latino children and youth: Policies and practice. *The High School Journal, 88*(2), 43–54.

TESOL. (2003). *Standards for the accreditation of initial programs in P–2 ESL teacher education.* Alexandria, VA: Author.

Tom, A. (1997). *Redesigning teacher education.* Albany, NY: SUNY Press.

Urban, W. J. (1990). Historical studies of teacher education. In W. R. Houston (Ed.), *Handbook of research on teacher education* (pp. 59–71). New York: Macmillan.

Verstegen, D. A., & King, R. A. (1998). The relationship between school spending and student achievement: A review and analysis of 35 years of production function research. *Journal of Education Finance, 24*(2), 243–262.

Waxman, H., & Téllez, K. (2002). *Research synthesis on effective teaching practices for English language learners.* Philadelphia, PA: Temple University, Laboratory for Student Success.

Chapter 2

Training Teachers Through Their Students' First Language

Liliana Minaya-Rowe
University of Connecticut

This chapter examines recent effective approaches and programs to train teachers how to teach English language learners (ELLs). In doing so, it draws from experiences of recent and ongoing collaborations with four university training programs at pre-service and in-service levels and with teachers of ELLs in several urban school districts enrolled in graduate teacher training programs. It illustrates both the approach and its usefulness in the professional development of all teachers of ELLs. The approach involves selected training courses designed to meet both the Spanish language proficiency needs of mainstream, bilingual and English as a second language teachers, and their common professional development needs to teach ELLs English, their second language, reading and the standards-based curriculum. The overarching goal of the training programs is to encourage teachers of ELLs to analyze the constraints and opportunities they perceive in teaching ELLs. Real-life experience takes the place of simulation, since teachers experience firsthand the difficulties and challenges faced by their own students when having to attend to new language and content at the same time. For most program students the language of instruction in selected courses is Spanish, their second language and the weekly or biweekly course meetings are conducted almost exclusively in this language guided by the theoretical framework for learning both language and content through sheltered instruction (SI) and the Sheltered Instruction Observation Protocol (SIOP). Students benefit from the courses and demonstrate command of the second language to the extent that they can function in relatively fixed linguistic exchanges (e.g., at school, with their students and their students' parents), awareness of the teaching and learning process, and apply SI and the SIOP strategies to promote linguistic literacy and academic success for their students. The chapter also discusses the role of programs with courses of this nature as a useful addition in professional development efforts and how teacher training institutions can use them to prepare all teachers of the increasing multilingual and multicultural American school population.

INTRODUCTION

ELLs' academic success depends on teachers' knowledge and applications of effective pedagogy in the classroom. To date, much of the professional development in schools on language and academic needs of ELLs has been addressed to bilingual and/or ESL teachers. Universities have developed undergraduate and graduate programs with curricula and courses to prepare these professionals. In turn, school systems have addressed professional development programs for furthering the continuing education of in-service teachers. However, comparatively little attention has been focused on mainstream teachers who have or will have ELLs in their classrooms (Menken & Antúnez, 2001). This is a cause for concern if we consider that the numbers of ELLs in the regular mainstream classroom are increasing, and will continue to increase at a very rapid pace, if demographic projections hold true (National Center for Education Statistics, 2003).

This chapter presents a strategy for introducing teachers and teachers-to-be to the same second language (L2) experiences that ELLs have during their schooling. It examines specific L2 principles and teaching practices to ascertain their usefulness in the professional development of all teachers of ELLs. Selected graduate courses are designed to meet both the Spanish language proficiency needs of mainstream, bilingual and English as second language (ESL) teachers, while providing for their common professional development needs to teach ELLs English, their L2, reading and the standards-based curriculum.

BACKGROUND

This chapter is based on current research on teacher education in social constructivism, current theories on L2 methodology, and the five standards for effective pedagogy posed by the Center for Research on Education, Diversity and Excellence (CREDE). This section focuses on language and content instruction pedagogy, and on fostering personally and academically meaningful language development. The four language modes—listening, speaking, reading, and writing—are taught as an integrated whole, lessons are learner-centered and meaningful to the students, and social interaction and collaborative learning are emphasized (Krashen, Candin, & Terrell, 1996). Furthermore, the philosophy of learning movement calls for a reduction in the amount of teacher talk in order to expose students to more opportunities for using language in creative, useful, and motivating ways (Schifini, 2000).

Social Constructivism

Research on learning processes in social contexts (e.g., schooling and professional development), has provided an explanation of how interaction impacts cognition. According to Shotter (1997), the learning process involves self and others in an exchange of ideas to deepen individual understanding. Vygotsky (1986) contends that learning is a sociocultural practice and that language gives and receives meaning from social activity. In other words, thought develops from undergoing changes produced by interactions. Vygotsky's theory assumes that cognitive development arises as a result of social interactions between individuals and that learning is a dynamic social process in which dialogue between the novice and the expert leads to the development of higher cognitive levels. His "zone of proximal development" (ZPD) is defined as the distance between the actual developmental level as determined by individual problem solving and the level of potential development as determined through problem solving in collaboration with more capable peers. It is the level of performance at which a learner is capable of functioning when there is support from interaction with a more capable individual. Interactions in the "zone" are those that use speech, visual representations such as modeling, and feedback.

Although the writings of Vygotsky were not directly related to L2 learning, the relationship drawn between learning and cognitive development offers valuable insights into the role of social interaction in language acquisition. Vygotsky (1978) asserted that ". . . language and consciousness are both lodged within a matrix of social activity, and that this activity system, rather than the isolated individual, should be the primary focus of study" (p. 21). Krashen's Input Hypothesis is reminiscent of Vygotsky's ZPD (Richard-Amato, 1996). According to Krashen (1989) comprehensible input is a key factor in acquiring a L2. Acquisition occurs when learners understand language that is slightly beyond their current level of competence through input that is made comprehensible by the context or a simplified linguistic message in a way that is meaningful. Krashen (1989) stated that learners ". . . move from *i* (their current level), to + *1* (the next level along the natural order), by understanding input containing *i* + *1*" as illustrated in Fig. 2.1.

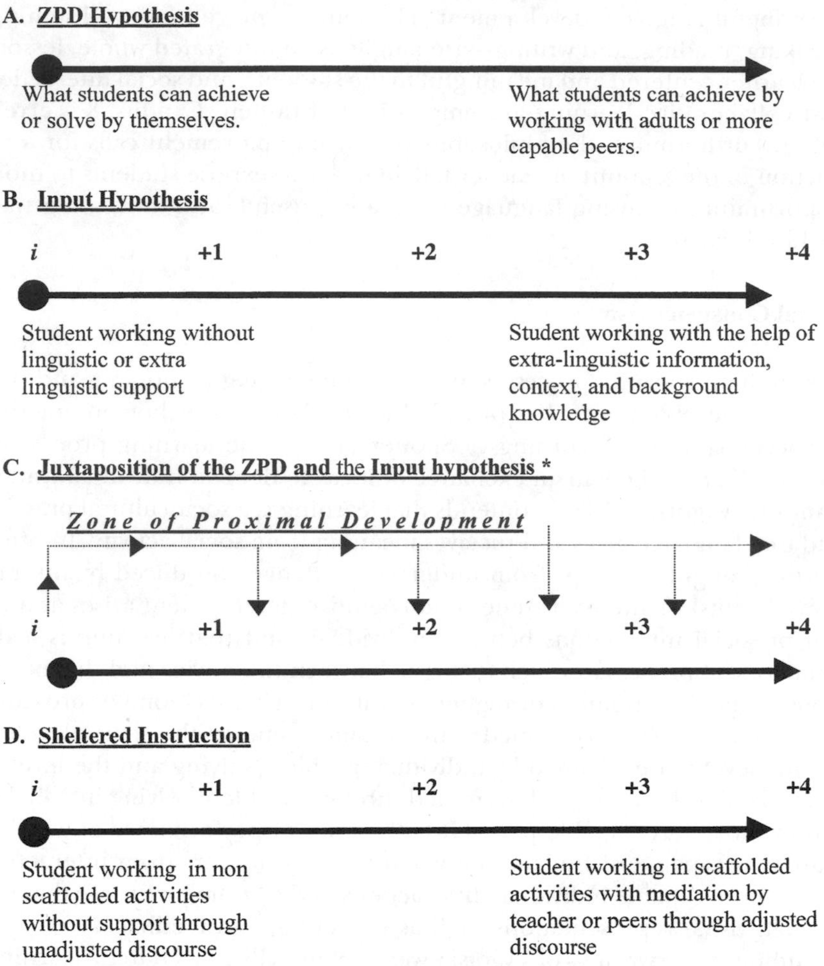
A. ZPD Hypothesis
What students can achieve or solve by themselves.
What students can achieve by working with adults or more capable peers.
B. Input Hypothesis
i
+1
+2
+3
+4
Student working without linguistic or extra linguistic support
Student working with the help of extra-linguistic information, context, and background knowledge
C. Juxtaposition of the ZPD and the Input hypothesis *
Zone of Proximal Development
i
+1
+2
+3
+4
D. Sheltered Instruction
i
+1
+2
+3
+4
Student working in non scaffolded activities without support through unadjusted discourse
Student working in scaffolded activities with mediation by teacher or peers through adjusted discourse

*There is a basis for comparison between Vygotsky's ZPD (dotted line) and Krashen's (i+1) theories (solid line). Both emphasize the distance between what a child does by himself or herself and what he or she can achieve by working in collaboration with an adult or more capable peer. In addition, sheltered instruction merges both concepts into a representation that describes properties that portray teacher behavior in the planning and delivery of effective lessons for second language learner.

FIG. 2.1. The input hypothesis and the zone of proximal development.

Theories of L2 Acquisition and Methodology

Language teaching methodologies have undergone a radical shift from the behaviorist methods of the 1960s to an interactive instructional approach in which the student takes an active (intrinsic) role (Gravelle, 2000). The process of developing L2 proficiency is an essential part of both learning and instruction. L2 learning depends on access to and participation in legitimate social activities in which students use multiple forms and functions of language with the goal of understanding and using new discourse appropriately to accomplish their purposes (Peregoy & Boyle, 2001). Collier (1995) posed a model with four major components to explain the process of L2 learning in the classroom: (a) Sociocultural, students learn the L2 in situations that occur in their everyday lives; (b) Language development, the subconscious and conscious aspects of language learning; (c) Academic development, academic knowledge and conceptual development in all content areas of the curriculum; and, (d) Cognitive development, the subconscious natural process that occurs developmentally from birth to schooling.

SI and the SIOP methodology provide L2 learners with a medium to develop the academic and linguistic demands in their L2. The key components of the SIOP are lesson preparation, comprehensibility, lesson delivery, and interaction (Echevarria, Vogt, & Short, 2000). All the components integrate listening, speaking, reading, and writing with the teaching of content. SI is scaffolded and mediated to provide refuge from the linguistic demands of L2 discourse, which is beyond the current level of comprehension of the students. The theoretical underpinning of the model is that L2 acquisition is enhanced through meaningful use and interaction. SI can be described as a melding of elements of L2 principles and elements of quality teaching. It is also influenced by sociocultural theory because it occurs within social and cultural contexts. This approach facilitates a high level of student involvement and interaction in the classroom.

The Five Standards for Effective Pedagogy

CREDE researchers have proposed five standards to provide teachers with tools to enact best teaching practices (Tharp, Estrada, Dalton, & Yamauchi, 2000). They are:

1. Joint Productive Activity, when experts and novices work together for a common product or goal;
2. Language Development, fostered best through meaningful use and purposeful conversation between teachers and students;
3. Contextualization, which utilizes students' knowledge and skills as a foundation for new knowledge;
4. Challenging Activity, ELLs are not often challenged academically on the erroneous assumption that they are of limited ability;
5. Instructional Conversation, promoted through dialogue, by questioning and sharing ideas and knowledge.

CREDE's researchers pose that these five standards have the potential to give all students the opportunity to obtain the language and the content necessary to succeed in school (Padrón & Waxman, 1999). The standards have been designed to generate activity patterns of collaboration, reflection, and activity involvement of teachers and students during classroom instruction (Tharp et al., 2000). These five principles went through a consensus defining process where researchers, teachers, parents, administrators, and policymakers had the opportunity to alter them when necessary. Tharp (1999) suggested that these standards ". . . are recommendations on which literature is in agreement, across all cultural, racial, and linguistic groups in the United States, at all age levels, and in all subject matters. Even for mainstream students, the standards describe the ideal conditions for instruction; but for students at-risk of educational failure, effective classroom implementation of the standards is vital" (p. 5). Furthermore, Rueda (1998) posed that the five standards can also be applied to professional development. He stated that ". . . the principles that describe effective teaching and learning for students in classrooms should not differ from those of adults in general and teachers in particular" (p. 1).

METHODS

Participants

The participants for this study are groups of master's or postmaster's degree students ($n = 15$ to 22) who work as teachers (bilingual, ESL, or mainstream) of Hispanic ELLs at all levels of instruction in various school districts across the state and who are enrolled in universities with bilingual or ESL graduate training programs. For the most part, bilingual teachers were born and raised in Puerto Rico, they are native speakers of Spanish and educated in Spanish and/or English. ESL and mainstream teachers are nonnative speakers of Spanish and have been educated in English with some high school or college Spanish training. Although the course(s) was/were a response to program students' requests, they were offered to all program teachers as an option to refine their Spanish language skills as well as to learn the training content with the same academic standards as other university courses. Selection of these courses was on a voluntary basis. Those who opted not to take the Spanish content course(s) were ESL or mainstream teachers who had not had previous Spanish training or did not feel they were ready for both the language and academic demands of courses of this nature. They opted to take similar courses in English instead.

The Graduate Programs

This chapter is based on efforts of four university programs to offer in-service courses in Spanish to teachers of large urban school districts across the state. The programs' goals are to enhance teaching skills and complete degree and bilingual and/or ESL certification requirements. The programs' specific objectives include: (a) Increase the number of qualified teachers of ELLs; (b) Improve teachers' first and L2 proficiency and competence; and, (c) Broaden career opportunities for teachers of ELLs. Their training programs include course work in literacy and biliteracy, assessment of bilingualism, ESL teaching methods and curriculum design, foundations of bilingual and bicultural education, linguistics and other courses meant to develop expertise in the education of ELLs. As a result of their training, teachers receive a Master of Arts Degree or a Sixth-Year Professional Diploma in Education, or Education Specialist Degree with Emphasis on Bilingual Bicultural/ESL Education and meet requirements to receive the Bilingual or ESL certification endorsements from the states' departments of education. In addition they become instructional teacher leaders or in-school trainers and offer professional development on SI methodology at district and/or school professional development days.

The Sheltered Spanish Courses

Three-credit graduate courses are offered to graduate students who work in various school districts as ESL, bilingual, and mainstream program teachers. At the beginning of the program or course, their level of Spanish language proficiency is assessed using informal measures and ranges from advanced beginner, to intermediate, to advanced level. For the most part, students have studied Spanish at school or in college for 1 to 6 years with native Spanish speaking instructors. The most commonly used method by their Spanish instructors then is identified as grammar based. Most students have expressed that learning Spanish is a positive experience overall. Some are open to learn the culture of their ELLs and to understand their students' cultural, social and linguistic "funds of knowledge."

Each course is designed to meet the students' varied language proficiency needs in addition to the SI pedagogy needed of teachers who are implementing literacy and content for ELLs in their classrooms. These courses, titles, descriptions, and course syllabi are approved courses by the universities and listed in the institutions' graduate schools catalogs. The sheltered Spanish instructors' task is to write the course syllabus (Prontuario del curso) with the same contents and requirements in Spanish, detail activities during the semester, select appropriate readings and textbooks in Spanish that focus on teaching strategies for reading, language, and content area development. The content objectives and the requirements for the Spanish courses are the same as those approved by the university.

The language objectives differ for course students. For bilingual students (native speakers of Spanish, most raised in Puerto Rico or the United States and schooled in English), the language objective is to improve facets of their Spanish proficiency (e.g., academic writing, and to increase vocabulary range in curriculum content areas). For ESL and mainstream teachers (nonnative speakers of Spanish with some high school or college Spanish training), the language objective is to increase their command of the L2 to the extent that they can function in relatively fixed linguistic exchanges (e.g., at school, with their students, and their students' parents).

The pedagogical objectives relate to literacy, SI and the SIOP, and to the notion of reflection. Students examine the myriad of factors that shape what they do in their classrooms in order to become effective practitioners. They are encouraged to analyze the constraints and opportunities they perceive in teaching ELLs (Joyce & Showers, 2002). What perhaps is uncommon in this approach is the means utilized to foster reflection and sensitization concerning the dynamic language, reading and content classroom contexts that they need to create. Real-life experience takes the place of simulation, since students experience first hand the difficulties and challenges faced by ELLs when having to attend to new language, content and same academic standards for all students at the same time. For most course students the language of instruction (Spanish) is their L2 and the course meetings are conducted almost exclusively in this language using the SI approach. Figure 2.2 presents a descriptive summary of the courses, the language, cultural and academic goals, students' background and requirements.

SI and the SIOP provide the frameworks for each course, their content selection and lesson preparation (Echevarria et al., 2000). The SIOP was developed to meet the needs of ELLs.

However, for these training programs, SI and the SIOP are adapted to meet the needs of Spanish as second language students. SI and the SIOP are based on the premise that L2 acquisition is enhanced through meaningful use and interaction. Through the study of content, students interact in Spanish with meaningful material that is relevant to their training.

Since language processes, such as listening, speaking, readings, and writing, develop independently, SI Spanish lessons incorporate activities that integrate those skills. These lessons mirror high quality nonsheltered teaching for native Spanish speakers and careful attention is paid to the students' distinctive L2 development needs.

Essential in this process is the articulation of different levels of Spanish used with and by the students and the provision of comprehensible input

Descriptors	Characteristics
1. College Status	• Graduate
2. Academic Content Goals	• Same as official syllabi for all graduate students
3. Language Goals	• Academic Spanish Proficiency • Functional Language • Academic Vocabulary • Reading Comprehension • Writing Process • Grammar Points
4. Entry Level	• Some knowledge of Spanish
5. Student Characteristics	• Mainstream, Bilingual and ESL Teachers (experienced and new teachers)
6. Levels of Spanish Proficiency	• Beginners, intermediate and advanced
7. Language of Instruction	• In Spanish with adaptations, visuals, props
8. Instructional Materials, Texts, Visual Aids, Handouts	• In Spanish with adaptations as needed, visuals, realia, culturally appropriate readings, tapes
9. Length of Student Participation	• By semester; follow-up during the program

FIG. 2.2. Descriptive summary of sheltered Spanish instruction. Based on Genesee (1999).

through the use of realia and meaningful activities such as visuals, props, modeling, demonstrations, graphic organizers, vocabulary previews, predictions, adapted texts, joint productive activities, peer tutoring, instructional conversations, and first language support. The goal is to create a nonthreatening environment where students feel comfortable taking risks with language. However, lesson activities are linguistically and academically challenging and the mandated course content syllabus is carefully followed. The objective is to make specific connections between the content being taught and students' experiences or prior knowledge while expanding their Spanish language base and to promote a high level of student engagement and interaction with the course instructor(s), with one another, and with text in order to promote elaborate discourse. Students are also explicitly taught functional Spanish language skills such as how to negotiate meaning, ask for clarification, confirm information, argue, persuade, and disagree. When requested, exercises on grammar points (e.g., identification and discussion of noun phrases in Spanish in a poem, adverbs of comparison) are practiced. Through meaningful activities, students practice and apply their knowledge of Spanish as well as their content knowledge. Diverse supplementary materials and resources are used to support the academic texts (Pérez & Torres-Guzmán, 2002). A sample of a class agenda for

Fundamentos de la Educación Bilingüe y Bicultural
(Foundations in Bilingual and Bicultural Education)
Agenda
10 de marzo del 2003 (March 10, 2003)
De las 6:30 a las 9:00 p.m. (From 6:30 to 9:00 p.m.)

Contenidos (Contents)

- Comentarios sobre sus reflexiones. (Comments on your written reflections.)
- Compartiendo con los amigos. (Sharing time.)
- Repaso del vocabulario + 5 palabras (charadas). (Vocabulary review and 5 new words, charades.)
- Dictado de oraciones. (Dictation of sentences.)
- Trabajo en grupos (centros). Reacción a la lectura *El Bialfabetismo para el Desarrollo Personal y La Participación Social.* (Group Work, Centers. Discussion on the reading entitled *Biliteracy for Personal Growth and Social Participation.*)
- Presentación del capítulo 6, *El Alfabetismo en las Areas de Contenido*—Informe, interpretación crítica y discusión. (A presentation on chapter 6, *Literacy in the Content Areas*—Reporting, interpretation and discussion.)
- Relación del capítulo 6 para la enseñanza de la lectura y las áreas de contenido. (Relating chapter 6 to the teaching of reading and the content areas.)
- Reflexión y recapitulación. ¿Qué hicimos hoy? (Reflection—What did we do today?)

  Comentarios sobre las actividades de hoy. (Comments on today's activities.)

  Continuar diario de palabras personales. (Continue building your own diary of new words.)

the course entitled Foundations of Bilingual Bicultural Education illustrates the SI methodology used.

The agenda's contents above are then broken down into activities for the day to accomplish it as illustrated below.

Fundamentos de la Educación Bilingüe y Bicultural
(Foundations in Bilingual and Bicultural Education)
Agenda
10 de marzo del 2003 (March 10, 2003)
De 6:30 a 9:00 p.m. (From 6:30 to 9:00 p.m.)

Actividades para implementer la agenda (Activities to implement the agenda)

1. Esta vez se les dictarán las oraciones con las palabras del vocabulario. Los estudiantes escribirán la oración completa tres veces.

   (Dictation consists of sentences with key vocabulary words. The students will write the complete sentence 3 times.)

2. La actividad de centros consta de cuatro grupos; el grupo 1 discute el tema del bialfabetismo, el grupo 2 describe las características del desarrollo personal; el grupo 3 desarrolla el tema de la participación social, y el grupo 4 propone soluciones curriculares para mantener el bialfabetismo.

   (The activity centers consist of four groups: Group 1 discusses the theme of biliteracy, group 2 describes personal growth in biliteracy, group 3 examines the social participation, and group 4 proposes curricular solutions to maintain biliteracy.)

3. Diseño de un diagrama que incorpora las estrategias necesarias en las áreas de lectura y matemática.

   (Design of a diagram that incorporates strategies in the areas of reading and math.)

4. El capítulo 6 se trabajará en grupos. Los estudiantes examinarán los resultados de los exámenes estatales e identificarán las estrategias que sus estudiantes necesitan para el aprendizaje de la lectura y para la matemática.

   (Chapter 6 will be done as a group project. Students will examine results from the state mastery tests and identify strategies their students need to be mastered in reading and math.)

A sample of the group product based on the agenda and the activities delineated above yields the following examples.

Estrategias para el Desarrollo de la Lectura y la Matemática en la Escuela Intermedia
(Strategies for Reading and Math Development in the Middle School)

Estrategias para aprender
(Strategies to be mastered)

La Matemática (Math)
- Interpretación de gráficas y cuadros. (Interpreting graphs and charts.)
- Práctica de la geometría. (Using geometry.)
- Usos de la estimación. (Using estimation.)
- Desarrollo del sentido de numeración. (Building number sense.)

La Lectura (Reading)
- Entendimiento de las sucesiones. (Understanding sequences.)
- Desarrollo de la interpretación. (Developing an interpretation.)
- Identificación del significado de una palabra en su contexto. (Finding word meaning in context.)
- Práctica de la comparación y el contraste. (Comparing and contrasting.)

Estrategias para el Desarrollo de la Lectura y la Matemática en la Escuela Intermedia
(Strategies for Reading and Math Development in the Middle School)

Objetivos para Aprender las Estrategias
(Objectives to Master the Strategies)

De Contenido (Content)
1. Crear una gráfica para trazar las coordenadas.
   (Make a graph for plotting coordinate points.)
2. Copiar grupos de pares ordenados y sus direcciones en el papel cuadriculado.
   (Copy sets of ordered pairs and directions onto their graph paper.)
3. Hacer una gráfica con las coordenadas y seguir las instrucciones para diseñar un cuadro geométrico.
   (Graph coordinate points and follow the directions in order to make a geometrical design.)

De Lenguaje (Language)

1. Explicar oralmente lo que son las líneas verticales y horizontales.
   (Articulate what vertical and horizontal lines are.)
2. Identificar los nombres de estas líneas como *eje y* y como *eje x* respectivamente.
   (Identify the names of these lines as the y-axis and the x-axis respectively.)
3. Encontrar el origen en la gráfica y entender que "origen" significa "comienzo".
   (Identify where the origin is on the graph and understand the "origin" as meaning the "beginning".)
4. Explicar cómo trazar una coordenada en un par ordenado.
   (Explain how to plot a coordinate point given an ordered pair.)
5. Describir la importancia de las coordenadas en situaciones de la vida real.
   (Describe how coordinate points are important in real life situations.)

Course Evaluation Results

The purpose of these SI and SIOP Spanish courses is to better understand the teaching–learning process of the L2, Spanish. Participants move from surface engagement with theory to an engagement that promotes reflective commitment to become more effective bilingual, ESL, or mainstream teachers of ELLs. The constructs of instructional and social interaction are examined as cultural phenomena reflecting the interactive process of the construction of meaning and the language of the learning process. Ethnographic techniques such as journals, focus group interviews, questionnaires, detailed record keeping, and surveys are used to describe these courses in terms of major categories. The rationale for the selection of techniques is based on the need to capture the insider's or "emic" point of view (Miles & Huberman, 1994).

In this study rich descriptions and multiple data sources are utilized (Bernard, 1994). Key themes are underlined and marginal notations are instrumental in this chapter. Through a constant comparative method, the data are reduced, and related themes of the reduced data are grouped together to form categories. For example, in the choice of quotes key themes were highlighted after words or phrases were repeated verbally or in writing at least 10 times; these were considered preliminary themes. The quotes were selected from a number of data sources: the end-of-course evaluations and questionnaires, surveys administered a year after participants took the course(s), focus group interviews, comments made by program students on the positive aspects of the course(s), and/or recommendations made for course improvement. Related themes were grouped together to form tentative categories. As more data were amassed, they were compared with previously coded data and broader categories were created to regroup and further organize themes and categories for all quotes. A summary of the results follows.

1. Interpretation is simple: Students are pleased with the courses and the nature of their instruction in the courses. In their view, instruction in these courses met their needs in (a) teaching strategies and methodology, (b) language and culture development, and (c) applicable classroom activities. These results coincide closely with the goals set for the Spanish courses, which focused on Spanish language communication related to the students' L2 development.

Participants' responses are so rich as to merit separate treatment elsewhere, but a few insights make possible a fuller understanding of the data obtained. Teachers who took the Spanish course(s) expressed orally and in writing about specific aspects of the course(s) and/or portions of it. They expressed their satisfaction as presented in the following verbatim (unedited) statements.

2. Students are satisfied with the nature of their Spanish course instruction. In their view, instruction in the courses could not get appreciably better.

First, students valued the SI methodology and classroom activities employed as expressed in the following statements.

> *This type of course should be offered to all educators. This is the way to learn a second language.*
>
> *This has been one of the best and most effective courses that I have taken in while at ______. The course was very successful at showing us how to make content comprehensible.*
>
> *En general, esta preparación me ha pulido como profesional y me ha motivado a mantenerme al día en mi campo de labor como nunca antes lo había estado. (In general, this course training has polished me as a professional and has motivated me to keep up to date in the field as I had never been so.)*

Second, the students expressed their feelings surrounding the Spanish SI experience and their desire to continue having exposure to the L2 in other courses of their graduate program.

> *The professors are very enthusiastic and obviously enjoy what they are doing. They make me feel very comfortable in a class where the language is unknown to me. I have come away with a great understanding of the Spanish language.*
>
> *This was the BEST Spanish course I ever took. (I took 5 classes prior!). The methods used were excellent.*
>
> *Very interactive. The instructor models best practices. The classes are excellent. I have improved on my Spanish and learned theory and the application of the theory.*

Third, the following statements illustrate the expansions in the students' thinking and conceptualization of their training program, relations with peers and instructors, minority–majority relations, and cultural identity.

> *Sin duda alguna mi vida profesional ha mejorado enormemente como educador de estudiantes bilingües desde que comencé a tomar estos cursos en "Sheltered Instruction". Me he puesto al día en cuanto a la investigación lingüística y he podido comprender fenómenos lingüísticos en mi salón de clases luego de haber sido expuesto a teorías e hipótesis que explican comportamientos lingüísticos en los ELLs y, por ende, he actuado mas inteligente y efectivamente para beneficio del alumno y su aprendizaje. (Without a doubt my professional life has improved enormously as educator of bilingual students since I began to take these courses in "Sheltered Instruction". I have been updated with regards to the linguistic research and have been able to understand linguistic phenomena in my classrooms after having been exposed to theories and hypotheses that explain the linguistic behavior of ELLs and, hence, I have acted more intelligently and effectively for the benefit of the student and his/her learning.)*
>
> *The instructor is extremely positive. Much time and effort is put into the development of this class. Personal relationships have been developed between the instructor and students—this created outstanding products.*
>
> *Continúen haciendo su labor como lo han hecho hasta ahora. Entre companeros americanos e hispanos se han hecho comentarios muy positivos de ustedes. ¡Ustedes son un orgullo hispano! ¡Felicitaciones! (Continue doing your job as you have done up to now. Among American and Hispanic classmates, very positive comments have been made about you. You are a Hispanic pride! Congratulations!)*

3. After a semester or two of taking Spanish SI courses, all students strongly agreed or agreed that the SI Spanish courses they took were very useful in the planning and delivery of their daily lessons to meet their ELLs' needs during the school year. They have incorporated SI and the SIOP to integrate concept and language opportunities. They still consider comprehensible input as an important lesson component and adjust their speech to their ELLs' proficiency levels. They also use scaffolding techniques, group work to support the language and content objectives of their SI and SIOP lessons, and provide a review of key concepts throughout the lesson. They wrote their continued satisfaction with the courses they took.

> *Many of the strategies that were modeled in the SI class were used in my classroom. In fact many other teachers in the school have been using strategies and techniques that I was exposed to during that class. The use of task cards, having students rewrite endings, and the variety of presenting work are just some of the things that are evident in my classroom after taking the course.*
>
> *I have implemented many of the strategies I learned throughout the year. My next challenge will be to incorporate all I have learned into my own 4th grade classroom . . . next year I will have my own mainstream classroom with all levels of ELLs in with main-*

stream! I am very excited about this new opportunity, but I will never forget the joys of being an ESL teacher. My new role will still allow me to use all the ESL strategies, just with a more varied group of students . . . Thank you again for enabling me to become a more sensitive, creative, and child-centered teacher . . .

Because of these courses I have been able to create a transformed classroom. I believe in the potential of my ELLs—or any student for that matter. I am taking on the challenge and provide my students with the necessary "i + 1" to empower them as future productive citizens in the global market.

CONCLUSIONS

In these Spanish SI courses, students use their L2 to talk and write about their own experiences and notions about L2 learning and to voice their changing perspectives. The experience of having to deal with academic demands in the L2 can provide valuable insights into the world as viewed by ELLs. Through carefully planned experiences in which intellectual activity is coupled with interactive participation, the course instructors practice a pedagogical approach that might help design more effective teacher education programs and facilitate the development of in-service and pre-service teachers of ELLs. Traditionally, SI has been part of an ESL program, a bilingual program, a dual language program, a newcomer's program, or a foreign language program. The goal is to extend its role to the implementation of graduate level university courses and programs with the purpose of developing a strong foundation in SI, the SIOP, and a common knowledge base related to the understanding of language and to sociocultural issues underlying effective instructional practices for all teachers of ELLs (Tharp, 1999).

The SI methodology and the SIOP have proved to be highly useful professional tools to aid in the planning of training units for professional development sessions. Students appear to benefit from these courses since their L2 achievement has improved. They also speak highly of the benefits of classroom collaboration and interaction in increasing their ability to speak Spanish, and sensitizing them to their students' learning process. They find the lessons interesting and comprehensible. They enjoy the courses because they feel relaxed and confident. They reiterate that their Spanish vocabulary has increased. Sometimes they feel nervous when they have to speak to the whole class and always are comfortable when they work in groups. They stress that they are using the techniques and routines introduced during the course in their own classrooms. The statement *Las horas de clase pasan rápido* (The class hours go by very fast.) is often made. A semester to a year after they took these courses, students strongly agreed or agreed that SI and the SIOP were very useful in the planning and delivery of their daily lessons to meet their ELLs' needs. They incorporated SI and the SIOP as important lesson components to integrate concept and language opportunities to teach their ELLs.

Overall, this study provides support for a number of key characteristics which professional development initiatives need to adopt in order to respond effectively to the needs of teachers of ELLs. Effective teaching requires an understanding of both social and school factors that influence L2 acquisition and academic learning (Tharp & Gallimore, 1988). This chapter has proposed an approach to professional development that is both interactive and exploratory (Scribner, 1999). Although the number of Spanish SI courses offered in these graduate programs is too small compared to the number of courses offered in English and included in the students' plans of study, the possibilities exhibited by these courses appear to be promising. These courses can become bridges between the theoretical content and the practical reality of the L2 classroom. No claim can be made that these courses are the answer to the problems posed by teacher education in these challenging times, but it is fair to state that courses of this nature have a valuable role to play in in-service, and perhaps pre-service, efforts.

POLICY AND PRACTICAL IMPLICATIONS

The 2001 No Child Left Behind federal legislation aims to close the achievement gap by measuring adequate yearly progress on test scores. In response to this legislation, education reforms have raised the bar to close the achievement gap for ELLs and other groups while increasing all students' mastery of state education standards. All students in the United States must finish school and participate in the economic and social world of the new century (Thomas & Collier, 2003). The reforms also place tremendous emphasis on the professional development of all teachers in schools across the nation who is continuously challenged to meet the needs of a widely diverse population. This pressure creates a greater gap between teacher training and the skills needed to teach ELLs nationwide. Most educators do not receive the preparation to teach this student population before entering the workforce and they have limited opportunities to update their knowledge and skills in an ongoing basis throughout their careers (Nieto, 2003).

Teachers currently joining the workforce face the challenge of teaching ELLs. When they enter teacher education programs, they tend to see diversity as a problem to be overcome rather than as an asset in promoting discourse and learning (Gay, 2004; Ladson-Billings, 1999). Furthermore, when teachers are not familiar with their students' culture they may have negative expectations or misinterpret their interaction patterns (Darling-Hammond & Sykes, 1999). To equip all teachers to work successfully with a growing ELL population requires continuing renewal and extension of the skills, knowledge, and awareness needed to remain effective in a culturally dynamic environment (Joyce & Showers, 2002; Waxman, 2004). New and experienced teachers are likely to have had little or no formal instruction on L2 acquisition and L2 teaching methodology and need to integrate these perspectives into the content and structure of their lessons to ensure their successful teaching of ELLs (Cummins & Fillmore, 2000).

An important group of professionals, who are responsible for the success of ELLs, as well as that of language majority groups in school, is the growing numbers of English monolingual teachers who are or will be part of two-way or dual language programs (Minaya-Rowe, 2002). These educators need to become familiar with the principles of additive bilingualism, SI, the SIOP, and language-rich environments. A working knowledge of the minority language can also prove to be an invaluable asset in these settings. Since ELLs' production in the L2 may lag behind their comprehension in the initial stages of language acquisition, they may occasionally fall back into their first language (L1) for communicative purposes. If teachers have some information about their students' L1 and the role it plays in L2 learning, they may be able to use it as an opportunity toward more successful schooling.

The current structure of university courses and of district-led professional development provide relatively few teachers or teachers-to-be with the opportunity to reflect and analyze the needs of ELLs going through the L2 acquisition process to the degree that is being accomplished in these courses (Rueda, 1998). There is rarely any occasion when teachers come together and collaborate on the teaching and learning process, certainly publications and resources are nonexistent that use the students' L2 as the language of instruction in a sustained way. The teachers who participate in these courses create learning communities in which they can explore their beliefs about their students and increase their repertoire of culturally relevant pedagogy. The application of these results can contribute to a better understanding of professional development needs of teachers of ELLs as they take on the task of preparing for the diversity they are sure to encounter in their classrooms (Moir & Bloom, 2003).

There is a quiet revolution when teachers are taught using their students' L1. It has the potential to change the way teacher educators prepare teachers to teach ELLs and to learn alongside their students' needs and strengths. Professional development programs need new ways to teach the standards-based curriculum so that ELLs can participate and benefit from classroom activities. An important consideration is that the current U.S. teacher population is approximately 90% White American, and monolingual female and no significant changes in the percentage are predicted despite education reform efforts. Furthermore, teacher education programs, for the most part, reflect the monocultural and monolingual circumstances of teachers, especially in daily instructional practices. For example, Ladson-Billings (1999) described the operation of schools (the textbooks, instructional practices, and the policies) as not substantially different from Anglo-American student teachers' own experience.

The SI Spanish courses can become part of a coherent and sustained graduate program, much like the two-way bilingual or dual language program to educate ELLs. Thomas and Collier (2003) posed that grade-level and accelerated instruction in two languages is the key to the successful future of U.S. education. Although their statements relate to K–12 education, they can also serve to pave the way to two-way programs (e.g., Spanish and English) at the college and university levels.

- The SI Spanish courses educate Spanish learners and native Spanish speakers together; the two-way programs educate English learners and native English speakers together.
- All students in the SI courses benefit from quality, meaningful, challenging, and accelerated instruction. All students in two-way programs benefit from the same and without being remedial or compensatory in nature.
- The SI Spanish courses develop proficiency in Spanish and mastery of the curriculum in Spanish. The two-way program offers full proficiency and mastery of the curriculum in two languages. The graduate training program could be revised to develop a balanced component of SI Spanish and SI English courses to compare with the two-way program.
- The SI Spanish courses use only Spanish and occasionally English to meet individual students' needs. The two-way program separates the two languages for instruction without translation or repeated lessons in the other language. The SI courses do not offer translations and lessons are not repeated in the other language.
- The SI Spanish courses cover approximately 20% of the graduate program offerings with 80% of coursework offered in English. The two-way program recommends optional distribution of both languages. For example, in a 50–50 model, students receive half of their instruction in English and the other half in Spanish. A revision of the graduate program needs to be undertaken to match the two-way program language distribution options (Calderón & Minaya-Rowe, 2003).
- Both the SI Spanish courses and the two-way programs are additive; they add or reinforce a new language at no cost to the students' first language.
- Both the SI Spanish courses and the two-way programs need high-quality personnel, not only proficient in the language of instruction but in the content areas.

- Both the SI Spanish courses and the two-way programs use target language speakers as a resource in the classroom. Both groups receive accelerated instructional benefits from their other language peers and from the instructor's/teacher's use of cooperative learning group strategies to capitalize on this effect. Learning together increases student interest and motivation to learn (Calderón & Minaya-Rowe, 2003).

Approaches of this nature need to have an evaluation component built into it for professional development and program implementation and improvement purposes. The broad evaluation of the SI and SIOP approach would provide the means for determining whether it is meeting its goals and objectives (i.e., how on target it is by comparing achieved outcomes with intended ones; Holcomb, 1999; Worthen, Sanders, & Fitzpatrick, 1997). Teachers, administrators, students, and university professors can play an important role in all areas; everyone's involvement can strengthen the approach and instill a sense of ownership of the approach.

The following four evaluation steps have been adapted for the SI and SIOP approach evaluation, as proposed by Airisian (1997):

1. Specify the outcomes of the approach and their measurement. Decide what you are trying to achieve in professional development courses that intertwine L2 development, content-based instruction paired with reflection and communities of learners.
2. Specify and evaluate inputs and process. Identify the elements of the SI and SIOP courses that you plan to evaluate.
3. Construct a design. Set the standards and identify the principles behind a design that will yield valid and generalizable conclusions for the SI and SIOP approach.
4. Carry out the evaluation. The approach evaluator develops or obtains existing evaluation measures to administer, analyze, interpret, and report on the SI approach.

A fifth step would add the following:

5. Use the evaluation results to improve the approach implementation. For the SI and SIOP approach to continue offering quality and innovative courses of this nature, a process of ongoing feedback must be set in place.

REFERENCES

Airisian, P. (1997). *Classroom assessment* (2nd ed.). New York: McGraw-Hill.

Bernard, H. R. (1994). *Research methods in anthropology: Qualitative and quantitative approaches* (2nd ed.). Thousand Oaks, CA: Sage.

Calderón, M. E., & Minaya-Rowe, L. (2003). *Designing and implementing two-way bilingual programs. A step-by step guide for administrators, teachers and parents.* Thousand Oaks, CA: Corwin Press.

Collier, V. P. (1995). *Promoting academic success for ESL students: Understanding second language acquisition for school.* Elizabeth, NJ: New Jersey Teachers of English to Speakers of Other Languages-Bilingual Educators.

Cummins, J., & Fillmore, L. W. (2000). *Language and education: What every teacher (and administrator) needs to know* (Cassette Recording No. NABE00-FS10A). Dallas, TX: CopyCats.

Darling-Hammond, L., & Sykes, G. (Eds.). (1999). *Teaching as the learning profession: Handbook of policy and practice.* San Francisco: Jossey-Bass.

Echevarria, J., Vogt, M. E., & Short, D. J. (2000). *Making content comprehensible for English language learners: The SIOP model.* Needham Heights, MA: Allyn & Bacon.

Gay, G. (2004). The importance of multicultural education. *Educational Leadership, 61*(4), 30–35.

Genesee, F. (1999). *Program alternatives for linguistically diverse students.* Santa Cruz, CA: Center for Research in Education, Diversity, & Excellence.

Gravelle, M. (2000). *Planning for bilingual learners. An inclusive curriculum.* Arlington, VA. Stylus Publishing.

Holcomb, E. L. (1999). *Getting excited about data: How to combine people, passion, and proof.* Thousand Oaks, CA: Sage.

Joyce, B., & Showers, B. (2002). *Student achievement through staff development* (3rd ed.). White Plains, NY: Longman.

Krashen, S. D. (1989). We acquire vocabulary and spelling by reading: Additional evidence for the Input Hypothesis. *Modern Language Journal, 73,* 440–464.

Krashen, S. D., Candin, C. N., & Terrell, T. D. (1996). *The Natural Approach: Language acquisition in the classroom.* New York: Simon & Schuster International Group.

Ladson-Billings, G. (1999). Preparing teachers for diverse student populations: A critical race theory perspective. In A. Iran-Nejad & D. P. Pearson (Eds.), *Review of Research in Education, 24,* 211–247. Washington, DC: American Educational Research Association.

Menken, K., & Antúnez, B. (2001). *An overview of the preparation and certification of teachers working with low English proficiency students.* Washington, DC: National Clearinghouse for Bilingual Education.

Miles, M. B., & Huberman, A. M. (1994). *Qualitative data analysis: An expanded sourcebook* (2nd ed.). Thousand Oaks, CA: Sage.

Minaya-Rowe, L. (Ed.). (2002). *Teacher training and effective pedagogy in the context of student diversity.* Greenwich, CT: Information Age.

Moir, E., & Bloom, G. (2003). Fostering leadership through mentoring. *Educational Leadership, 60*(8), 58–61.

National Center for Education Statistics. (2003). *The Condition of Education. 2003.* Washington, DC: U.S. Department of Education, Institute of Education Sciences.

Nieto, S. (2003). What keeps teachers going. *Educational Leadership, 60*(8), 14–19.

Padrón, Y. N., & Waxman, H. C. (1999). Classroom observations of the Five Standards for Effective Teaching in urban classrooms with ELLs. *Teaching and Change, 7,* 79–100.

Peregoy, S. F., & Boyle, O. F. (2001). *Reading, writing, and learning in ESL* (3rd ed.). New York: Longman.

Pérez, B., & Torres-Guzmán, M. E. (2002). *Learning in two worlds. An integrated Spanish/English biliteracy approach* (2nd ed.). Boston: Allyn & Bacon.

Richard-Amato, P. A. (1996). *Making it happen: Interaction in the second language classroom.* White Plains, NY: Longman.

Rueda, R. (1998). *Standards for professional development: A sociocultural perspective.* Santa Cruz, CA: Center for Research in Education, Diversity, & Excellence.

Schifini, A. (2000). *Second language learning at its best. The stages of language acquisition.* Carmel, CA: Hampton Brown Publishers.

Scribner, J. P. (1999). Professional development: Untangling the influence of work context on teacher learning. *Educational Administration Quarterly, 35*(2), 238–266.

Shotter, J. (1997). *Talk of saying, showing, gesturing, and feeling in Wittgenstein and Vygotsky.* [Online]. Available: http://www.massey.sc.nz/~Alock/virtual/wittvyg.htm

Tharp, R. G. (1999). *Proofs and evidence: Effectiveness of the five standards for effective teaching.* Santa Cruz, CA: Center for Research in Education, Diversity, & Excellence.

Tharp, R. G., Estrada, P., Dalton, S. S., & Yamauchi, L. A. (2000). *Teaching transformed: Achieving excellence, fairness, inclusion, and harmony.* Boulder, CO: Westview Press.

Tharp, R. G., & Gallimore, R. (1988). *Rousing minds to life: Teaching, learning, and schooling in social context.* New York: Cambridge University Press.

Thomas, W. P., & Collier, V. P. (2003). The multiple benefits of dual language. *Educational Leadership, 61*(2), 61–64.

Vygotsky, L. S. (1978). *Mind in society: The development of higher psychological processes.* Cambridge, MA: Harvard University Press.

Vygotsky, L. S. (1986). *Thought and language.* Cambridge, MA: MIT Press.

Waxman, H. (2003, November). *Quality teachers for English language learners: The premise of the conference.* Opening session presented at the National Invitational Conference Improving Teacher Quality for English Language Learners, Arlington, VA.

Worthen, B. R., Sanders, J. R., & Fitzpatrick, J. L. (1997). *Program evaluation: Alternative approaches and practical guidelines* (2nd ed.). New York: Longman.

Chapter 3

Proposition 227 in California: Issues for the Preparation of Quality Teachers for Linguistically and Culturally Diverse Students

Eugene E. Garcia
Arizona State University

Tom Stritikus
University of Washington

As a typical teacher looks at the students in her classroom, she sees a picture quite different from the classroom of her childhood. Today 1 in 3 children nationwide is from an ethnic or racial minority group, 1 in 7 speaks a language other than English at home, and 1 in 15 was born outside the United States. The linguistic and cultural diversity of America's school population has increased dramatically during the past decade, and is expected to increase even more in the future. The concept of "minority" group will soon become obsolete as no group will be a majority (Garcia, 2001a).

Educating children from immigrant and ethnic minority group families is a major concern of school systems across the country. For many of these children, American education is not a successful experience. While one tenth of non-Hispanic White students leave school without a diploma, one fourth of African Americans, one third of Hispanics, one half of Native Americans, and two thirds of immigrant students drop out of school.

Confronted with this dismal reality, administrators, teachers, parents, and policymakers urge each other to do something different—change teaching methods, adopt new curricula, allocate more funding. Such actions might be needed, but will not be meaningful unless we begin to think differently about these students. In order to educate them, we must first educate ourselves about who they are and what they need to succeed. Thinking differently involves viewing these students in new ways that may contradict conventional notions, and coming to a new set of realizations.

The reality of teaching students that are culturally and linguistically diverse in the variety of schools and programs in which they reside is complex and perplexing. Following is a dramatic but real example of this challenge (Hull-Cortes, 2003):

> It is a warm June afternoon, and I am invited to sit in on a 2nd grade level meeting, the purpose of which is to "do the pink and blues," or to sort the current students into groups and assign them to teachers for the following school year. I enter the classroom to find six men and women seated on child-sized chairs around a low kidney shaped table, each studying their four by six inch, pink and blue cards. Several teachers hold their cards fanned out in their hands, others have them laid out neatly in columns and rows on the table in front of them. They are already well into their task of configuring the next years' 3rd grade classes. In front of them in the middle of the table is a hand written list, to which they refer as they create and negotiate their hands:
>
> third grade classes:
> EO/sheltered
> Mien IA/sheltered
> Cambodian/sheltered
> Fung
> EO/sheltered
> Viet/sheltered
>
> As I pull up a small red chair, one teacher says to the group: "I'll see you one Spanish girl, raise you one Mien boy." As she offers a pink card to the center of the table, she explains to me, "We first focus on language in making the decision—but the decision whether to put kids in bilingual classes is made by the parents." She motions to a large stack of cards at the opposite end of the table, mixed pink and blue, bound by rubber bands, separated from the others. These cards do not come into play, as they contain the names of the students designated by their parents and the school as "Spanish Bilinguals." This stack remains separate—isolated from the others—rubber bands in place.
>
> Someone else calls out, "Give me a girl." A pink card is then tossed into the center of the table. The teacher who discarded "the pink" from her hand leans toward the teacher seated next to him, and says, "She can read, but she's a problem though." The trading and configuring of cards continues in this way, as each teacher revises his or her stack, counting how many pinks and how many blues they are each accumulating. "Here's another EO," one teacher says as he discards a blue card with the name of an African-American student into the center of the table. Two of the other teachers explain to me that they "try to make even abilities in the classes" but that the task is challenging as "language trumps everything." (p. 7)

Historically, there has been much tension and political debate over the issue of how to best educate language minority children and, in turn, how to prepare professional educators to serve these same students. Although much has been written about different language education policies (Crawford, 1992; Gutierrez, Baquedano-Lopez, & Asato, 2000; Rumberger & Gándara, 2000; Stritikus, 2003) and best practices for language minority children in the classroom (August & Hakuta, 1997; Cummins, 2000; Garcia, 1999), very little attention has been devoted to the processes of how teachers are sorted into various programs or to the lives and academic outcomes of the actual students who are participating in these classrooms targeted at English language learners (ELLs). The research literature is also lacking in studies that explicitly explore the relationship between these two important areas of inquiry, and how they may inform each other.

Due to a variety of changes in educational demographic landscapes, such as urban demographics (Garcia, 2001a) and current bilingual education practices, elementary students are often identified, sorted, labeled, and subsequently grouped according to their home language background (see Rumberger & Gándara, 2000; Valdés, 1998). Teachers are also sorted regarding their specific training and experience to meet the demands of the students. In the name of providing bilingual education and/or "Structured English Immersion," students attending schools with much linguistic diversity may be placed in a classroom together with other students of their same ethnicity, year after year, in what we refer to as "language tracking." In some of these same schools, students of African-American descent and other English-speaking students are labeled as "EOs" (derived from speaking "English Only") and are either used as fillers in completing classrooms where there are not sufficient numbers of ELLs to fill a class, or are segregated out and taught separately from their peers of immigrant origins.

The schooling experience is a critical time for low-income, minority-status students as it is within this school context where one's identity and commitment to staying in school is either fostered and encouraged, or possibly discouraged, often depending on the school setting as a critical factor. It is this set of circumstances that suggest to us what realities must be addressed as we prepare teachers to succeed in such circumstances.

THESE ARE NOT THE STUDENTS WE EXPECTED TO TEACH

In contrast to racial, ethnic, and linguistic diversity among students, the vast majority of teachers and administrators are White and speak English as their native and only language. Many are experiencing the daunting personal and professional challenge in adapting in adulthood to a degree of diversity that did not exist during their childhood.

The average teacher and administrator in his 30s and 40s grew up in the 1950s and 1960s. People who were raised in the postwar period, before desegregation, were likely to have attended school with those of their own ethnic group. Not until young adulthood did they encounter the Civil Rights Movement and other expressions of ethnic presence on a national level. Nor did they experience the swift increases in diversity that has occurred recently. They and their parents grew up expecting a much different world than they now face. The parents and teachers of today's teacher grew up in the 1930s and the 1940s, after the period of massive immigration from Europe to the United States had ended. Today's senior teacher entered school at a time when the United States had a much larger proportion of foreign-born persons than today. But this diversity was perhaps not so evident because of segregated ethnic enclaves in housing and schooling and less widespread mass communications. And over the course of their lifetime, people now in their 70s experienced decreasing diversity. The melting pot ideology matched their own observations; the children of immigrants abandoned their native language and culture as they were urged to become 100% Americans.

But the 30-year period straddling the mid-century mark was an anomaly in our history. Until the 1930s, the story of the United States was a tale of immigration. The grandparents of today's teacher, who grew up in the early 1900s, and many of whom were immigrants themselves, experienced increasing ethnic and linguistic diversity during their formative years.

THE UNITED STATES HAS ALWAYS BEEN A MULTICULTURAL, MULTILINGUAL SOCIETY

To many Americans, the immigration movement that brought our ancestors to this country is a closed chapter, part of our national past. But from the perspective of the entire spectrum of American history, immigration has been the norm rather than the exception. Two generations of adults have grown up in a very unusual low-immigration period, an environment that has shaped our perceptions of our country. The new reality is that the America of 2000 will resemble the America of the 1900s more than the America of the 1950s. Today's kindergartners will experience increasing diversity over their lifetime, as the generation of their great-grandparents did.

From 1900 to 1910, nearly 9 million immigrants entered the United States, increasing the entire population by 10%. In the 1980s, about the same number of immigrants came to the United States, but they accounted for only a 4% increase in a now much larger U.S. population. In the early decades of this century, and back as far as 1850, as many as 1 in 7 people in the United States were foreign-born. The current rate of 1 in 13 is high only in comparison to the low-immigration decades of the 1950s and 1960s, when 1 in 20 Americans were foreign-born. By 2020, when today's kindergartners are in the workforce, the foreign-born population of the United States is again projected to reach 1 in 7 people.

Because the United States is so closely identified with the English language, many people assume that Anglo-Americans have always formed the majority group in U.S. society. But the 1990 census reveals that only 13% of Americans claim English ancestry. They are outnumbered by the 15% whose families originated in Ireland, many of whom did not speak English as a native language. An additional 5% identify their ancestry as "American"; many of these are Scottish-Americans whose families have been in the United States for 9 or 10 generations. Thus, at most, about one third of Americans trace their ancestry to the various cultures and languages of Great Britain.

Today, nearly 1 in 5 Americans live in households in which a language other than English is spoken. Half of these households are Spanish-speaking; the other more common languages are French, German, Italian, and Chinese. Educating students from immigrant families may seem like an entirely new challenge, but it is not; such students have always been in U.S. schools in large numbers. Throughout most of our history, 1 in 4 or 5 White Americans grew up in an immigrant family.

WHAT WORKED IN THE PAST MAY NOT WORK NOW

One mission of educators is to prepare young people for an occupational life. The economic environment in which today's students will seek employment has changed radically in the past few decades. Manufacturing jobs used to provide a good living for ethnic minority group members and for immigrants. Most jobs in the industrial sector did not require a high level of education, or academic competence in English.

But those jobs have disappeared. The new economy will require workers who have more than basic skills; employees must be able to think critically and engage in group decision making, communicate effectively orally and in writing, and be able to adapt to changing conditions by learning new skills. A larger proportion of jobs in the future will require the kind of educational preparation that has traditionally been provided to only the top students.

The American economy is now intertwined with the global marketplace; workers who can interact easily with people of different cultural and linguistic backgrounds will be prized. Even the domestic workplace that today's students will enter is changing as employees and customers are becoming more diverse. Business leaders are well aware that most of their new employees will be minorities and women. Observers of American business trends comment that many companies have gone beyond debating whether they need to change; they are now actively managing diversity. If one of the purposes of education is to train young people for productive work lives, then schools will need to prepare all students for employment in a more ethnically, culturally, and linguistically diverse occupational environment than in the past.

ONE SIZE DOESN'T FIT ALL STUDENTS

Students from immigrant families are often defined by the characteristics they share—a lack of English fluency. But such a definition masks their diversity, and underestimates the challenge facing schools. Schools serve students who are new immigrants, ignorant of American life beyond what they have seen in movies, as well as African Americans, Mexican Americans, Asian Americans, Native Americans, and European American students whose families have lived here for generations. Students representing dozens of native languages may attend a single school; in some school districts more than 125 languages are spoken by students. In many schools, a majority of the students come from immigrant or ethnic minority families. Some schools face a mobility problem; student turnover is high and the ethnic mix shifts radically from year to year.

Along with linguistic diversity comes diversity in culture, religion, and academic preparation. Some students visit their home country frequently, while others lack that opportunity. Some immigrant students have had excellent schooling in their home country before coming to the United States, others have had their schooling interrupted by war, and still others have never attended school. Some are illiterate in their own language, and some have languages that were only oral until recently; others come from cultures with long literary traditions.

The complexity of the task for schools can be illustrated by five hypothetical students from two families. Each of these students has very different needs. The Escalonas immigrated from Colombia and the Nguyens from Vietnam. All four parents work together on an electronics assembly line. The Escalonas are both college graduates, and taught high school math in their homeland. The Nguyens were farmers in their native country, and attended school through the fourth grade:

Maria Escalona—Eighth Grade. She had excellent schooling through the seventh grade in Colombia. The math and the science curriculum in her school was more advanced than in the U.S. system. She studied English in school for 3 years.

Raul Escolana—Fifth Grade. He had good prior schooling, but had not yet begun to study English. Because he is only 10, his academic mastery of Spanish is incomplete.

Teresita Escolana—Kindergarten. She attended preschool in Colombia, and knows the Spanish alphabet as well as songs, stories, numbers, shapes, and colors. Maria, Raul, and Teresita will have many language compatriots in their classes.

Binh Nguyen—Tenth Grade. He has good schooling through the seventh grade, but has attended school only sporadically in refugee camps since then.

Tui Nguyen—Third Grade. She has had no prior formal education. Taught by her brother, she can read and write a little Vietnamese. Binh and Tui have had little exposure to English. They will have a few classmates who speak their native language, but many whose native language is Spanish.

The differences between these students—their age and entry into U.S. schools, the quality of their prior schooling, their own and their parents/family/community native language and number of native language compatriots in their class, their parents' education and English language skills, and their family history and current circumstances—will affect their academic success much more than their common lack of English.

THEORIES OF TEACHING AND LEARNING AS A CRITICAL VARIABLE

For teachers, theories play a central role in guiding the intellectual work that they have chosen to perform. Teachers are guided by theories which they use to interpret, analyze, and take action in their professional worlds. In their practice, teachers are like other learners in the sense that they interpret new ideas and attempts to change their practice based on their existing understandings. The manner in which teachers modify new ideas is based upon their guiding extant theories about their profession and their students (Cohen & Barnes, 1993; Kennedy, 1991; Woods, 1994).

The importance of teachers' theories and world views has been highlighted by empirical research. In a recent study of effective teachers for language minority students, teachers reported that they have very well articulated theories of how children develop and learn, and the role education plays in such processes (Garcia, 1999). In short, whether we articulate them or not, we all have theories that guide us in making meaning of the world we live in.

Consequently, it is important to look more explicitly at conceptual frameworks—theories—which might help us understand the educational circumstances of language minority students and their teachers. This is particularly the case when a host of competing theories attempt to drive policy and practice for language minority students. Such is the case with California's Proposition 227 and its attempt to end bilingual education in that state. Specifically, we consider the following two questions: First, how might teachers' theories be complimented or contrasted by the underlying theoretical position of Proposition 227? Second, how do teachers' theories about their students mediate the manner in which they react and respond to policy shift away from native language instruction? To consider these questions, we examine the theoretical and policy-based positions currently competing to shape the nature of educational practice for language minority students. Then, to consider the empirical implications of these questions, we examine select findings from Walton Unified School District's implementation of Proposition 227. We use the experiences of three teachers from the small rural district to illustrate how teachers' theories regarding the needs of their students, bilingual education, and language maintenance influenced their reaction to Proposition 227. We conclude by considering what implications competitive structures have for the future of policy and practice for language minority students in the United States.

COMPETING THEORIES FOR THE EDUCATION OF LANGUAGE MINORITY STUDENTS

Proposition 227, known by its proponents as the "English for the Children Initiative," passed with a 61% majority of California voters on June 2, 1998. The initiative was an example of "people making law," written in response to apparent widespread discontent with the state's theories/policies regarding the education of non-English speaking children in public schools. Its intent was to inject more English instruction for these students in California's public schools. Some 25% of California's students currently fall into this student category and are referred to as Limited English proficient (LEP), English language learners (ELL), and/or as language minority students. The assumption which lay under the initiative was that teaching children in their native language served only to hold them back in their acquisition of English and therefore in their future educational success.

Immediately upon its passage, Proposition 227 became a part of the California Education Code (#300–340). As it required within its text, districts throughout the state were given only 60 days to implement it. Under this new education code, children entering California public schools with very little English must be "observed" for a period of 30 calendar days. After 30 days, school personnel must decide if children have enough fluency in English to manage in a mainstream English classroom. If not, they are eligible to receive 1 year of "Sheltered English Immersion," also referred to as "Structured English Immersion," a program of English language instruction not described in detail in the law except to require that instruction be "nearly all" in English (with a definition for the term *nearly all* left up to the district's discretion). After 1 year, children are normally expected to integrate into mainstream English classrooms, where instruction is required to be "overwhelmingly" in English (again, with a definition for the term *overwhelmingly* left up to the district's discretion). If parents or legal guardians find that district or school personnel, including classroom teachers, "willfully and repeatedly refuse" to provide the English instruction as required, they have the right to sue for damages. This aspect of the law has not yet been fully tested in the courts.

The only legal alternative to placing an ELL student in a Sheltered English Immersion or mainstream English classrooms is the utilization of the parental waiver process. According to the new law, children who have special language needs, or whose parents specifically request it, can be placed in "alternative programs," most likely some form of bilingual program which includes instruction in the child's primary language. In order for a child to be enrolled in such a program, the parent or guardian must visit the school annually and sign a waiver requesting the placement. However, the first year a child enters California schools she or he must go through 30 days of "observation," generally conducted in English language classrooms, even if the child has a signed waiver. Once the 30 days is completed, the child can enroll in an alternative program.

Along with the changes outlined earlier, the law allocates $50,000,000 per year to train adult English learners, parents or members of the community, to serve as tutors for children learning English. Finally, the new law is careful to state that if any conflicts are uncovered between its requirements and federal, state, or constitutional law, those conflicts are resolved by following the "higher authority" of that previous law.

There are some areas of the California State Board of Education's policy regarding the instruction of language minority children that were not at all affected by the passage of Proposition 227. Teacher credentialing has remained the same, as have the requirements regarding the assessment of LEP children in English and in their native language (Garcia, 2001a). It is still required by law that schools and districts communicate with language minority families in their primary language whenever necessary. Children who are identified as in need of Special Education and operate under an Individual Education Plan are not touched by the changes.

Proposition 227 and the Move Toward Subtractive Schooling

Proposition 227 certainly altered basic elements of policy toward language minority children in California's public schools. There had been a 20-year tradition, through legislative and executive actions, encouraging, even mandating bilingual education programs in California. In 1987, these laws officially sunset, leaving districts less clear on the mandate from the state. Nonetheless, even since 1987, there had been a climate of increasing openness toward bilingual programs and other special services for language minority students among California school districts. Although state level support of bilingual education existed, multiple districts and schools across the state had taken steps to limit or weaken bilingual education programs (Wong Fillmore, 1992).

Bilingual education is not, and never has been, a neutral process. The education of linguistically diverse students is situated in larger issues about immigration, distribution of wealth and power, and the empowerment of students (Cummins, 2000; Heller, 1994). Policy and practice questions are situated in debates surrounding the legitimacy of the language and culture of diverse groups (Olsen, 1997). The subtractive and additive frameworks advanced in this literature review offer a way to situate the nature of teacher theories, educational practice, and educational policy in these broader debates surrounding the place of culturally and linguistically diverse students in the United States—a debate intensified by the changes in the California Education Code brought about by the voter initiative Proposition 227 and its reversal of the state's official support of primary language instruction.

Garcia (1995, 2001b) and Garcia and Gonzalez (1995) serve as exemplars of the theoretical/policy/practice position that was overturned by Proposition 227. Imbedded in this additive perspective for language minority students is the understanding that language, culture, and their accompanying values, are constructed in the home and community environments, that children come to school with some constructed knowledge about many things, and that children's development and learning is best understood as the interaction of previous and present linguistic, sociocultural, and cognitive constructions. An appropriate perspective of teaching language minority students is one that recognizes that learning becomes enhanced when it occurs in contexts that are socioculturally, linguistically and cognitively meaningful for the learner (Garcia, 1995; Moll, 1994). Moreover, policies should reflect these conceptual underpinnings. It was the case that reauthorization of federal policy did exactly that, recognizing the importance of native language instruction and supporting those programs that were additive in nature (Garcia & Gonzalez, 1995; Wiese & Garcia, 2001). Table 3.1 exemplifies the attributes of schoolwide and teacher prac-

TABLE 3.1
Additive Conceptual Dimensions of Addressing Cultural and Linguistic Diversity

Schoolwide Practices
• A vision defined by the acceptance and valuing of diversity—Americanization is NOT the goal
• Professional development characterized by collaboration, flexibility and continuity with a focus on teaching, learning, and student achievement
• Elimination (gradual or immediate) of policies that seek to categorize diverse students thereby rendering their educational experiences as inferior or limiting for further academic learning
• Reflection of and connection to surrounding community—particularly with the families of the students attending the school
Teacher Practices
• Bilingual/bicultural skills and awareness
• High expectations of diverse students
• Treatment of diversity as an asset to the classroom
• Ongoing professional development on issues of cultural and linguistic diversity and practices that are most effective
• Basis of curriculum development to address cultural and linguistic diversity
• Attention to and integration of home culture/practices
• Focus on maximizing student interactions across categories of Spanish and English proficiency and academic performance
• Focus on language development through meaningful interactions and communications

tices associated with this conceptual framework. This is clearly contrasted with the conceptual framework that is at the foundation of Proposition 227: a disregard for non-English skills and circumstances outside of school and a focus on the instruction of English in English. Table 3.2 articulates the schoolwide practices and teacher practices following from this conceptual framework. The distinction between additive and subtractive conceptions of cultural and linguistic diversity is not meant to be a strict dichotomy of policies and practices, but rather a framework for understanding the range of possible educational alternatives which exist for cultural and linguistically diverse students. The subtractive position advanced by Proposition 227—as summarized by the practices embodied in Table 3.2—is contrasted by multiculturalist and multilingualist notions that English-only instruction is deeply problematic. Rather than view the home language and culture through a lens of deficit, multiculturalist and additive perspectives urge schools to see these as valuable educational resources (Banks, 1995; Garcia, 1999; Gutiérrez et al., 2000; Olneck, 1995). Proposition 227 presents a direct challenge to the notion that languages other than English have a legitimate and valuable place in the education of diverse students. Hence, the

TABLE 3.2
Subtractive Conceptual Dimensions of Addressing Cultural and Linguistic Diversity

Schoolwide Practices
• A vision defined by the learning of English—Americanization/assimilation is the goal • Professional development characterized by a focus on direct teaching, emphasizing instruction of phonology, grammar, and phonics in reading • Elimination (gradual or immediate) of policies that seek to provide special instruction to a category of students marked by their non-English proficiency • Connection to surrounding community—particularly with the families of the students attending the school emphasizing the development and use of English
Teacher Practices
• English development skills and awareness • Expectations that English proficiency by students will enhance academic achievement • Treatment of linguistic diversity as a characteristic that must be minimized • Ongoing professional development and direct enforcement of direct teaching practices • Basis of curriculum development to address cultural and linguistic assimilation • Attention to and integration of diverse cultures into the "norm" • Focus on maximizing student academic English development as assessed by English language development and academic testing—in many cases, "high stakes" testing • Focus on English language, reading and literacy development through methods of direct instructions of skills

normative assumptions underlying Proposition 227 position the language and culture of diverse students in a subordinate and inferior role to English (Auerbach, 1995; Cummins, 2000; Kerper-Mora, 2000).

These normative assumptions have important consequences that extend beyond the classroom. The nature of the law works to position certain groups in a peripheral role in American society. Sekhon (1999), in an article assessing the legal and political implications of the proposition, argued that Proposition 227 positions immigrants on the outside of mainstream America:

> Proposition 227 positions English as "our" language by constructing it as our unlearned capacity: It is our birthright. The proposition differentiates "us" from "them" by denominating them in terms of an essential inability to call English their own. They must learn it. Proposition 227 not only demands that they learn our language, it demands that they forget their own. In so demanding, the proposition not only unleashes a salvo in the bilingual education debate, but is a crucial moment in the broader debate over assimilation and acculturation. (p. 1445)

Thus, in its scope, focus, and ideological implications, Proposition 227 differs markedly from past educational reforms. Teachers were not only told to shift educational practice, but forced to participate in an evolving debate about which theory would hold prominence in the education of language minority students. The distinction between additive and subtractive conceptions becomes a useful device for probing teachers' existing theories regarding their students, and how those theories interacted with district and school decisions regarding Proposition 227 to establish a context for classroom practice.

COMPETING THEORIES IN ACTION: A DISTRICT'S RESPONSES TO 227

To understand how competing theories regarding the education of language minority students materialize into action, we examine select findings from one district's implementation of Proposition 227. Focusing on the responses of three teachers in the district, an examination of how additive and subtractive theories influenced and shaped the nature of Proposition 227 implementation is conducted.

Walton Unified School District

Despite its attempt to prescribe a very uniform solution for the education of linguistically and culturally diverse students across the state of California, the law's impact on education of ELL students has varied widely from district to district, school to school, and in some cases classroom to classroom. Garcia and Curry-Rodriguez (2000) and Gandara et al. (2000) report that certain districts across the state have used the waiver clause of the law to pursue district wide waivers, others have implemented the English Only provisions of the law, and a third group has left the primary decisions up to individual schools. The implementation decisions made by "Westway" and "Open Valley," the two elementary schools which are the focus of this research, represent a microcosm of what occurred across the state.[1] Each school took actions based upon "competing ideologies" about how schools should respond to the challenge of linguistic and cultural diversity.

Walton Unified School District devised a plan that maximized flexibility for Westway and Open Valley. Under the plan, the schools could choose between maintaining their bilingual programs through the parental waiver process, or, developing a program for ELL students called "English Language Development" (ELD).

At Westway Elementary, all students who had been in bilingual programs were placed in self-contained ELD classes. The context for Proposition 227 implementation at Westway Elementary was shaped by the school's positive

[1]All names of people and places are pseudonyms.

orientation toward English-only instruction and curricular control arrangements. The decision to shift to English-only was made by the school's veteran principal, Beverly Elmherst, who in the past had tended away from hiring certified bilingual teachers. Consequently, the school had only three teachers who held the Bilingual Crosscultural Language and Academic Development (BLCAD) certificate. This hiring pattern meant there were very few strong advocates for maintaining the school's program.

The school's movement away from primary language use coincided with the state-wide decade-long movement toward phonics-based reading instruction and away from meaning-based or whole language instruction. A series of laws passed throughout the 1990s culminated in the California Reading Initiative (CRI), a collaborative effort between the state legislature, the Governor, and the California Department of Education. The new policy advocates a *balanced* approach to literacy instruction. It defines balanced literacy instruction with a definitive nod toward decoding and direct phonics instruction:

> A balanced approach involves considerable time and effort dedicated to basic decoding while attention is given to important meaning-based aspects of reading. For most students, however, intensive direct teaching of phonemic awareness, sound-symbol relationships, blending skills, and reading fluency is of primary importance. (CRI, 1996, p. 4)

The changes in literacy policy have positioned phonics and phonemic awareness as the primary concerns for early literacy instruction.

Consistent with the move on the state level toward phonics-based instruction, in February of 1998, the school adopted Open Court Collections for Young Scholars (hereafter, Open Court) as the schoolwide language arts series. Open Court uses explicit teacher-directed instruction to teach phonemic awareness, phonics, and reading comprehension. During the instructional components of the program, which include teacher-directed writing and reading exercises, and skills practice drills, teachers use scripts for all teacher questions, prompts, and responses. During blending, a centerpiece of the program, teachers read all sounds of a word and have students repeat them. Reading and writing activities are tightly controlled by the teacher.

Whereas the schoolwide context at Westway was characterized by a lack of curricular freedom and a climate favorable to English-only, the local school context at Open Valley was quite different. First, the overall climate of the school showed an overwhelming commitment to the goals of bilingual and multicultural education. Second, teachers at Open Valley experienced a great deal of curricular freedom. In the fall of 1999, the teachers at the school mobilized to secure parental waivers in order to maintain the school's bilingual program. Nearly every child who was in a bilingual program prior to the proposition was in a bilingual program in the fall of 1999. To avoid a second year of the waiver process in the spring of 1999, the teachers and administration of Open Valley applied for and received Charter status. Under California law, Charter status gave the school curricular flexibility and freedom from the direct mandates of Proposition 227.

TEACHERS

The research on the implementation of Proposition 227 focused on four teachers—two at both Open Valley and Westway. At Open Valley, the research focused on two teachers, Elisa and Angelica.

Angelica, a fifth-year teacher, came to teaching through her involvement in a migrant education program as an undergraduate. Although she was only in her late-20s, she had taught Sunday School for 12 years. She credited her experience with the migrant education program and her work in Sunday School as having a large influence on her teaching. She was born in Mexico, but attended school in California when her parents immigrated. During the year of the study, Angelica taught a second-grade bilingual class of approximately 18 students. The second-grade students in her class received language arts and math instruction in Spanish. Instruction in the afternoon, which included art, ESL, and social studies, occurred in English.

Born in Mexico, Elisa was educated in California and grew up in the Central Valley. She had been a teacher for 4 years—all of them at Open Valley and each in a different grade. During the 1999–2000 academic year, Elisa taught a third-grade bilingual classroom of approximately 14 to 20 students. Elisa's decision to enter teaching was closely related to her experiences as a child. She had worked in the fields of the Central Valley, and felt that experience helped her to identify with the instructional and social needs of her immigrant students.

Two teachers, Celia and Connie, were the focus of the research at Westway, but in this chapter we present findings only related to Connie. We have chosen to focus on Connie to examine the manner in which existing deficit orientations in teachers interact with a subtractive policy context. Additionally, Celia's rather complex and multifaceted reaction to Proposition 227 implementation has been examined in another article (Stritikus, 2003).

Connie, a Portuguese-American with 11 years of teaching experience, had always been assigned a bilingual classroom but never remembers requesting to be a bilingual teacher. Because the structure of the bilingual program prior to Proposition 227 placed native language instructional responsibility in the hands of teaching aides, Connie never worked directly with her immigrant students in the area of primary language instruction.

During the study, Connie taught a third-grade, self-contained *English Language Development* class of 20 students.

FINDINGS

The manner in which the two teachers responded and reacted to Proposition 227 is illustrative of the way that subtractive and additive theories compete to shape the nature of the policy to practice connection. In large part, teachers' guiding theories about their students influenced the way they mediated and negotiated the policy shifts brought about by changes in bilingual education policy. In the following sections, we explore the connection between classroom practice and policy shifts by examining the role that teachers' theories played in the process. We highlight how aspects of a subtractive policy context brought certain aspects of teachers' additive or subtractive theories to the surface in their decision-making process.

Teachers' Theories in Programs That Retained Bilingual Education

For Elisa, a guiding theory drove her intellectual work at the school. She believed that native language instruction provided significant academic, cognitive, social, and cultural benefits for her students. For her, the academic and cultural benefits of bilingualism were inextricably linked and strengthened her resolve and commitment to bilingual education. She described her theory on the manner in which language minority students could most attain academic success:

> Yes, it is hard to remain a bilingual. But, if you don't give students a base—the foundation that the child needs to use against the second language—success in the second language is not going to happen. Basically, we are all here in this America. And, we do all need to speak the language of this country, but that doesn't mean that we have to let go of our language. (Interview, May, 2000)

For Elisa, academic success and participation in American society did not mean that students had to sacrifice elements of their social and cultural identities. For her, these identities served as the basis for student success. She believed that Proposition 227, and its supporters, were asking Latino student to leave crucial elements of their culture and language behind. She saw her role as a teacher to ensure that this didn't happen at Open Valley.

In addition, Elisa saw the use of native language instruction as a direct part of a strategy of the advancement of Latino students. The genesis of this theory was related to her own experiences as a migrant farm worker:

> The sun was coming out at five o'clock in the morning. I was there alone. There was nobody in the field. I was just left there and I was waiting for the people to get there. I was maybe fourteen or fifteen. I kept thinking: What I am going to do? I didn't want to work in the fields for the rest of my life. That's actually what brought me up wanting to teach. It's like: I want to do something productive for my people—for the kids and parents who work in the fields because I saw how hard they work and they really didn't make any money. So, I wanted to make a difference. That's why I became a bilingual teacher. (Interview, April, 2000)

This teacher's guiding theory saw bilingualism as a social and academic resource and viewed tapping into students' existing linguistic capacity as the best way to ensure their academic success. The teachers possessed theories which allowed for students to be multilingual and still play valuable and meaningful roles in U.S. society. This theory had its roots in personal experiences and the benefits of bilingualism they had gained as well as hardship they experienced in schools that did not value their linguistic diversity.

FROM THEORY TO ACTION: TEACHING IN A BILINGUAL SCHOOL

For Elisa, theories about language minority students led to particular types of responses to policy shifts. Elisa became a very vocal proponent for bilingual education after the passage of Proposition 227. She used her standing in the school to rally support for the school's bilingual program and helped secure the parental waivers necessary to continue bilingual education at the school. In practice, she used native language instruction in real and substantial ways in her classroom, which included assessments done in English and Spanish. She was clear to comment that Proposition 227 had renewed her commitment to bilingual education. She continually looked for opportunities to defend the school's program and petitioned the district for resources related to bilingual education.

For Elisa, her renewed commitment was directly related to the manner in which she saw language use in her classroom:

> Creo que me hizo un poco mas rebelde [I think it has made me a bit more rebellious] about using Spanish. Before I was like I shouldn't speak in Spanish, because we are being asked to move away from bilingual education. But, now, I don't feel that way. (Interview, April, 2000)

Her commentary illustrates the manner in which the subtractive policy context brought certain elements of teachers' theories to the surface as they negotiated aspects of Proposition 227.

To understand the manner in which teachers' theories serve to mediate their responses to policy shifts, we outline data from the first day of English-guiding reading groups in Elisa's third-grade classroom. The event illustrates her attempt to create an additive context for learning in her classroom. Elisa commented that the debate over Proposition 227 had made her more committed to making sure that her the students saw their home language as a resource. The nature of teacher and student interaction on the first day of English-guided reading was very telling. The message of the exchange was clear: "If you can do it in Spanish, you can do it English." Students were eager participants in these types of conversations and shared stories about bilingual relatives or about community members who spoke English and Spanish fluently.

Elisa's decision to establish an instructional context in which Spanish was presented to the students as a direct way to make sense of English also had important consequences in terms of the way students approached learning tasks in the guided reading group. During the interaction of this group, the students eagerly explored the new ways they would be able to use English. Her framing of learning English as an activity created a sense of excited energy for the students. This excitement surfaced as the students discussed what they would one day be able to do with English. Daniel proclaims that he "will know the words that he has to know to respond [to questions]." And, Betty, unsolicited, offers her English knowledge to the group suggesting that Elisa substitute "the tree" for the Spanish word "arbol." Elisa created an additive context in which she encouraged students to capitalize on their existing linguistic resources during their acquisition of English. The context established by Elisa made it clear to the students that Spanish was viewed as a language-learning resource by their teacher. Because the focus of the study was to understand teachers' conceptions of bilingualism, we can not with certainty claim that this additive conception had a direct impact on students' conceptions of their own bilingualism. For Elisa, however, her additive conceptions of bilingualism had influenced the manner in which she reacted to the subtractive policy context created by Proposition 227.

SUBTRACTIVE THEORIES OF EDUCATION FOR LANGUAGE MINORITY STUDENTS

To understand the connection between subtractive theories for language minority students and classroom practice, we present the case of Connie, a third-grade teacher at Westway Elementary. Connie's case is illustrative of how teachers' existing subtractive theories materialize in classroom practice. Her case is instructive because her theory regarding the education of language minority students mirrored the theories of many school and district leaders who eliminated their bilingual education programs after the passage of Proposition 227 (Garcia & Curry-Rodriguez, 2000). Proposition 227 did not *cause* her subtractive orientation but rather *reinforced* it and gave her new opportunities to act upon it.

Connie's theories surrounding her students were undergirded by two major beliefs about the education of language minority students. First, she believed that the English language served as a unifying force in the United States that was undermined by multilingualism. In this sense, Connie was in striking agreement with much of the political discourse surrounding both the English-only and antibilingual education movements. In an interview, Connie commented, "I totally agree that English should be *the* language of this country. You need to have some base and I think English needs to be the base here." A child of Portuguese immigrants, Connie resented the "special treatment" that she felt Latino children and families received. She viewed bilingual education as one such special treatment.

Second, Connie believed that her students' academic progress was severely limited by their use of Spanish. Thus, rather than seeing students' primary language as a resource, she saw it as one their primary weaknesses:

> My students' problem is that they rely too much on their Spanish. I know a lot of them came from second-grade classes where they spoke Spanish all the time to the teacher. It makes a big difference. My goal is that they learn as much vocabulary as they can, learn to speak grammatically correct, and have their adjectives and nouns in the right places. (Interview, December, 1999)

Connie felt that the students' use of Spanish interfered with their acquisition of English. This subtractive theory differs shapely with the important theoretical work done in the area of second language acquisition stressing the transfer of academic and cognitive skills independent of language (Cummins, 1979).

FROM SUBTRACTIVE THEORY TO SUBTRACTIVE PRACTICE

Connie's theory about language minority students resulted in a particular kind of educational practice which did not focus on the cultural, social, and linguistic resources brought by her students. Watered-down and deficit-based literacy practice in the new policy environment reflected Connie's instructional goals and expectations for her students (Gersten & Woodward,

1992). A significant amount of instructional time focused on phonetic exactness—moments in instruction when Connie focused on the components and sounds of words. During these interactions Connie's emphasis was on correct pronunciation and strict adherence to following directions. Coding of literacy events revealed that Connie's literacy practice centered on the following types of interactions:

- *Word Meaning.* Connie asked the students about the meaning of an individual word. She used the word in a sentence until the students could supply a synonym.
- *Conventions.* Connie asked the students about the punctuation of a particular sentence, or she asked students to identify words that were particular parts of speech in the text.
- *Phonetic Exactness.* Connie worked with the students to ensure the proper pronunciation of English words and phonemes.

Her emphasis on these three types of interactions was influenced by the nature of the Open Court program and its literacy material. During teacher-run reading events, Connie seldom asked questions regarding the story events or the plot. Connie often asked students to identify compound words or to circle long vowels. Such interaction contributed to the treatment of text as a puzzle. Texts were viewed as little more than the sum total of their phonetic or grammatical values. During literacy instruction, Connie closely adhered to the script of the Open Court teacher's manual. Open Court activities dominated her instructional day. Beyond the 40 minutes that Connie spent in math instruction, the entire day was occupied with Open Court literacy activities.

The following literacy event, highlights the nature of literacy instruction in Connie's classroom and the manner that Connie's beliefs about her students, which were in large part influenced by her own familiar experience, seemed to influence the enactment of such literacy practice.

> Connie stood at the front of the class and had just read the first problem of the worksheet. She instructed students that they were supposed to circle each long vowel sound in each of the sentences and write the word in the long vowel column. This was the third in a series of worksheets the class had done that day. Connie completed the first three sentences with the students. In each sentence, her pattern was fairly consistent. She read the sentence and asked the students which words in the sentence had a long vowel sound. Students were not allowed to pick up their pencils until the class had identified all the long vowel sounds. During the first three sentences, a few student called answers without being officially recognized. When this happened on the 4th sentence, Connie said, "Since you seem to have no problem with this activity you can do it on your own."

Ruben and Miguel, who were seated on the opposite side of the room from where I was, excitedly rubbed their hands together. I got up from my seat and sat behind Miguel, a child who always seemed to have a smile on his face.

Miguel: (Reading number 5) (Reads in a flat tone with no questioning intonation.) Will Pat go to the store. (Pauses for a moment) Will Pat **go to** the store. (Flat intonation). Will Pat . . . Pat go to the store? (An almost raised but unnatural intonation on store). [He raises his head from the text]. That doesn't make any sense. (almost smugly) Don't matter. [He picks up his pencil and writes the words "go" and "store" in the Long O column.]

This literacy event highlighted many of the themes which emerged from the study in Connie's classroom. Classroom instruction focused on the component parts of reading. Connie's comfort with this focus was related to her views about the instructional needs of her students. The event also highlighted the tightly controlled nature of literacy events. In the activity—as was the case with many others—students were allowed to do the work independently only as a form of punishment. Lastly, the event indicated the nature of students' experiences of literacy curriculum which stressed skills over meaning.

Connie believed that her students would experience success if they stopped speaking Spanish in the classroom. During grade level teacher meetings, Connie voiced this position. Her comments generally related to "deficits" in the students (Lipman, 1998). Although it is highly likely that Connie's deficit perspectives of her students existed prior to Proposition 227, she noted that Proposition 227 had allowed her to act on her beliefs about the needs of her students in ways that she had not been able to. Because she was convinced that several issues outside the realm of her classroom contributed to the academic failure of the students, she took no actions to the change the programmatic and curricular actions at the school.

Connie's ideological alignment with the law and her views about her students played a large role in the connection between policy and practice in her classroom. The following literacy exchange taken from a field note entry occurred early in the year and was indicative of her priorities and perceptions:

Connie told the class that she wants them to work on their reading comprehension, and that to do so they are going to read stories on worksheets that will help them understand other stories better. Connie told the students to place their fingers under the first word and called on individual students to read a story about a snow flake. The story was a part of the first-grade skills practice of Open Court. She called on Sonia, who struggles to read the first sentence of the eight-sentence story.

Connie said, "OK, Sonia, since Luis is ready to read I am going to give him a chance." Luis, a recent immigrant in the class with very strong decoding skills

> did not understand Connie's request as a request to read because he wasn't called on directly. He stared at Sonia and then turned his gaze back to the teacher. Connie nodded at him, and he still looked confused. A student sitting next to him said in a quiet voice, "Tienes que leerlo" [You have to read it]. Connie clinches her fist, "Ugh," she said with great exasperation, "Don't say it in Spanish!" (October 21, 2000).

The event which was similar to many literacy events in Connie's classrooms speaks to two beliefs that guided her approach to classroom literacy instruction: Spanish was a detriment to her students' academic progress; and what her students needed most were the "basics." Connie's interaction with the local school context influenced the way these beliefs surfaced in her classroom literacy practice. She noted that the move to English-only made her feel more comfortable in stopping her students from speaking Spanish in the classroom.

For Connie, Proposition 227 offered an opportunity to enact a subtractive version of language and literacy practice in her classroom. Literacy instruction in her classroom was heavily influenced by her theories about her students and their bilingualism. Proposition 227 and its subtractive implications for the schooling of culturally and linguistically diverse students complemented Connie's existing views of her students and gave her liberty to attempt to restrict and limit students' use of Spanish in her classroom. Although we do not claim that Connie's use of the Open Court literacy series is representative of all uses of the program, her case illustrates how teachers with subtractive theories of their students might utilize and implement aspects of similar skills-based scripted literacy programs.

CONCLUSION

California has begun a weighty experiment in the instruction of language minority students based on subtractive theories of education. The underlying theory of Proposition 227 suggests that linguistic diversity is a problem in need of correction, and instruction exclusively in English provides the best therapy for such deficiencies. Such a theory of instruction suggests that the primary role of schooling is Americanization.

Proposition 227 is not just a theory, but one of the dominating policy voices in California and the nation guiding the schooling of linguistically diverse students. Given that teachers will continue to be the last line of implementation in this growing policy trend, it is important to consider various aspects of the roles they play. In this chapter, we have chosen to focus on the role that teachers' existing theories about their students play in the way they reacted to aspects of Proposition 227. To understand the range of teachers' theories, we have presented distinctions between additive and subtractive conceptions of language minority students.

The distinction between additive and subtractive conceptions of schooling for culturally and linguistically diverse students are a useful tool for understanding how teachers' existing theories were complemented or contrasted by Proposition 227 implementation. For Elisa, Proposition 227 served to strengthen her commitments to bilingual education. These renewed commitments were evident in the manner in which she framed their classroom practice in relation to Proposition 227. Elisa asserted that Proposition 227 made her more determined to use students' primary language as a resource; and compared Proposition 227 to getting knocked down in a soccer game:

> Proposition 227 really pushed the people that did believe in continuing fighting for our dream. It's like a soccer game; you didn't make the goal. Oh, well. You have a chance of getting up and trying again. Soccer players fall many times during a game. They trip over each other. We can trip over these polices and fall over these laws. You can trip me, and I'll fall, but I'm going to get up again. I'll keep going. When things like Proposition 227 happen, just don't trip, fall, and stay laying down. (Interview, May, 2000)

She saw Proposition 227 as one major impediment to enacting an additive conception of education, but she saw it as a challenge she could and would overcome.

For Connie, her subtractive conceptions of her students were complimented by the political and pedagogical implications of Proposition 227. In many senses, the subtractive policy context served to clarify her pedagogical purpose. As she interacted with the local policy context, the result was an enactment of practice which was a direct match of the intent of the new law. As her students became more resistant and distant based on their experience of Open Court, she became more convinced that her students needed more "basic" instruction. As her experience as part of family that "made it" without any special programs influenced her views of the policy, she become more convinced that any Spanish usage in her class was detrimental to student learning. She enacted punitive rules for students who used Spanish and noted that Proposition 227 had given her the feeling that this was a proper course of action to take.

The importance of teachers' theories and beliefs has been supported by Wiese's (2001) examinations of a policy and practice at a dual language immersion school after the passage of Proposition 227. She found that the manner in which Federal and State educational policy is reconstructed at school level was highly influenced by teachers' theories about their students, instruction, and the world around them.

Seeking the day when all language minority students will conclude that what they do in their classrooms does matter, we suggest that the theories that teachers hold about their students and instruction play a monumental role in the face of educational polices designed to lead to specific practices. Theories can bolster the intent of the policy, as was the case with Connie, or theories can provide teachers with a powerful basis to resist and reshape the intended consequences of certain policies as was the case with Elisa. If teachers are to capitalize on the linguistic, cognitive, and cultural resources which language minority students bring to the classroom, then those concerned with education must continue to pursue and develop substantial ways to support and develop additive conceptions of linguistic diversity in teachers. This will be the case in Arizona and Massachusetts, where propositions like California's 227 are being implemented, as well as nationally, as public schools address the mandates of No Child Left Behind and the determination of "highly qualified teachers."

REFERENCES

August, D., & Hakuta, K. (1997). *Improving schooling for language-minority children: A research, policy and practice.* Chicago: Charles C. Thomas.

Auerbach, E. (1995). The politics of the ESL classroom: Issues of power in pedagogical choices. In J. Tollefson (Ed.), *Power and inequality in language education* (pp. 9–33). New York: Cambridge University Press.

Banks, J. (1995). Multicultural education: Historical development, dimensions, and practice. In J. A. Banks & C. A. McGee-Banks (Eds.), *Handbook of research on multicultural education* (pp. 3–34). New York: Macmillan.

California Reading Initiative. (1996). Sacramento: California Department of Education.

Cohen, D. K., & Barnes, C. A. (1993). Pedagogy and policy. In D. K. Cohen, M. W. McLaughlin, & J. E. Talbert (Eds.), *Teaching for understanding; Issues for policy and practice* (pp. 207–239). San Francisco, CA: Jossey-Bass.

Crawford, J. (1992). *Hold your tongue: Bilingualism and the politics of "English only."* Reading, MA: Addison-Wesley.

Cummins, J. (1979). Linguistic interdependence and the educational development of bilingual children. *Review of Educational Research, 34,* 46–49.

Cummins, J. (2000). *Language, power and pedagogy: Bilingual children in the crossfire.* Great Britain: Multilingual Matters.

Gandara, P., Maxwell-Jolly, J., Garcia, E., Asato, J., Gutierrez, K., Stritikus, T., & Curry-Rodriguez, J. (2000). *The initial impact of Proposition 227 on the instruction of English learners* [Online]. Available at www.uclmrinte.ucsb.edu

Garcia, E. (1995). Educating Mexican American students: Past treatments and recent developments in theory, research, policy, and practice. In J. Banks & C. A. McGee-Banks (Eds.), *Handbook of research on multicultural education* (pp. 372–426). New York: Macmillan.

Garcia, E. (1999). *Understanding and meeting the challenge of student cultural diversity* (1st ed.). Boston, MA: Houghton Mifflin.

Garcia, E. (2001a). *Hispanics education in the United States: Raices y alas.* Lanham, MD: Rowman & Littlefield.

Garcia, E. (2001b). *Understanding and meeting the challenge of student diversity* (3rd ed.). Boston, MA: Houghton Mifflin.

Garcia, E., & Curry-Rodriguez, J. E. (2000). The education of limited English proficient students in California schools: An assessment of the influence of Proposition 227 in selected districts and schools. *Bilingual Research Journal, 24*(1–2), 15–36.

Garcia, E., & Gonzalez, G. (1995). Issues in systemic reform for culturally and linguistically diverse students. *College Record, 96*(3), 418–431.

Gersten, R. M., & Woodward, J. (1992). The quest to translate research into classroom practice: Strategies for assisting classroom teachers' work with "at risk" students and students with disabilities. In D. Carnine & E. Kameenui (Eds.), *Higher cognitive functioning for all students* (pp. 201–218). Austin: Pro-Ed.

Gutierrez, K., Baquedano-Lopez, P., & Asato, J. (2000). "English for the Children"; The new literacy of the old world order, language policy and educational reform. *The Bilingual Research Journal, 24*(1 & 2), 87–105.

Heller, M. (1994). *Crosswords: Language education and ethnicity in French Ontario.* Berlin and New York: Mouton de Gruyter.

Hull Cortes, K. (2004, May). *I'll see you one Spanish girl, raise you one Mien boy: The sorting mechanisms at work in an urban elementary school.* Paper presented at the University of California Language Minority Institute Conference, Santa Barbara, CA.

Kennedy, M. (1991). *An agenda for research on teacher learning.* East Lansing, MI: Michigan State University, National Center for Research on Teacher Learning.

Kerper-Mora, J. (2000). Policy shifts in language-minority education: A mismatch between politics and pedagogy. *The Educational Forum, 64,* 204–214.

Lipman, P. (1998). *Race, class, and power in school restructuring.* Albany, NY: SUNY Press.

Moll, L. C. (1994). *Vygotsky and education: Instructional implications and applications of sociohistorical psychology.* Cambridge, England: Cambridge University Press.

Olneck, M. R. (1995). Immigrants and education. In J. A. Banks & C. A. McGee-Banks (Eds.), *Handbook of research on multicultural education* (pp. 310–327). New York: Macmillan.

Olsen, L. (1997). *Made in America: Immigrant students in our public schools.* New York: The New York Press.

Rumberger, R., & Gándara, P. (2003). Has Proposition 227 reduced the English learner achievement gap? *UCLMRI Newsletter, 13*(1), 1–2.

Sekhon, N. (1999). A birthright rearticulated: The politics of bilingual education. *The New York University Law Review, 74*(5), 1407–1445.

Stritikus, T. (2003). The interrelationship of beliefs, context, and learning: The case of a teacher reacting to language policy. *Journal of Language, Identity, and Education, 2*(1), 29–52.

Valdés, G. (1998). The world outside and inside schools: Language and immigrant children. *Educational Research, 27*(6), 4–18.

Wiese, A. M. (2001). *"To meet the needs of the kids, not the program": Teachers constructing policy, program, and practice in a bilingual school.* Unpublished doctoral dissertation, University of California, Berkeley.

Wiese, A., & Garcia, E. (2001). The Bilingual Education Act: Language minority students and equal educational opportunity. *Bilingual Research Journal, 22*(1), 1–6.

Wong Fillmore, L. (1992). Against our best interests: The attempt to sabotage bilingual education. In J. Crawford (Ed.), *Language loyalties: A source book of the official English controversy.* Chicago: University of Chicago Press.

Woods, P. (1994). Adaptation and self-determination in English primary schools. *Oxford Review of Education, 20*(4).

Chapter 4

Lessons Learned From a Research Synthesis on the Effects of Teachers' Professional Development on Culturally Diverse Students

Stephanie L. Knight
Texas A&M University

Donna L. Wiseman
University of Maryland

Recent research in Tennessee and Texas (see e.g., Haycock, 1998) focuses our attention on the teacher as the key to student learning. Although we have a fairly substantial knowledge of what constitutes teacher effectiveness for certain kinds of outcomes and certain groups of students (see e.g., Good & Brophy, 2000), we have not yet determined how best to increase the effectiveness of teachers. The challenge intensifies in settings populated by teachers who may have been prepared for very different kinds of children, families, and classrooms than they encounter in classrooms today. Because quality of teaching makes a difference in student performance (Haycock, 2003), this chapter focuses on teacher professional development that makes a difference in the performance of students from traditionally underrepresented populations, particularly those from diverse cultural and linguistic groups. More specifically, the chapter reviews the status of research on professional development for teachers of diverse students and summarizes selected findings from a recent synthesis of research on that topic (see Knight & Wiseman, in press).

THE CONTEXT OF PROFESSIONAL DEVELOPMENT FOR DIVERSITY

The most recent census substantiates the demographic trends that teachers and administrators have noted in their schools and districts: The U.S. population is becoming increasingly diverse and this trend is particularly noticeable in PreK–12 classrooms. Although these statistics appear in various forms in almost any text that focuses on improvement of education of any type, they provide an important aspect of the rationale for the focus on professional development of teachers targeted in this review. Unlike classrooms of recent generations, one third of the elementary and secondary school population can claim racial or ethnic minority status and a third of these students are considered to have limited English proficiency.

Factors related to poverty, educational attainment, and low achievement have created a gap between Hispanics and their White, Asian, and African-American peers (Padron, Waxman, & Rivera, 2002). Statistics representing Hispanic students' school performance indicate the complex nature of the problem. In general, Hispanic students score considerably below Whites on national tests, drop out of school at a higher rate, and attend college at a lower rate than their peers in other ethnic groups. Furthermore, they are more likely to live in poverty and attend high-poverty urban schools with the most severe educational problems (Garcia, 1994). Differences in language background and literacy attainment, in Spanish as well as English, further confound the problem. Almost half of all Hispanics live in urban areas, presenting additional problems related to meeting their linguistic needs. These conditions are of concern as Hispanic students will constitute almost a fourth of the school-age population by 2005. Some states, such as Texas and California, are experiencing more marked demographic changes due to immigration and minority birthrate patterns.

Despite the increase in classroom diversity, the demographics of the teachers in our nation's classrooms have changed little over the past decades, creating a mismatch between students and teachers. Teachers are predominantly White, English speaking, middle class, and female. Problems associated with the mismatch between teachers and students in their classes are particularly acute when dealing with linguistic minority students. Although a debate exists over what kinds of language programs best serve English language learners (ELLs), educators typically agree that teachers need an understanding of the important academic and social goals for linguistic minority students in addition to literacy goals; well-developed intercultural competencies; and in the case of bilingual teachers, adequate native and second-language proficiency (Garcia, 1990). However, shortages of minority teachers, and in particular bilingual and ESL teachers, present a challenge in cities and states with large numbers of Spanish-speaking students. Furthermore, many teachers of Hispanic ELLs may not have received any specific preparation for linguistic minority students. Professional development that focuses on intercultural skills and knowledge for teachers of linguistically and culturally diverse students may be needed to address the mismatch between conditions in current classrooms and the characteristics of diverse students.

MODELS OF PROFESSIONAL DEVELOPMENT

Generic professional development models typically specify the processes, but not the content of professional development. Sparks and Loucks-Horsley (1990) specified the following five models or components of professional development that capture differences in processes or approaches:

- *Individually Guided Staff Development*: Teachers design their own professional growth activities. From this perspective, teachers' selection of their own goals for growth and how they will accomplish them motivates them to work harder and allows them to focus on meaningful local problems. Furthermore, self-direction increases teacher professionalism.
- *Observations and Assessment*: In this approach, a colleague or another person observes a teacher in his or her classroom and provides feedback in order to improve instruction. The observers also benefit since they learn from their observations of others' practice.
- *Involvement in a Development or Improvement Process*: The new wave of systemic school-improvement innovations involves teachers in assessment of current teaching practice and student performance and identification of problems related to student outcomes. Teachers subsequently participate in creation and implementation of solutions such as developing curricula, designing or identifying programs to address problems, and/or changing classroom behaviors. Reading and discussion with peers, observations of others' classroom practice, workshops and experimentation contribute to acquisition of skills and knowledge needed to implement the solution.
- *Training*: In this approach, an expert presenter determines the objectives, teacher activities, and outcomes addressed. Outcomes typically include development of awareness, knowledge, and skills. However, issues related to change in attitudes and beliefs of teachers and transfer of training to the classroom setting require attention also. Highly effective training programs also include presentation of theory, demonstrations of skills, practice of new skills with feedback on performance, and coaching within the classroom.
- *Inquiry*: Teachers engage in reflective action in this model—they pose questions about their practice and investigate answers to those questions. While models vary, inquiry includes steps for identification of a problem, data collection and analysis, and development of interventions followed by evaluation of the intervention. The inquiry can be done individually or collaboratively with other colleagues and professionals. (http://www.ncrel.org/sdrs/areas/issues/educatrs/profdevl/pd2fimo.htm)

Although each model or component may be used alone, there is some overlap (e.g., effective training draws on observation/assessment) and they are often combined in professional development approaches. For purposes of this review, training is considered information or assistance provided by experts who determine the objectives, activities, and outcomes of training. Coaching and other extensions are noted when they occur in order to differentiate between "one shot workshop" approaches and more effective training approaches.

As can be seen in the definitions presented earlier, professional development models for teachers differ in their processes and activities; orientations of the source of activity (teacher or staff developer); where that activity takes place (at or near the site of the teacher's classroom or away from the school campus); and duration (length of professional development). For example, traditional models of professional development, similar to the training model in Sparks' conceptualization of professional development, often consisted of workshops delivered by outside experts with little consideration for teacher needs or preferences and little collaboration among teachers after the workshop. This kind of conventional training (i.e., isolated workshops that expose teachers to new ideas or train them in new practices) is often considered unsuitable and ineffective for adult learners and lacking the complexity needed for teachers to help all students succeed (Hawley & Valli, 1999). The one-shot session, "expert" presenters, passive listening stances, and specific skills development out of context may facilitate short-term results rather than lasting change.

Whereas generic models of staff development provide an organizational structure to study professional development in general, several reviews suggest some important content components to consider when preparing teachers for diverse classrooms. Effective teachers of diverse populations recognize and accept their own culture, commit to equity for all students, maintain high expectations for all students, develop strong relationships with students, provide academically challenging curriculum, establish collaborative learning environments, include connections to different cultural groups, scaffold between academic curriculum and cultural resources students bring to school, involve parents and community, and understand the political issues outside the classroom (Zeichner, 1992). But the question remains: How do we provide effective professional development to enable teachers, particularly in urban and high need settings, to acquire the knowledge, skills, and attitudes to succeed with students from culturally and linguistically diverse backgrounds?

Although there are many professional development options that suggest what constitutes cultural diversity and intercultural sensitivity, there is little theoretical agreement about which inservice teacher education strategies and practices will actually promote the development of intercultural competence for teachers (Zeichner & Hoeft, 1996). This chapter summarizes selected findings from a synthesis of research on professional development for teachers of diverse students conducted for the Center for Research on Education, Diversity, and Excellence (CREDE). Although the original synthesis of research investigated a broader range of professional development for teachers of diverse students, this chapter narrows the scope to focus on linguistically and culturally diverse student populations.

We utilized two approaches to the review. First, we focused on identification of instructional models considered effective for linguistically and culturally diverse students and examination of the student outcomes and professional development associated with their implementation. Then, we conducted a traditional search of research to identify studies that focused on professional development of teachers of diverse student populations to determine to what extent the professional development and programs represented in the traditional search were consistent with the descriptions of professional development in exemplary models. We reasoned that areas of convergence in the two approaches would provide the most compelling support for the strategies and content of professional development and that areas of divergence would provide promising directions for further research. The following sections provide descriptions of the two approaches and their findings as well as lessons learned about professional development for teachers of diverse students.

PROFESSIONAL DEVELOPMENT IN INSTRUCTIONAL APPROACHES FOR DIVERSE STUDENT POPULATIONS

Several criteria were used as the basis for selection of instructional models or approaches developed specifically for students from underserved populations described in this section. First, instructional models or approaches selected were specifically developed for culturally and linguistically diverse student populations. Second, target teachers in diverse K–12 classrooms were the primary implementers of program components, rather than researchers or implementers external to the classroom. Next, each instructional model or approach selected for examination in this chapter reflects a research basis in one or both of two ways. Some models base their strategies and approaches on empirical evidence of student learning and/or they have evidence of the impact of the model or model components on student outcomes of interest. Many studies included student impact data, but fewer included evidence to make the link between professional development components and student or teacher outcomes. In fact, we found very few explicit studies of professional development associated with models or approaches of interest and, for this reason, adopted the current two-pronged approach to identification of effective professional development for teachers of linguistically and culturally diverse students.

In order to reflect recent research on effective instruction for culturally and linguistically diverse students, instructional models and approaches selected for review exhibit one or more of the standards for effective pedagogy developed by the Center for Research on Education, Diversity, and Excellence (CREDE; Rueda, 1998; Tharp, 2001, http://www.crede.ucsc.edu/research/pdd/rb2.shtml). Although teachers may or may not use strategies consistent with the standards without training, we are assuming that programs adhering to these standards would include professional development components for teachers to assure that the standards could be implemented appropriately. Finally, the models or approaches selected for review are recognized by experts in strategies for diverse students as effective models or approaches for their target populations. For the first four criteria, we relied on examination of websites, articles, books, journals, and technical reports for evidence of the criteria. For the fifth criterion, we polled the members of our National Synthesis Advisory Team for respected and well-known or promising programs that meet the criteria for inclusion previously described.

STANDARDS FOR EFFECTIVE PEDAGOGY

CREDE has synthesized the research and sociocultural theory focusing on "improving the academic success of students at-risk for failure due to poverty, limited English proficiency, and/or background knowledge and experiences which do not map easily onto school expectations . . ." (Rueda, 1998, p. 1) into the five standards for teaching and learning listed below (Rueda, 1998; Tharp, 2002; Tharp, Estrada, Dalton, & Yamauchi, 2000). Tharp described the skeletal model as one consisting of a teacher and small group of students engaging in instructional conversation while collaborating on a cognitively challenging activity grounded in students' knowledge and experience (Doherty et al., 2003, p. 5). Other students would be simultaneously engaged in a variety of other activities. Complex thinking and literacy development comprise the desired student outcomes. More specifically, the model involves operationalization of the following five standards.

1. *Teachers and students producing together.* Experts and novices in educational settings work together for a common product or goal, engaging in discussion about their activity as they engage in the process. All participants offer and receive assistance, considered the basic act of teaching. Teaching and learning take place in the form of joint activity between teachers and

individual students or in cooperative learning groups guided or facilitated by teachers.

2. *Developing language and literacy across the curriculum.* Language development at all levels constitutes the most important curriculum of schooling. Language development includes everyday social discourse, formal academic language, literacy associated with individual content areas such as math or science, and language for thinking and problem solving. In this sense, teaching for specific content knowledge is similar to teaching a second language and many of the same principles apply. In order to meet this standard, teachers provide students with many opportunities to use varieties of language in written and oral form and receive natural feedback during conversation.

3. *Making meaning—connecting school to students' lives.* In order to promote student understanding, teachers situate new learning in the context of students' previous learning and experiences including those provided by families and cultural and geographic communities. While much school learning is based on "rules, abstractions, and verbal descriptions," teachers need to help students understand how academic learning is related to the world as they know it (Tharp et al., 2000, p. 26). The translation of informal understandings to more abstract understanding can be accomplished by embedding instruction in familiar, practical problems encountered in their everyday lives. This contextualization encompasses three levels: the pedagogical level featuring relation of students' existing schema to new information; the curriculum level drawing on cultural materials and skills through personal and community-based experiences; and the policy level focusing on contextualization of the entire school within the community in which it exists. Approaches that exemplify this standard include Instructional Conversation, culturally compatible or responsive instruction for Hawaiian students known as KEEP (Tharp, 1982).

4. *Teaching complex thinking.* Standard IV refers to teaching in a *way* that is cognitively challenging as well as teaching *content* that is cognitively challenging. This does not preclude teaching of basic skills, but goes beyond the skills level to involve students in use of facts and skills to think analytically and engage in problem solving. Often, groups of students are excluded from challenging instruction due to teacher perceptions of their ability to experience success in these activities (Waxman, Padron, & Knight, 1991). Students considered at risk or those who speak another language often receive a heavy dose of drill, lecture, and seatwork with worksheets, resulting in the "pedagogy of poverty" used by Haberman (1991) to describe instruction in many urban settings. Restriction of expectations for some students to acquisition and practice of routine skills denies them access to meaningful learning. On the other hand, with varying degrees of teacher assistance, tools, and resources, all students can apply information and rou-

tine skills to achieve complex outcomes. The higher expectations, coupled with teacher support or "scaffolding," result in increased academic success for all students (see e.g., Knapp, 1995).

5. *Teaching through conversation.* Teaching through dialogue is an instructional strategy that relies on authentic teacher and student questions and sharing of knowledge and ideas within a classroom "community of learners" (Tharp & Gallimore, 1988; Tharp et al., 2000). Teachers adjust their conversation to assist individual students in their efforts to form and express ideas in speaking and writing and also help contextualize teaching and learning in the experiences and culture of the learner. The concept of teaching through dialogue is supported by research and development in several instructional models developed independently, including the KEEP program, teaching literacy through dialogue (Lee, 1995), and dialogic teaching in math and science (Lee & Fradd, 1998). (http://www.crede.ucsc.edu/research/pdd/5stand_evidence.html)

Padron and her colleagues (2002) have identified a number of effective teaching practices congruent with the standards as well as approaches that incorporate sensitivity to language and cultural differences and therefore promote educational success for Hispanic students. They suggest five successful teaching practices or approaches that specifically address needs of Hispanic students who are often learning a second language as well as a different culture. These include culturally responsive teaching, cooperative learning, instructional conversation, cognitively guided instruction, and technology enriched instruction. Each approach may encompass a variety of specific programs used by teachers that vary somewhat in type or sequence of activities. In addition, more than one approach may be combined for a specific program implemented in schools. Examination of the professional development for teachers associated with these models is a necessary step in improvement of academic outcomes for Hispanic students. Because research on these specific standards has been primarily with ELL, this chapter examines research on professional development for teachers of this particular population.

CREDE researchers hypothesize that the five standards also apply to professional development of teachers (Rueda, 1998). Although they recognize that children and adults may learn differently, principles describing effective teaching and learning in classrooms should not differ for teachers and students. In order to teach in a manner consistent with the standards, teachers must experience professional development that mirrors these principles. Therefore, professional development theoretically should employ joint productive activity among participants characterized by meaningful discourse within a community of learners. Activities and collaborative problem-solving tasks would be connected to issues and problems that participants encounter in their everyday professional lives. In keeping with the focus on teaching complex thinking, professional development experiences would focus on on-going problem solving rather than short-term "quick fixes." Instructional conversations within professional development could facilitate the connection of practical knowledge and experiences with more formal knowledge and the opportunity to give and receive responsive assistance. In this manner, the five standards for effective pedagogy provide a theoretical bridge from classroom teaching and learning to professional development. Professional development within the studies described in the remainder of this chapter can be characterized in relation to consistency with the standards.

Although connection to the five standards provides an organizing mechanism, we did not limit our search to studies of programs or approaches specifically based on the standards. As Tharp and his colleagues point out, the standards do not represent the totality of teaching and do not exclude use of other instructional strategies such as direct instruction, nor should they be used to the exclusion of other strategies. Therefore, the search for professional development studies outlined as the second strategy of this review included attempts to locate professional development for teachers of ELLs for other kinds of instructional models or strategies as well as those based on CREDE's five standards.

RESEARCH SYNTHESIS OVERVIEW

A National Advisory Team for Professional Development for Diversity established by CREDE agreed on several questions that constituted key aspects of professional development for teachers of diverse populations: the nature of professional development for teachers of diverse populations, its impact on both teacher and student outcomes, and contextual characteristics that impact professional development for diversity. This review reports findings from the question related to the impact on teacher and student outcomes for linguistically and culturally diverse students and compares the findings to the effective programs identified for ELLs in the previous sections.

Manual and database searches using relevant keywords yielded studies for the synthesis. Manual searches of current literature, including reference lists of relevant studies, books, literature reviews, and reports; relevant chapters in the handbooks of educational research; and tables of contents and abstracts of relevant education journals and web sites of research centers and reform models for teaching and learning of diverse populations supplemented the electronic searches. Criteria for selecting abstracts for further review included: evidence of empirical data; inservice as opposed to preservice professional development; and culturally diverse student populations. In addition, only studies conducted in the United States and published in peer-reviewed journals from 1986 to the present qualified for the second strategy used in this review. The review includes both qualitative and quantitative studies.

FINDINGS

Research on the five standards, individually and in combination, suggest a relationship between their classroom implementation and various student outcomes (see Appendix A). Each approach is reviewed in the following sections. Studies of professional development related to these approaches as well as others that emerged during the search are also reported in this section.

Five Standards of Effective Pedagogy

The research used as a basis for development of the model as a whole has been reviewed in a series of CREDE technical reports (see e.g., Tharp, 2001, 2002). The basis for the Five Standards model originated in studies of the original Kamehameha Elementary Education Program and its extensions that are reviewed as a separate program in this chapter.

Research on the impact of the five standards as a whole has been conducted primarily by CREDE researchers who report their findings in one book, three book chapters, and three journal articles. Correlational studies have found relationships between use of the five standards and student time on task, perceptions of classroom cohesiveness, and academic self-concept (Padron & Waxman, 1999), and reading and language scores on standardized tests (Estrada, 2003). A quasiexperimental study documented improvement in eighth-grade Native American students' attitudes toward math and higher math conceptual learning and retention in comparison with students in classes taught by traditional whole class instruction approaches (Hilberg, Tharp, & DeGeest, 2000).

The standards represent instructional principles to promote active student learning, but not models or programs per se, and would need to be adapted to different contexts according to characteristics of settings, content, and students. In addition, the components of the model might be implemented separately, resulting in different outcomes than the model as a whole. For this reason, programs focusing on one or more of the components, but not all five equally, are included in the following section. Programs not related to the five standards also emerged and are included.

Effective Instructional Approaches for ELLs

In addition to the Five Standards model, efforts to locate effective approaches for ELLs resulted in identification of eight models including the KEEP model which formed the basis of the Five Standards model (see Appendix A). The first four models (KEEP, Instructional Conversations, O.L.A., and SI) illustrate either all or several of the five standards and have been specifically targeted by CREDE researchers. The remaining four (Culturally Responsive Instruction, CGI, Cooperative Learning, and FOK) are compatible with the five standards but were not developed by CREDE researchers.

Kamehameha Elementary Education Project (KEEP). KEEP is a research and development project aimed at improving the literacy of students of Native Hawaiian heritage through culturally congruent instructional practices. Although the program was officially ended in 1997 due to problems related to expansion, reduction of resources, and subsequent loss of fidelity to the original model (Doherty et al., 2003), extensions and adaptations of KEEP have persisted. Writers' and Readers' Workshops within a whole-language approach provide the vehicle for literacy development. KEEP has evolved over time and several current related or similar programs such as Culturally Based Education (CBE) have been developed from the model.

Instructional Conversations. This approach forms an important component of the Five Standards approach but can be used alone or in combination with other approaches. Teachers contextualize the formal content of instruction within students' individual, home, and community lives and provide students with comprehensible input during dialogs. The conversations or discussions typically take place between teachers and small groups of students, are goal directed, and focus on academic content. Teachers listen carefully, pose questions, assess student understanding, and help students make elaborations and associations related to the content. Although there is a focus on students' cultural knowledge, the approach explicitly targets formulation and expression of ideas through oral language and can be used prior to, during, and after reading and in combination with other approaches such as Writer's Workshop, Reciprocal Teaching, and Literature Logs. The results of a series of experimental studies indicate that ELL students taught through Instructional Conversations or through IC combined with contextualization demonstrated better reading comprehension and story theme understanding than students taught using direct instruction methods (Saunders & Goldenberg, 1999). In addition, the combination of IC with contextualization achieved better results than use of IC alone.

Opportunities Through Language Arts (O.L.A.). O.L.A. is included separately in the list of effective programs in Appendix A since it was suggested by a number of experts in the field as an example of a promising program for ELLs. O.L.A. is an example of a specific language arts program based on use of instructional conversations that is targeted for middle school students in transitional bilingual education programs. The program features contextualization, cognitive complexity, and instructional conversation for middle grade students. Contextualization in this case closely resembles culturally responsive teaching described in a subsequent section.

Sheltered Instruction (SI). SI is an approach involving specific strategies for teaching content to ELLs that promote their English language development and make the subject matter content comprehensible. Researchers at CREDE have developed a model of sheltered instruction and are currently conducting research to investigate teacher change as well as the effects of sheltered instruction on ELLs' English language development. Although the evidence of effectiveness at this time is somewhat sparse in comparison with models such as *Exito Para Todos,* SI was recommended by several experts in the study and is one of two programs, together with O.L.A. described previously, listed by CREDE as effective programs for ELLs based on the five standards (Tharp, 2002). Initial findings with middle school students indicate significant improvement in comparison with control groups on expository writing including language production, focus, elaboration, organization, and mechanics (Tharp, 2002).

Culturally Responsive Instruction for ELLs. Culturally responsive instruction is a learner-centered approach that includes aspects of the students' social, cultural, and linguistic knowledge in classroom activities, texts, and instruction to facilitate their learning. Whereas the approach has been used with various other student populations (see e.g., Gay, 2000), it has also been used with ELLs, typically in combination with other approaches such as Instructional Conversations. The standard associated with contextualization of instruction draws heavily on culturally responsive teaching approaches as a means of making school concepts more meaningful to students' everyday lives. There is a body of knowledge regarding culturally responsive instruction associated with other populations, but programs in this area need to be tailored to specific ethnic and language groups as well as to specific contexts, and take into consideration the match between the teachers' cultural background and that of his or her students (see e.g., Darder, 1993).

Cognitively-Guided Instruction (CGI). CGI features development and explicit instruction of students' cognitive strategies, cognitive monitoring, and metacognition with the goal of transferring control of their use to students. Reciprocal Teaching is an example of a CGI approach focusing on summarizing, questioning, clarifying and predicting. Research comparing strategy use of ELLs in comparison with their monolingual peers has indicated differences that may impact literacy acquisition negatively (Chamot, Dale, O'Malley, & Spanos, 1993; Padron, Knight, & Waxman, 1986). However, intervention studies with ELLs have resulted in greater strategy use and better text comprehension (Padron & Waxman, 1988).

Cooperative Learning. Cooperative learning involves students working together in small groups for a common purpose such as learning content or skills, discovering information, or creating products. Perhaps the best known program incorporating this approach is the Spanish version of *Success for All* translated as *Exito Para Todos.* While much of the benefit may be from the individual tutoring included in the program (see e.g., Wasik & Slavin, 1993), cooperative learning is one of the instructional strategies used in the English and Spanish versions of the model. Numerous technical reports and refereed journal articles document the success of the program for basic skills in reading (see summaries of research in Slavin et al., 1996 and Weiler, 1998). However the effects vary for ELL students (Weiler, 1998). ELL students participating in adapted SFA (Slavin & Yampolsky, 1992) and the bilingual SFA called *Exito Para Todos* (Slavin & Madden, 1998) show improved reading achievement, but those ELLs in regular SFA experience less benefit (Weiler, 1998).

Funds of Knowledge (FOK). "Funds of knowledge" is an approach that differs from the others reviewed in the focus of the program and the context in which it occurs, but is compatible with the Five Standards. FOK capitalizes on the knowledge, skills, abilities, and practices that promote the functioning of families, particularly those of diverse ethnic and linguistic backgrounds. In the original model, researchers and teachers worked together to use participant–observer methodology during visits to minority student households to identify and record family and cultural knowledge. More recently, through activities associated with the Puente project, precollege students have participated in order to validate their identities and to use the knowledge as a basis for future learning (Gonzalez & Moll, 2002). The knowledge obtained in this way can be used by teachers and students to create culturally congruent classrooms and to change perceptions of teachers and students.

Professional Development

As described previously the second strategy of the review involved the search for research focusing on professional development for teachers of culturally and linguistically diverse students. The intent was to determine the extent and focus of the research on professional development in this area and to investigate the extent to which programs considered effective for ELLs are represented in the professional development research. The results of the search yielded 19 studies of professional development for teachers of culturally and linguistically diverse students that could be divided into three categories (see Appendix B): Professional development for specific programs, Professional development for multicultural or culturally relevant instruction, and Professional development through learning communities and inquiry. The following sections summarize the findings from each category.

Professional Development for Specific Programs. Eight studies involved examination of specific programs targeted for bilingual or ESL students or that included teachers of bilingual/ESL students in the sample. Three of the studies describe bilingual programs (dual language immersion, teaching bilingually, and the Natural Approach) and one describes teachers' perceptions in a TESOL program. Two of the three bilingual program studies used training models of professional development, while the dual language immersion and TESOL approaches were acquired through a development/improvement and inquiry process spearheaded by a teacher leader and study group comprised of other teachers in one case and a school-university team in the other. All noted positive teacher change in perceptions as outcomes. Running records of students' reading in the dual immersion study showed improvement in Spanish literacy for all students without a detriment to their English literacy.

In addition to the four studies just described, four studies of specific instructional programs targeted professional development in four of the effective instructional approaches for culturally and linguistically diverse students identified in the previous section—KEEP, cooperative learning/SFA, CGI, and Instructional Conversations. The KEEP study reported results of professional development for whole language approaches within the KEEP model. Utilizing consultants for support throughout the year, full implementation of KEEP components by teachers was related to improvements in students' writing achievement. However, consultants concentrated their efforts and support on teachers who they thought were most likely to obtain full implementation by the end of the year and therefore did not reflect a representative mix of teachers in the professional development.

Another study focused on 36 teachers in two Success for All (SFA; *Exito Para Todos*) schools. As previously described, SFA is a whole school reform model for reading success in the early grades that includes cooperative grouping. *Exito Para Todos* is the Spanish bilingual version. Teachers implemented the reform after training with follow-up classroom visits by trainers. Despite demands of fidelity to the model, teachers made various adaptations to the program. The qualitative data revealed that teachers exhibited four categories of support for SFA, ranging from strong to resistance. Although teachers generally felt that the model limited their creativity and was too rigid in its parameters, nevertheless, they supported the model because they perceived it was beneficial to the students.

The third study featured professional development for teachers in the metacognitive instructional approach for mathematics problem solving, a form of Cognitively Guided Instruction. The researcher conducted a 3-day workshop featuring lecture, demonstration, discussion, simulation, and preworkshop observations. The experimental group of primarily low-achieving Hispanic students who had teachers trained in this method performed significantly better than the control on criterion-referenced mathematics achievement tests and assessments of attitudes toward mathematics. Although teachers varied in their degrees of implementation of the approach, students still exhibited similar gains. This finding is somewhat perplexing since the degree of implementation of the model should impact its outcomes. It is unclear whether the finding signifies that something other than the training received by teachers was affecting student performance or that the model is robust and can tolerate variations without detrimental effects on student performance.

The fourth instructional approach study in this group used Instructional Conversations (IC) to train nine mainstream and bilingual teachers in the use of IC in their classrooms. Teachers participated in eight 2-hour professional development sessions over the period of 1 month. Sessions included provision of the theoretical basis of the strategy, demonstrations, practice in implementing the strategy, and observations of strategy implementation with another educator. In addition, part of each session was devoted to reflection. All teachers demonstrated an understanding of the strategy in interviews and exhibited classroom behaviors consistent with their training. As a result, the researcher concludes that IC can be used as an effective means of professional development as well as instructional strategy for ELLs. The study is an example of the five standards applied to professional development of teachers. However, little is known about the impact of the approach on classrooms of the participants.

Professional Development for Multicultural/Culturally Relevant Instruction. Only two studies emerged during the search that involved professional development for multicultural instruction. One study operated within a project designed to develop and field test professional development modules to prepare teachers to work more effectively with diverse students. Prior to participation, teachers typically ignored the effects of culture and reflected a deficit approach when referring to culturally and linguistically diverse students and families. After participation, they became more aware of the impact of culture and made fewer stereotypical or negative comments about students and families. In addition, they tended to stress the importance of valuing and addressing cultural differences in their instruction.

The second study in this set focuses on teacher application of a professional development experience in multicultural education to their mathematics instruction. Four themes provided the linkage between culture and instruction: use of students' cultural backgrounds as an instructional resource, high expectations for mathematics achievement for culturally diverse students, view of mathematics as a culturally created construct, and connection of mathematics to students' lives. Thirty teachers participated in 9 full-day sessions of professional development to enhance multicultural teaching in the first year and 5 all-day sessions in the second year. No particular content area in mathematics was emphasized. Classroom observations over the 2 years revealed little impact on teachers' mathematics instruction despite claims by teachers that they learned a great deal. They taught mathematics as a decontextualized, sequential set of skills and did not apply content from their workshops to mathematics teaching. The researcher concludes that teachers are unlikely to change mathematics instruction in short workshop formats and without specifically connecting multicultural knowledge, skills, and attitudes to mathematics teaching and learning.

Professional Development Through Learning Communities Engaged in Inquiry. Nine studies comprise the category of professional development involving participation in inquiry within the context of learning communities and represent the efforts of the past 10 years to involve teachers and external partners in the systemic reform of schools. Professional or learning communities share common beliefs and values; a focus on student learning; and collaboration, deprivatized practice, and reflective dialogue as tools for growth (Louis, Marks, & Kruse, 1996). Professional development embodied in this research includes Development/Improvement approaches in conjunction with collaboration between schools and universities or within reform networks, and Inquiry in the form of study groups and teacher research or sharing of life histories. Teachers and their external partners in networks or school–university partnerships often choose to participate in workshops on particular topics within the learning community, but the primary means of professional growth is through participation with others in order to address problems or study teacher and school practices, curriculum, and/or policy. Research associated with these models is typically qualitative case study design and focuses on stakeholders' satisfaction with their professional growth, participant empowerment, and primarily anecdotal reports of positive student outcomes. Positive findings from these studies relate to increased professionalism of teachers and perceptions of improved student learning. Negative findings highlight the wide variation in impact across schools and settings and unevenness of stakeholder understandings within a reform setting.

LESSONS LEARNED

The research synthesis yielded several lessons related to the impact of professional development on culturally and linguistically diverse students. These are necessarily tentative due to the small number of studies that met the criteria for inclusion. In fact, the first lesson learned refers to the paucity of research in the area.

Lesson #1: Studies about professional development for teachers of culturally and linguistically diverse students provide little guidance for transforming the effectiveness of inservice teachers of these populations. Few studies that focus on professional development exist in journals accessible to researchers and educators in this area. While we found several studies in which we inferred that professional development for teachers of diverse learners took place, no description or an incomplete description of the professional development was given. For example, a study hypothetically could have investigated the impact of an instructional strategy for reading on Hispanic students' performance as measured by the reading section of a standardized test. If a number of teachers were involved in implementation of the strategy, it seems logical that some type of professional development must have taken place to enable them to implement the presumed innovation. In fact, guidelines and manuals for professional development of teachers exist for each of the approaches outlined in the first part of the review. However, many studies utilizing these approaches neglected to describe how—or even whether—teachers acquired the particular strategy. Although research on the impact of instructional programs or approaches exists, little attention has been given to the link between professional development of teachers in the instructional strategy and the impact of the professional development on teachers or students. Even among the studies in this review, few devoted more than a few paragraphs to the processes and activities of professional development targeted by the study. Furthermore, many studies of professional development neglected to describe the populations taught by teachers in the study.

Lesson #2: Training models of professional development, a common approach for professional development of teachers of culturally and linguistically diverse students, have mixed impact on teacher and student outcomes. Surprisingly, given recent criticism of the passive training model of professional development, almost half of the studies that emerged used some form of training or workshop for professional development. Those that augmented the workshops with follow-up coaching or consulting and designed more interaction and reflection in the typically passive approach, appeared to have more positive outcomes. Success for All/*Exito Para Todos* provides extensive follow-up of training and requires strict adherence to implementation guidelines. However, in another study, use of extended workshops for culturally responsive teaching over a period of time failed to translate to classroom behaviors, even when teachers reported that they had learned a great deal in the training. More attention needs to be given to behavioral outcomes of training and to retention of these behaviors over time.

Lesson #3: Current trends in professional development for teachers of culturally and linguistically diverse students favor collaborative models of professional development that involve learning communities in inquiry into practice, but little is known about their impact on students. Almost half of the studies included in the review featured the development/improvement approach to professional development and inquiry embedded in networks, study groups or collaborative teacher research. The five standards described for instructional programs for students appear to be mirrored in these two types of professional development for teachers. This new generation of professional development features joint productive activity among participants (Standard 1) characterized by meaningful discourse within a community of learners (Standard 5). Collaborative problem solving is connected to issues and problems identified by participants (Standard 4). In opposition to many of the training models, professional development experiences from this perspective focus on complex, on-going problem solving rather than short-term quick fixes (Standard 3). However, the nature of the qualitative case study research reported in many of these studies makes it difficult to link the conclusions drawn to the qualitative data presented since methodology is not well described. Furthermore, few studies focus on the student outcomes associated with this type of professional development.

Lesson #4: While a number of student instructional models or approaches have a research base (albeit in some cases somewhat limited and emergent) to support their effectiveness for ELLs, little is known about how to enable ELL teachers to acquire these skills and knowledge. The effective programs for ELLs identified by experts and through literature on the topic, varied in the extent and quality of research conducted to determine their impact. Emergent programs such as the Five Standards, O.L.A., and Sheltered Instruction had few studies reported in peer-reviewed journals and relied primarily on book chapters or books with summaries of research used to develop the model and technical reports of research just completed or research in progress. This is understandable in relatively new approaches and should be remedied over time, but it is difficult at this point to draw definitive conclusions about their success. Programs of longer duration, such as KEEP and Success for All, were characterized by more research in more types of outlets including peer-reviewed journals, books, book chapters, technical reports, and summaries of research. Nevertheless, they have been scrutinized and criticized despite the relatively large number of studies conducted. For example, SFA studies have been almost exclusively conducted by the developers in conjunction with implementers, may lack objectivity in interpretation of findings, and are limited in outcomes (see e.g., Pogrow, 2000).

Studies of professional development emerged for only 4 of the 8 instructional models listed in the previous section. Clearly, professional development for teachers of culturally and linguistically diverse students is a neglected area of research. Even if providers of professional development evaluate the impact of their approaches on teachers, it does not appear that they do so in a systematic way or that they disseminate their findings beyond the immediate context. Although quality of teaching continues to be a major factor in the success of diverse students and in the implementation of needed reform, teacher professional development is a neglected area of study.

CONCLUSIONS

Professional development for diversity is complex, requiring an understanding of the context of current classrooms, adult development, institutional change, views of diversity, and professional development approaches. Although the research is scanty, disparate, and even contradictory at times, this review suggests some directions that may help organize work in the area. Perhaps of highest importance, program implementers need to join with researchers to fully describe and assess the impact of professional development on teachers of culturally and linguistically diverse students and disseminate their findings to other researchers, policymakers, and consumers. Because the instructional approaches for ELLs and other cultural groups involve specialized knowledge and skills, the generic professional development for teachers that dominates in this area may be inappropriate and ineffective. However, we have little research to support or refute this claim. In addition to the paucity of research on professional development in general, there is little research on the relation between the content of professional development and outcomes for teachers of diverse populations. Intensive study of the conditions and approaches for development of effective teachers is considerably less well developed in this area than studies of student outcomes in relation to interventions.

The nature of the study of professional development also needs to be considered. Studies of professional development need to focus on classroom outcomes including impact on teacher classroom behaviors and student performance. Weaknesses in this area include a lack of connection between professional development and student outcomes and inclusion of largely anecdotal accounts of teacher and student impact. In particular, careful reasoning from evidence to interpretation within and across studies is critical (National Research Council, 2001). For professional development studies, this indicates making linkages from professional development to teacher behaviors as well as other cognitive and affective outcomes and then from teacher behaviors to student outcomes. For intervention studies, this means assessing the degree of implementation of an innovation in relation to teacher and student outcomes. The connection is more easily made with less complex approaches to professional development, perhaps leading to a false conclusion that training is a more effective means of improving teaching. Complex professional development models, particularly those that feature a great deal of teacher autonomy and multiple, integrated approaches and activities, may require collecting additional evidence to make the linkages (see e.g., Knight & Wiseman, 2003). Nevertheless, given the importance of the teacher in the success of innovations (Elmore, 2002), the knowledge gained would be well worth the effort expended.

APPENDIX A: EFFECTIVE INSTRUCTIONAL APPROACHES FOR ELLs

Five Standards for Effective Pedagogy

Description

A model of instruction characterized by teacher facilitation of joint productive activity among teacher and students, student complex thinking, teaching through conversation, language and literacy development and contextualization of teaching in homes and communities of students.

Research

Estrada, P. (2003). Patterns of language arts instruction activity: Excellence, inclusion fairness, and harmony in first and fourth grade culturally and linguistically diverse classrooms. In H. Waxman, R. G. Tharp, & R. S. Hilberg (Eds.), *Observational research in U.S. classrooms.* New York: Cambridge University Press.

Estrada, P., & Imhoff, B. (2003). One road to reform: Professional development, pedagogy, and student achievement in the context of state reform of literacy instruction. In S. Stringfield & A. Datnow (Eds.), *The imperfect storm: Successes and failures of school reform efforts in multicultural/multilingual settings.* Cambridge, MA: Cambridge University Press.

Doherty, R., & Hilberg, R. (2003). The standards performance continuum: a performance-based measure of the standards for effective pedagogy. In H. Waxman, R. G. Tharp, & R. S. Hilberg (Eds.), *Observational research in U.S. classrooms.* New York: Cambridge University Press.

Doherty, R., Hilberg, R., Pinal, A., & Tharp, R. (2003). Five standards and student achievement. *NABE Journal of Research and Practice, 1*(1), 1–24.

Elmore, R. F. (2002). *Bridging the gap between standards and achievement: The imperative for professional development in education.* American Federation of Teachers: Albert Shanker Institute.

Hilberg, R. S., Tharp, R. G., & DeGeest, L. (2000). The efficacy of CREDE's standards-based instruction in American Indian Mathematics classes. *Equity and Excellence in Education, 33*(2), 32–39.

Padron, Y., & Waxman, H. (1999). Classroom observations of the Five Standards of Effective Teaching in urban classrooms with English language learners. *Teaching and Change, 7*(1), 79–100.

Tharp, R., Estrada, P., Dalton, S., & Yamauchi, L. (2000). *Teaching transformed: Achieving excellence, fairness, inclusion, and harmony.* Boulder, CO: Westview.

Kamehameha Early Education Program (KEEP)

Description

The Kamehameha Elementary Education Project (KEEP) is a research and development project to improve literacy outcomes of Native Hawaiian elementary students through culturally congruent instructional practices. Although formally terminated in 1997, several current related or similar programs such as Culturally Based Education (CBE) have been developed from the model.

Research

Au, K., & Carroll, J. H. (1997). Improving literacy achievement through a constructivist approach: The KEEP demonstration classroom project. *Elementary School Journal, 97*(3), 203–221.

Au, K., & Kawakami, A. (1994). Cultural congruence in instruction. In E. Hollins, J. Kirg, & W. Hayman (Eds.), *Teaching diverse populations: Formulating a knowledge base* (pp. 5–23). Albany, NY: State University of New York Press.

Demmert, W., & Towner, J. (2003). *A review of the research literature on the influences of culturally based education on the academic performance of Native American students.* Portland, OR: Northwest Regional Education Laboratory.

Tharp, R. (1982). The effective instruction of comprehension: Results and description of the Kamehameha Early Education Program. *Reading Research Quarterly, 17*(4), 503–527.

Instructional Conversations

Description

In this approach, teachers contextualize the formal content of instruction within students' individual, home, and community lives and provide students with comprehensible input during dialogs. While there is a focus on students' cultural knowledge, the approach explicitly targets formulation and expression of ideas through oral language.

Research

Duran, B., Dugan, T., & Weffer, R. (1992). Increasing teacher effectiveness with language minority students. *The High School Journal, 84,* 238–246.

Goldenberg, C. (1993). Instructional conversations: Promoting conversation through discussion. *The Reading Teacher, 46*(4), 316–326.

Goldenberg, C., Sanders, B., & Gallimore, R. (1998). Making the transition from Spanish to English instruction. *Talking Leaves. CREDE, 2*(2), 1&6.

Saunders, W., & Goldenberg, C. (1999). *The effects of instructional conversations and literature logs on the story comprehension and thematic understanding of English proficient and limited English students.* Santa Cruz, CA: Center for Research on Education, Diversity & Excellence, University of California.

Opportunities Through Language Arts (O.L.A.)

Description

O.L.A. is a language arts program that incorporates aspects of the Five Standards targeted specifically toward students in transitional bilingual education programs. The program features contextualization, cognitive complexity, and instructional conversation for middle grade students.

Research

Saunders, W. (1999). Improving literacy achievement for English learners in transitional bilingual programs. *Educational Research and Evaluation, 5*(4), 345–381.

Saunders, W., & Goldenberg, C. (1999a). *The effects of instructional conversations and literature logs on the story comprehension and thematic understanding of English proficient and limited English proficient students.* Santa Cruz, CA: Center for Research on Education, Diversity, and Excellence, University of California.

Saunders, W., & Goldenberg, C. (1999b). *The effects of comprehensive Language Arts/Transition program on the literacy development of English learners.* Santa Cruz, CA: Center for Research on Education, Diversity, and Excellence, University of California.

Saunders, W., O'Brien, G., Lennon, D., & MacLean, J. (1998). Making the transition to English literacy successful: Effective strategies for studying literature with transition students. In R. Gersten & R. Jimenez (Eds.), *Promoting learning for culturally and linguistically diverse students.* Monterey, CA: Brooks Cole.

Sheltered Instruction (SI)

Description

SI is an approach involving specific strategies for teaching content to ELLs that promote their English language development and make the subject matter content comprehensible.

Research

Echevarria, J. (1998, December). *Teaching language minority students in elementary schools.* CREDE Research Brief No. 1.

Echevarria, J., & Goldenberg, C. (1999, October). *Teaching secondary language minority students.* CREDE Research Brief No. 4.

Echevarria, J., & Graves, A. (1998). *Sheltered language protocol: Teaching language minority students.* Boston: Allyn & Bacon.

Echevarria, J., & Short, D. (2000, April). *Using multiple perspectives in observations of diverse classrooms: The Sheltered Instruction Observation Protocol (SIOP).* Paper presented at the annual meeting of the American Educational Research Association, New Orleans, LA.

Culturally Responsive Instruction for ELLs

Description

Culturally responsive instruction is a learner-centered approach that includes aspects of the students' social, cultural, and linguistic knowledge in classroom activities, texts, and instruction to facilitate their learning.

Research

Darder, A. (1993). How does the culture of the teacher shape the classroom experience of Latino students? The unexamined question in critical pedagogy. In S. Rothstein (Ed.), *Handbook of schooling in urban America* (pp. 195–221). Westport, CT: Greenwood.

McCollum, P. (1989). Turn-allocation in lessons with North American and Puerto Rican students: A comparative study. *Anthropology and Education Quarterly, 20,* 133–158.

Cognitively-Guided Instruction (CGI)

Description

CGI features development and explicit instruction of students' cognitive strategies, cognitive monitoring, and metacognition with the goal of transferring control of their use to students. Reciprocal Teaching is an example of a CGI approach focusing on summarizing, questioning, clarifying, and predicting.

Research

Chamot, A., & O'Malley, J. (1989). The cognitive academic language learning approach: A bridge to the mainstream. *TESOL Quarterly, 21,* 227–249.

Chamot, A., Dale, M., O'Malley, J., & Spanos, G. (1993). Learning and problem solving strategies of ESL students. *Bilingual Research Journal, 16*(3&4), 1–34.

Padron, Y., Knight, S., & Waxman, H. (1986). Analyzing bilingual and monolingual students' perceptions of their reading strategies. *The Reading Teacher, 39,* 430–433.

Padron, Y., & Waxman, H. (1988). The effect of students' perceptions of their cognitive strategies on reading achievement. *TESOL Quarterly, 22,* 146–150.

Cooperative Learning

Description

Cooperative learning involves students working together in small groups for a common purpose such as learning content or skills, discovering information, or creating products.

Research

Johnson, D., & Johnson, R. (1991). Classroom instruction and cooperative grouping. In H. Waxman & H. Walberg (Eds.), *Effective teaching: Current research* (pp. 277–293). Berkeley, CA: McCutchan.

Ross, S., Smith, L., Madden, N., & Slavin, R. (1997). Improving the academic success of disadvantaged children: An examination of Success for All. *Psychology in the Schools, 34*(2), 171–180.

Slavin, R. et al. (1996). Success for all: A summary of research. *Journal of Education for Students Placed At Risk, 1*(1), 41–76.

Slavin, R. (1991). Synthesis of the research on cooperative learning. *Phi Delta Kappan, 48*(5), 71–82.

Weiler, J. (1998). *Success for all: A summary of evaluations.* ERIC/CUE Digest Number 139.

Funds of Knowledge

Description

"Funds of knowledge" is an approach that capitalizes on the knowledge, skills, abilities, and practices that promote the functioning of families. Researchers and teachers originally worked together to use participant-observer methodology during visits to minority student households to identify and record this knowledge. More recently, the approach has been extended to include precollege students.

Research

Gonzalez, N., & Moll, L. (2002). Cruzando el Puente: Building bridges to Funds of Knowledge. *Educational Policy, 16*(4), 623–641.

Gonzalez, N., Moll, L., Tenery, M., Rivera, A., Rendon, P., Gonzales, R., & Amanti, C. (1995). Funds of knowledge for teaching in Latino households. *Urban Education, 29*(4), 444–471.

Moll, L. C. (1992). Literacy research in community and classrooms: A sociocultural approach. In R. Beach, J. L. Green, M. L. Kamil, & T. Shanahan (Eds.), *Multidisciplinary perspectives on literacy research.* Urbana, IL: NCATE.

Moll, L. C., Amanti, C., Neff, D., & Gonzalez, N. (1992). Funds of knowledge for teaching: Using a qualitative approach to connect homes and classrooms. *Theory Into Practice, 31,* 132–141.

Moll, L., & Greenberg, J. (1990). Creating zones of possibilities: Combining social contexts for instruction. In L. Moll (Ed.), *Vygotsky and education: Instructional implications and applications of sociohistorical psychology* (pp. 319–348). New York: Cambridge University Press.

Moll, L. C., & Greenberg, T. (1992). Creating zones of possibilities: Combining social contexts for literacy instruction. In L. Moll (Ed.), *Vygotsky and education* (pp. 319–348). Cambridge, England: Cambridge University Press.

APPENDIX B: SYNTHESIS OF RESEARCH ON PROFESSIONAL DEVELOPMENT FOR TEACHERS OF CULTURALLY AND LINGUISTICALLY DIVERSE STUDENTS

Professional Development for Specific Programs

Au, K., & Carroll, J. Improving literacy achievement through a constructivist approach: The KEEP demonstration classroom project. *Elementary School Journal, 97*(3), 203–220.

Cardelle-Elawar, M. (1995). Effects of metacognitive instruction on low achievers in mathematics problems. *Teaching and Teacher Education, 11*(1), 81–95.

Cooper, R., Slavin, R. E., & Madden, N. A. (1998). Success for all: Improving the quality of implementation of whole-school change through the use of a national reform network. *Education and Urban Society, 30*(3), 385–408.

Datnow, A., & Castellano, M. (2000). Teachers' responses to success for all: How beliefs, experiences, and adaptations shape implementation. *American Educational Research Journal, 37*(3), 775–799.

Faltis, C. (1996). Learning to teach content bilingually in a middle school classroom. *Bilingual Research Journal, 20*(1), 29–44.

Fradd, S., & Lee, O. (1997). Teachers' voices in program evaluation and improvement: A case study of a TESOL program. *Teaching and Teacher Education, 13*(6), 563–577.

Solis, A. (1999). Research-informed teaching in bilingual education: Does it happen? How does it help? *Bilingual Research Journal, 23*(1), 89–96.

Quinones-Benitez, A. (2003). Training teachers of English language learners through instructional conversations: A metalogue. *NABE Journal of research and Practice, 1*(1), 25–49.

Professional Development for Multicultural or Culturally Relevant Instruction

Betsinger, A., Garcia, S., & Guerra, P. (2001). Up for scrutiny. *Journal of Staff Development, 22*(2), 24–27.

Sleeter, C. (1997). Mathematics, multicultural education, and training of teachers. *Journal for Research in Mathematics Education, 28*(6), 680–694.

Professional Development Through Learning Communities Engaged in Inquiry

Allexsaht-Snider, M. (1996). Windows into diverse worlds: The telling and sharing of teachers' life histories. *Education and Urban Society, 29*(1), 103–119.

Grant, S., Peterson, P., & Shojgreen-Downer, A. (1996). Learning to teach mathematics in the context of systemic reform. *American Educational Research Journal, 33*(2), 509–541.

Greenleaf, C., Hull, G., & Reilly, B. (1994). Learning from our diverse students: Helping teachers rethink problematic teaching and learning situations. *Teaching and Teacher Education, 10*(5), 521–541.

Harthun, M., Drapeau, A., Dustman, P., & Marsiglia, F. (2002). Implementing a prevention curriculum: An effective researcher–teacher partnership. *Education and Urban Society, 34*(3), 353–364.

King, M. (2002). Professional development to promote schoolwide inquiry. *Teaching and Teacher Education, 18,* 243–257.

Nevarez-La Torre, A. (1999). Developing voice: Teacher research in bilingual classrooms. *Bilingual Research Journal, 23*(4), 451–470.

Reyes, L. (2002). Professional development in a bilingual adult learning community: The case of P.S. 24. *Bilingual Research Journal, 26*(1), 181–192.

Zeitlin, A., & MacLeod, E. (1995). A school-university partnership working toward the restructure of an urban school and community. *Education and Urban Society, 27*(4), 411–420.

Zeitlin, A., MacLeod, E., & Michener, D. (1998). Professional development of teachers of language minority students through university-school partnership. *Teacher Education and Special Education, 21*(2), 109–120.

REFERENCES

Chamot, A., Dale, M., O'Malley, J., & Spanos, G. (1993). Learning and problem solving strategies of ESL students. *Bilingual Research Journal, 16*(3&4), 1–34.

Darder, A. (1993). How does the culture of the teacher shape the classroom experience of Latino students? The unexamined question in critical pedagogy. In S. Rothstein (Ed.), *Handbook of schooling in urban America* (pp. 195–221). Westport, CT: Greenwood.

Doherty, R., Hilberg, R., Pinal, A., & Tharp, R. (2003). Five standards and student achievement. *NABE Journal of Research and Practice, 1*(1), 1–24.

Elmore, R. (2002). *Bridging the gap between standards and achievement: The imperative for professional development in education.* District of Columbia: Albert Shaker Institute.

Estrada, P. (2003). Patterns of language arts instruction activity: Excellence, inclusion fairness, and harmony in first and fourth grade culturally and linguistically diverse classrooms. In H. Waxman, R. G. Tharp, & R. S. Hilberg (Eds.), *Observational research in U.S. classrooms.* New York: Cambridge University Press.

Garcia, E. (1990). Educating teachers for language minority students. In R. Houston (Ed.), *Handbook of research on teacher education* (pp. 717–729). New York: Macmillan.

Garcia, E. (1994). *Understanding and meeting the challenge of student cultural diversity.* Boston: Houghton Mifflin.

Gay, G. (2000). *Culturally responsive teaching: Theory, research, and practice.* New York: Teachers College Press.

Gonzalez, N., & Moll, L. (2002). Cruzando el Puente: Building bridges to Funds of Knowledge. *Educational Policy, 16*(4), 623–641.

Good, T., & Brophy, J. (2000). *Looking in classrooms.* New York: Longman.

Haberman, M. (1991). The pedagogy of poverty versus good teaching. *Phi Delta Kappan, 73*(4), 290–294.

Hawley, W. D., & Valli, L. (1999). The essentials of effective professional development: A new consensus. In L. Darling-Hammond & G. Sykes (Eds.), *Teaching as the learning profession* (pp. 127–150). San Francisco: Jossey-Bass.

Haycock, K. (1998). *Good teaching matters: How well-qualified teachers can close the gap. Thinking K–16.* A Publication of The Education Trust, 3, No. 2, 1–14.

Haycock, K. (2003). Toward a fair distribution of teacher talent. *Educational Leadership, 60*(4), 11–15.

Hilberg, R. S., Tharp, R. G., & DeGeest, L. (2000). The efficacy of CREDE's standards-based instruction in American Indian Mathematics classes. *Equity and Excellence in Education, 33*(2), 32–39.

Knapp, M. (1995). *Teaching for meaning in high-poverty classrooms.* New York: Teachers College Press.

Knight, S. L., & Wiseman, D. (2003). Making the case: Lessons learned from school-university partnership research. In D. Wiseman & S. Knight (Eds.), *Linking school university collaboration and K–12 student outcomes* (pp. 166–200). Washington, DC: American Association of Colleges of Teacher Education.

Knight, S., & Wiseman, D. (in press). Professional development for teachers of diverse students: A summary of the research. *Journal for Education of Studies Placed At Risk.*

Lee, O. (1995). Subject matter knowledge, classroom management, and instructional practices in middle school science classrooms. *Journal of Research in Science Teaching, 32*(4), 423–440.

Lee, O., & Fradd, F. (1998). Science for all, including students from non-English language backgrounds. *Educational Researcher, 27*(3), 1–10.

Louis, K., Marks, H., & Kruse, S. (1996). Teachers' professional community in restructuring schools. *American Educational Research Journal, 33*(4), 757–798.

National Research Council. (2002). *Scientific inquiry in education.* Washington, DC: National Academy Press.

Padron, Y., Knight, S., & Waxman, H. (1986). Analyzing bilingual and monolingual students' perceptions of their reading strategies. *The Reading Teacher, 39,* 430–433.

Padron, Y., & Waxman, H. (1988). The effect of students' perceptions of their cognitive strategies on reading achievement. *TESOL Quarterly, 22,* 146–150.

Padron, Y., & Waxman, H. (1999). Classroom observations of the Five Standards of Effective Teaching in urban classrooms with English language learners. *Teaching and Change, 7*(1), 79–100.

Padron, Y., Waxman, H., & Rivera, H. (2002). Issues in educating Hispanic students. In S. Stringfield & D. Land (Eds.), *Educating at-risk students, One hundred-first yearbook of the National Society for the study of Education* (pp. 66–89). Chicago: University of Chicago Press.

Pogrow, S. (2000). The unsubstantiated "success" of Success for All. *Phi Delta Kappan, 81*(8), 596–600.

Rueda, R. (1998). *Standards for professional development: A sociocultural perspective* (Research Report #2). Santa Cruz, CA: CREDE.

Saunders, W., & Goldenberg, C. (1999). *The effects of instructional conversations and literature logs on the story comprehension and thematic understanding of English proficient and limited English students.* Santa Cruz, CA: Center for Research on Education, Diversity & Excellence, University of California.

Slavin, R., & Madden, N. (1998). Success for all/exito para todos: *Effects on the reading achievement of students acquiring English.* Eric Document ED423327.

Slavin, R., & Yampolsky, R. (1992). *Success for all: Effects on students with limited English proficiency: A three-year evaluation.* Eric Document ED346199.

Slavin, R., Madden, N., Dolan, L., Wasik, B., Ross, S., Smith, L., & Dianda, M. (1996). Success for all: A summary of research. *Journal of Education for Students Placed At Risk, 1*(1), 41–76.

Sparks, D., & Loucks-Horsley, S. (1990). Models of staff development. In R. Houston (Ed.), *Handbook of research on teacher education* (pp. 234–250). New York: Macmillan.

Tharp, R. (1982). The effective instruction of comprehension: Results and description of the Kamehameha Early Education Program. *Reading Research Quarterly, 17*(4), 503–527.

Tharp, R. (2001). *Claims and evidence: Effectiveness of the five standards for effective pedagogy.* Santa Cruz, CA: CREDE.

Tharp, R. (2002). Research evidence: *Five standards for effective pedagogy and student outcomes* (Technical Report No. G1). Santa Cruz, CA: CREDE.

Tharp, R. G., Estrada, P., Dalton, S. S., & Yamauchi, L. A. (2000). *Teaching transformed: Achieving excellence, fairness, inclusion, and harmony.* Boulder, CO: Westview.

Tharp, R., & Gallimore, R. (1988). *Rousing minds to life: Teaching, learning, and schooling in social context.* Cambridge, England: Cambridge University Press.

Wasik, B., & Slavin, R. (1993). Preventing early reading failure with one-to-one tutoring: A review of five programs. *Reading Research Quarterly, 28*(2), 178–200.

Waxman, H., Padron, Y., & Knight, S. (1991). Risks associated with students' limited cognitive mastery. In M. Wang, M. Reynolds, & H. Walberg (Eds.), *Handbook of special education research and practice* (Vol. 4, pp. 235–254). New York: Pergamon.

Weiler, J. (1998). *Success for all: A summary of evaluations.* ERIC/CUE Digest Number 139.

Zeichner, K. M. (1992). *Educating teachers for cultural diversity.* East Lansing MI: National Center for Research on Teacher Learning.

Zeichner, K. M., & Hoeft, K. (1996). Teacher socialization for cultural diversity. In J. Sikula (Ed.), *Handbook of research on teacher education* (pp. 525–547). New York: Macmillan.

Chapter 5

Critical Issues in Developing the Teacher Corps for English Learners

Patricia Gándara
Julie Maxwell-Jolly
University of California, Davis

In the last decade the total U.S. population grew by about 12%.[1] During this same period, the limited English proficient (LEP) population nearly doubled. English learners (ELs) now make up almost 10% of the country's K–12 students. Ten years ago, 1 out of 6 middle- and high-school students in the United States was from a linguistic minority background (Blanton, 1999). The 2000 Census places that number at 1 out of 4 nationally, and 1 out of 2 in California. English learners account for 1.5 million of California's nearly 6 million students. The state has slightly under 1 million additional linguistic minority students who come from homes where English is not the dominant language. Overall, then, students who speak a language other than English at home account for 40% of California's K–12 school population (California Department of Education, 2003). The state's English learners, students who are not yet proficient in English, represent 32% of the nation's English learners, followed by Texas with 12% and Florida and New York with 5% each. As the poet Richard Armour wryly noted,

> So leap with joy, be blithe and gay
> Or weep my friends with sorrow,
> What California is today,
> The rest will be tomorrow. (*Economist*)

[1]National language statistics can be found at http://www.ncela.gwu.edu/states/index.htm

Most of the languages on the planet are spoken in some school in the United States, Spanish is the language spoken by the great majority, with 79% of nonnative English speakers. The next largest concentration of English learners is among Vietnamese and Hmong students, with only 1.9% and 1.6%, respectively. For most schools serving English learners, the challenge is primarily one of providing an equitable education to students who speak Spanish.

In 2002 Federal *No Child Left Behind* (NCLB) legislation brought the challenge of providing EL students with an adequate education into even greater focus by mandating that all states test their English learners annually and hold schools accountable for the educational progress of these students. The stakes are higher than they have ever been for bringing EL students into the academic mainstream.

The primary key to successfully educating any students, particularly those who are especially vulnerable such as English learners, is providing them with a well-qualified teacher. Adequate facilities, reasonable class size, good curriculum and materials, and a safe place to learn are all important components of the education of ELs, but as for all students, nothing is more important for educational outcomes than the qualifications of the teacher. Yet, while NCLB has forced states to grapple with the definition of a "highly qualified teacher" for all students, there has been little attention at either the state or federal level to defining what constitutes a highly qualified teacher for English learners. This suggests that any teacher who meets the general high professional standards could be effective with ELs. But we do not think this is the case.

ABSENCE OF NATIONAL POLICY RATIONALE FOR RECRUITING AND PREPARING TEACHERS FOR ENGLISH LEARNERS

A fundamental impediment to the development of a teacher corps for ELs in this country is the absence of any national policy to provide direction for schools and communities. There is no local or national consensus about what an ideal education for English learners should look like. In fact there is very little policy discussion at all with regard to educating these students. In the absence of serious discussion about our educational goals for ELs, self-serving political entrepreneurs, like Ron Unz, have filled the policy void with political solutions to educational problems. The common discourse focuses on "closing the achievement gap" rhetoric for ELs without any real attention to what would be required to actually do this. For some, simply closing the achievement gap is not enough. These visionary educators would like to think that ELs might actually raise the educational bar by achieving mastery of two languages. In public polls, a majority of respondents think it is a good idea for students to be given the opportunity to become bilingual (Huddy & Sears, 1990; Krashen, 1996). Without question, neither high achievement, nor mastery of two languages will occur unless students can be assured of teachers with the attributes, skills, and knowledge to meet their academic needs. But there are many questions regarding what appropriate EL teacher preparation should consist of. What kind of teacher is best suited to teach these students—must it be someone from the same ethnic or linguistic background, or is this irrelevant if the teacher is highly qualified? How should we go about recruiting these teachers, and should there be extra compensation for the additional skills they possess? Should we provide special incentives to keep them in the workforce, given the high turnover of teachers and the shortage of individuals with these skills? And if so, what would these incentives be? For teachers of English learners already in the workforce, how should we support them? What should be the content of professional development?

WHY TEACHER QUALIFICATIONS MATTER FOR EL STUDENTS

An increasingly large body of research has established that teachers with good professional preparation can make a significant difference in students' learning (Darling-Hammond, 2002; Haycock, 1998; Sanders & Horn, 1995; Sanders & Rivers, 1996). The evidence suggests that this is equally true for teachers of ELs. Hayes and Salazar (2001) recently conducted a study in Los Angeles Unified School District (LAUSD) of the relationship between EL student achievement gains and the credential held by the teachers who taught them in 29 schools and 177 classrooms with large numbers of EL students. They found that teachers with EL authorization have a positive impact on student outcomes. For example, [Model B[2]] students of teachers holding no state or district authorization made largely negative or very small positive . . . adjusted gains in reading and language (see Table 5.1). A follow-up study of Grades 1–3 classrooms in the same schools during the subsequent school year (2001) found again that "students of credentialed teachers out-performed students of emergency permitted teachers" (Hayes, Salazar, & Vukovic, 2002, p. 90).

[2]LAUSD divides its Structured English Immersion classes into two types: Model A, which is English only and Model B, which allows some primary language support. Data are more difficult to interpret for Model A because cell sizes are smaller and the authors report a lack of confidence in these small numbers.

TABLE 5.1
Actual and Adjusted Gains by Teacher Authorization Grade 2, Selected Schools, LAUSD

	Reading Actual Gains	Adjusted Gains	*Language* Actual Gains	Adjusted Gains
BCLAD[a]	**1.8** (*n* = 142)	**1.6** (*n* = 142)	**4.1** (*n* = 148)	**2.4** (*n* = 148)
CLAD/LDS	**2.0** (*n* = 32)	**2.7** (*n* = 32)	**1.0** (*n* = 34)	**0.4** (*n* = 34)
SB1969	*	*	*	*
A Level@	**1.8** (*n* = 155)	**1.6** (*n* = 155)	**0.3** (*n* = 155)	**–1.5** (*n* = 155)
No Authorization	**–2.4** (*n* = 74)	**–2.9** (*n* = 74)	**0.5** (*n* = 93)	**–1.8** (*n* = 93)

*Actual and adjusted gains were not reported here due to the small sample size.
[a]BCLAD refers to Bilingual Cross-cultural, Language and Academic Development credential; CLAD refers to Cross-cultural, Language, and Academic Development credential, LDS refers to Language Development Specialist certification, SB 1969 refers to a "grandfathering" provision allowing teachers with considerable classroom experience to obtain a certification to teach English learners on the basis of a 45-hour course; A Level refers to LAUSD certification of language competency for its teachers if they do not already hold a BCLAD, but can demonstrate that they are fluently bilingual.

THE ENGLISH LEARNER TEACHER WORKFORCE

A study by Zehler et al. (2003) gives us a picture of the teacher workforce that is providing instruction for English learners. Forty percent of all teachers nationwide have at least one English learner in their classrooms. While in 1992 nearly two thirds of English learners received some instruction in their native language, in 2003 only about 41% were provided with such instruction. Most ELs today receive all of their instruction in English, whether they understand any English or not. Likewise, in 1992 two thirds of English learners were reported to receive a curriculum that was designed specifically to meet their needs, while in 2003 only slightly more than half (52%) were reported to receive instruction that was designed for them in particular. Teachers who taught at least three English learners in 2003 reported they had received a median of 4 hours of in-service training in working with these students over the previous 5 years. Only 18% of teachers working with English learners reported having an English as a Second Language (ESL) certification, and 11% reported having a bilingual certification nationally. In sum, the picture that emerges nationally is one of enormous growth in the numbers of teachers who are teaching ELs in their classrooms, yet relatively few with certification that is geared to this task. Moreover, a smaller percentage of these students than in years past are receiving a curriculum geared to their needs and their teachers, by and large, have had very little in-service training on how to provide appropriate instruction for them.

Because we have studied in great depth the preparation provided for teachers of English learners in California, we also present data for this state.

Our assumption, which is supported by the demographic data, is that ELs in California do not vary greatly with regard to their education needs from those in most other states.[3] The evidence suggests that the educational picture for these students is not dramatically different in other parts of the country, although some other states provide more instructional options for ELs than does California under Proposition 227, the antibilingual education initiative passed in 1998.

THE SHORTAGE OF QUALIFIED TEACHERS WITH SPECIALIZED KNOWLEDGE

In spite of the critical importance of a good teacher for the academic progress of English learners, this remains one of the most elusive features of their education. Nationwide, 98% of teachers reporting that they have English learners in their classrooms state that they hold a valid teaching credential in their state. However, this is not the case in California, where such a large percentage of the nation's English learners are educated. English learners in California are more likely than *all other* children to be assigned to teachers who have only an emergency credential. Whereas 14% of teachers statewide were not fully credentialed, this was true of 25% of teachers of ELs (Gándara, Rumberger, Maxwell-Jolly, & Callahan, 2003). Figure 5.1 shows that as the concentration of ELs in a California school increases, so too does the percentage of teachers holding emergency credentials. Inasmuch as Fig. 5.1 holds poverty constant, we would expect to see a flat line if the discrepancy in credentialed teachers were purely a function of poverty. However, these data show that ELs are significantly less likely to have a fully credentialed teacher than other low-income non-EL students.[4] We know that this is due to higher mobility of teachers in poor areas, flight to schools with better working conditions, and seniority rules that allow more experienced teachers to select schools of their choice in more attractive areas outside of the inner city (Borhnstedt & Stecher, 2002). Most teachers prefer to work in schools close to where they live, and that are similar to those they attended (Zeichner, 1996). As result, teachers tend to move to the suburbs when the opportunity presents itself.

Although the Development Associates study (Zehler et al., 2003) indicates that 82% of teachers of English learners do not possess even the mini-

[3]In California, the majority of English Learners are Spanish dominant (85%); the next most prevalent languages are Vietnamese and Hmong, accounting for 2.4% and 1.7% respectively. National K–12 educational statistics mirror California's language distribution.

[4]By fully credentialed we are referring to a teacher who has a state authorized "regular" credential: a multiple subject (elementary) or single subject (secondary) teaching credential, that is, the bare minimum. We are *not* referring to any additional certification or specialized credential granted to those with expertise in working with ELL students.

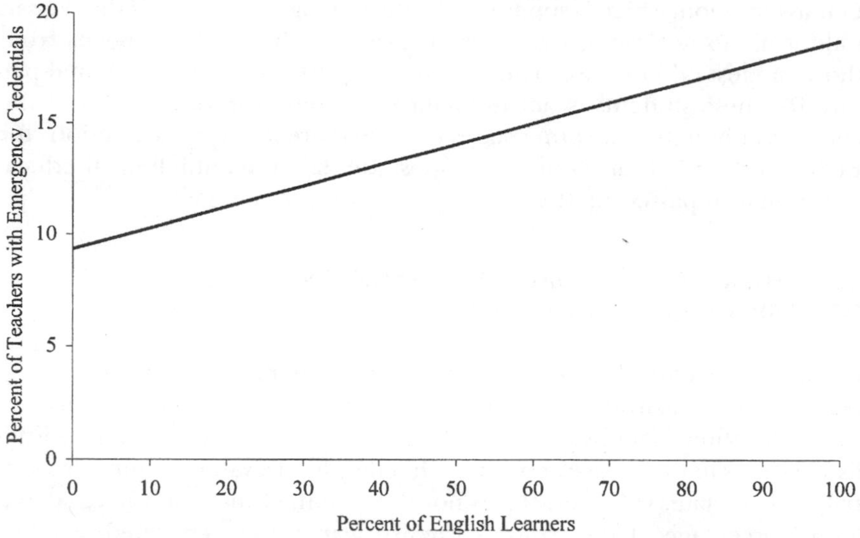

FIG. 5.1. The relationship between the percent of English learners and the percent of teachers with emergency credentials, holding constant the percent of students on free or reduced lunch, California schools, 1999–2000. Note: Relationship estimated from the regression equation: 3.553 + .119*LUNCH + .095*ELL (N = 6039), with LUNCH = 48.6 (sample mean). Source: 1999–2000 API Growth Data File. Retrieved October 4, 2000 from WWW: http://api.cde.ca.gov/datafiles.html

mal certification of ESL training, California data indicate a statewide average of only 4.2 such minimally prepared teachers per 100 English language learners (California Department of Education, Education Demographics Office, Spring 1999 Language Census). Comparing the numbers of teachers with the most rigorous training to teach ELs—those with a bilingual credential—the picture changes dramatically. There are only 1.9 fully credentialed bilingual teachers for every 100 EL students.

REASONS FOR THE SHORTAGE OF SPECIALIZED TEACHERS

The reasons for the shortage of teachers with specialized qualifications for ELs are multiple, but certainly much of the problem stems from the way that the education of English learners has been framed. During the 1970s several states passed laws regulating the education of English learners. New York, Massachusetts, and California were prominent among these. California, in particular, was considered to have a progressive law (the Chacon-Moscone Bill), which provided for "bilingual education" for the state's English learners whenever there was a critical mass of limited English speakers in the same school from the same language group. However, this 1976 legislation framed the issue facing these children as a language "problem" with the solution being to transition them as quickly as possible into English via a transitional bilingual education program (TBE). The California law reflected the driving philosophy of the federal Bilingual Education Act which viewed Limited English Proficient (LEP) students as suffering from a cultural and linguistic deficit that was to be remedied with the transition to English and away from the home culture and language (Crawford, 1999).

Given that the goal of most bilingual education programs was *not* to create fully bi-literate students, the role of most teachers of English learners was that of a bridge from one language to another. To be effective at this bridging function, oral skills in the non-English language was all that was needed to be a highly qualified teacher in this context. Thus, no urgency was created to develop a corps of *bi-literate* teachers who were highly qualified instructors of two languages. And, consistent with this, there were no major incentive programs mounted anywhere in the country to develop a corps of highly qualified bilingual teachers. Furthermore, the transition approach promoted a philosophy that emphasized bilingual instruction in Grades K–3 only, further limiting the potential pool of teachers. Had the instructional goal for English learners been framed as one of developing primary language as a resource (Ruiz, 1984), with the "solution" being to teach English alongside the primary language, thus maintaining the primary language and developing fully bi-literate students, a greater urgency for highly qualified bilingual teachers would have been created and the educational system would have been expected to respond to the mandate. However, the political compromise allowed the passage of seemingly progressive legislation, which did little to strengthen the capacity of the teaching force to meet the needs of these students. In fact, the lack of sufficient numbers of highly qualified bilingual teachers was often cited as an excuse for abandoning the approach in many locales (Crawford, 1998).

A second major reason for the shortage of highly qualified teachers of ELs is the abysmal record of moving language minority students successfully through high school, into college, and finally through teacher credentialing programs. Although qualified bilingual teachers of ELs do not have to come from the same language group that they teach—and most do not—this is the most likely pool of such teachers, since they are proficient in the language and familiar with the culture without any special training. Yet, data indicate that nationwide, only about 10.6% of Hispanics (the largest language minority group) achieve a bachelor's degree (Harvey, 2002). Thus, nearly 90% of all Hispanics are not even eligible to become teachers. However, even if many more bilingual individuals were ready and willing to become teachers for English learners, it is not clear that the educational system would be prepared to train them, as, aside from small federal Title III (previously Title

VII) seed grants, there is little funding to assist institutions of higher education to significantly increase their bilingual teacher training capacity. Special funds earmarked for this purpose were eliminated in 2000. Recent initiatives passed in California, Arizona, and Massachusetts curtailing bilingual education appear to be reducing the available pool of qualified bilingual teachers (Rumberger & Gándara, 2000).

THE ELEMENTS OF ADEQUATE PREPARATION OF EL TEACHERS

The question of what constitutes a highly qualified teacher for an English learner remains hotly debated in California and elsewhere. This issue has become all the more salient under federal regulations enacted in the 2002, No Child Left Behind legislation, which requires that every child have a highly qualified teacher by 2005–2006.[5] While the states must meet federal standards for "highly qualified teachers," for all students including EL children, there is no discussion of any special qualifications for teachers of ELs in the overall federal law. There is however, in Title III, the section of the federal law that funds various state programs serving EL students, a provision allowing—but not requiring—school districts to spend some of their Title III funds on the professional development of EL teachers. Among the authorized activities are: pre-service and in-service professional development programs for teachers, administrators, and other personnel providing educational services to LEP (EL) children; mentoring assistance to beginning teachers of LEP children; programs supporting effective teacher use of education technologies to improve instruction and assessment; and developing curricular materials and assessments for teachers appropriate to the needs of LEP children (Educational Testing Service, 2003). Thus, states enjoy considerable latitude in defining the qualifications for EL teachers.

The literature on English learner (EL) teaching and learning identifies unique attributes of effective teachers for these students in addition to the general characteristics of good teachers overall. Milk, Mercado, and Sapiens (1992) focused their discussion on aspects of good teaching for bilingual contexts that create optimal conditions for students to learn English as a second language distilled from a variety of sources. Their list suggests a set of fundamental skills, knowledge, and attitudes that all teachers working with language minority students (including mainstream teachers) should possess:

- An awareness of the kinds of special instructional services that second language learners experience at different stages of participation in bilingual and ESL programs.

[5]Public Law 107-110, No Child Left Behind, January 8, 2002. Full text available at http://www.ncela.gwu.edu/miscpubs/legislation/nclb/nclb.pd

- The ability to work collaboratively in teams that include specialists and nonspecialists in bilingual and ESL programs.
- An understanding of how classroom settings can be arranged to support a variety of instructional strategies.
- Knowledge of how pupils "use their existing knowledge to make sense of what is going on in the classroom and an awareness of ways in which pupils might misunderstand content that seems clear (even obvious) to the teacher."
- The ability to draw parents into classroom-related activities and tap into the knowledge and experience they can contribute to enhancing instruction.
- The ability to deliver an instructional program that includes ample opportunity for speaking, listening, reading and writing and provides scaffolding of new concepts to help guide students through the learning process.
- The ability and desire to include students in classroom dialogue.
- The ability to provide ongoing assessment of students' abilities in order to provide instruction aimed at an appropriate level above what students currently know.
- Tolerance of student responses that diverge from the teacher's point of view.
- Ability and desire to incorporate the culture of students into the curriculum.

In addition to these elements, Garcia (1996) noted others revealed by Tikunoff's (1983) study of effective teachers for English learners. Although they are similar in intent to those described by Milk, Mercado, and Sapiens (1992), they are sufficiently different to warrant inclusion here. According to Garcia, these teachers use the students' native language and English for instruction alternating between the two languages when necessary to provide clarity, but not translation. They specifically explain tasks and the expected outcomes and communicate high expectations for student learning while maintaining students' engagement by pacing instruction appropriately. Effective teachers for ELs use "active" teaching behaviors, including communicating clearly when giving directions, specifying tasks, and presenting information. They constantly monitor students' progress and provide immediate feedback on student success. Finally, these teachers have a sense of efficacy regarding their own ability to teach.

Although many of these competencies are valuable for instructing all students, some closely relate to the task of teaching ELs. In addition to the deeper understanding of second language development and the ways in which native language competency can bridge to, and support, English language acquisition, awareness of special services for English learners, ability to access and work with specialists in the field, understanding how to assess the academic progress of EL students and to discriminate between learning and language problems are all competencies that are key to effective instruction of this population. They are also competencies that are seldom, if ever, taught in standard teacher preparation programs.

Given the controversy over primary language versus English immersion programs with regard to the instruction of EL students, we think it essential to discuss the role of a teacher who speaks the home language of the students—no matter what the classroom program model. We believe that a teacher who is bilingual in English and the students' home language has the greatest likelihood of successfully teaching these students. For example, assessment of EL students is a notoriously difficult challenge, and because of this, these students are chronically overrepresented in special education classes (Gándara, Rumberger, Maxwell-Jolly, & Callahan, 2003). Teachers who know a student's home language are much better equipped to distinguish a language difficulty from a learning disability (Solano-Flores, Trumball, & Nelson-Barber, 2002). Multilingual teachers also have a better understanding of the challenges and complexities of learning a second language, as well as the ways in which the primary language can be used as a bridge to English (Wong Fillmore & Snow, 2002). Finally, research on appropriate programs and strategies for working with ELs often discusses the importance of "checking for understanding" (Solis, 1998). Clearly, a teacher who can speak to the student in a language that the student understands is able to do this more effectively than one who does not.

Speaking the language of the students one teaches also provides important access to understanding the social and cultural context in which students are learning. A teacher who is not able to understand student-to-student interactions is at a disadvantage in interpreting the dynamics of the classroom. The same might be said of the larger community. A teacher who understands the language and culture of the community has a much better grasp of the larger context in which his or her students live, and thus the potential effects of this context on their school experience (Cahnmann & Hornberger, 2000). In addition, ample research points out the important role that parental involvement can play in student success. In the case of EL children, teacher knowledge of the home language is critical to effective communication with and support of parents (Villarreal & Solis, 1998).

BUILDING A CORPS OF THE BEST TEACHERS FOR ENGLISH LEARNERS

Although scholars tell us something about the important attributes, skills, and knowledge of quality teachers for linguistically and culturally diverse students, less is known about how to build a corps of teachers who possess these qualities. One means of building a corps of teachers who are effective with diverse English learners is to recruit individuals who already have the language and other experience that enables them to effectively teach these students. As Haberman (1996) suggested, it may be easier to recruit the "right" person from the beginning than to try to change the "wrong one." He notes that an important consideration in preparing those he calls the "best and the brightest" for urban schools is that these individuals may be older with family responsibilities and therefore are likely to need flexible programs. For example, many paraeducator programs "grow their own" teachers by seeking paraprofessionals who have the community knowledge, language skills, and teaching and life experience to become effective teachers. His conclusion is that institutions must offer alternative preparation programs in order to encourage individuals who have the most potential for success with culturally and linguistically diverse students to consider the teaching profession.

The "right" teachers are not necessarily those from the same underrepresented communities as the students, but more often than not, these individuals have insights, experiences, and skills that are difficult to replicate in the short space of time that teacher preparation programs have to train new teachers. Certainly, the acquisition of a second language will rarely occur in that time frame. Moreover, these individuals may be the "right" teachers because they tend to come from the same geographic areas where many of the teachers who are currently graduating from teacher preparation programs do not want to work. Because teachers are drawn to teaching in near proximity to where they live (Murnane, Singer, Willett, Kemple, & Olsen, 1991; Shields, Marsh, & Powell, 1998a), the inclusion of more teachers from these underrepresented communities could have a salutary effect on the problem of unequal distribution of the teacher force. There is also reason to believe that teachers who share the backgrounds of these students are more likely to persist both in the teacher corps and in schools with high minority populations. For example, Murnane and his associates (1991) found that Black teachers teaching in largely Black inner cities were twice as likely to remain in the teaching force after 5 years as White teachers who taught in those schools.

INCENTIVES AND DISINCENTIVES TO BECOMING A BILINGUAL TEACHER

It is not necessarily true that "if we build it (larger bilingual teacher preparation programs) they will come." The job of a bilingual teacher is seldom compensated at a higher rate than regular teachers, yet the demands are considerably greater. These teachers often must develop their own curriculum because of inadequate materials (Gándara, Rumberger, Maxwell-Jolly, & Callahan, 2003); they must teach English at the same time that they teach subject matter content; and the challenges associated with teaching ELs are even greater than for the typical student. The large number of ELs who are immigrants frequently come from circumstances in which their early lives and education have been disrupted by war, loss or estrangement of family members, poverty, and residential mobility (Ruiz de Velasco & Fix, 2000; Olsen, 1998). As such, teachers must know how to intervene educationally with students whose personal and educational backgrounds are significantly different from the mainstream English-speaking student. Moreover, the age and grade placements of these students in U.S. schools often do not match their skill levels because of varying educational experiences in their countries of origin (Ruiz-de-Velasco & Fix, 2000).

Recent research suggests that working conditions influence teachers' decisions about where to teach more than do salaries (Hanushek, Kain, & Rivkin, 2001; Loeb & Page, 2000). Data for California demonstrate this clearly. Table 5.2 demonstrates that the differences between conditions in schools with high and low concentrations of EL students are dramatic, even with respect to characteristics that would not intuitively seem to be related to the concentration of English learners. However, it is evident that when working and learning conditions are poor, they affect the attitudes of staff, and no doubt the ability of the school to attract the most competent people to work there. For example, teachers of English learners are more apt than teachers of English speakers to respond that they do not have facilities that are conducive to teaching and learning. In a recent survey conducted in California, close to half of teachers in schools with higher percentages of ELs reported the physical facilities at their schools were only fair or poor, compared to 26% of teachers in schools with low percentages of English

TABLE 5.2
Condition of Facilities of California Schools by Percentage of English Learners in Teachers' Schools, January 2002
(percent of teachers reporting condition)

	25% or less	*Over 25%*	*Total*
The adequacy of the physical facilities is ONLY FAIR OR POOR	26	43	32
Bathrooms ARE NOT clean and open throughout the day.	13	23	17
HAVE seen evidence of cockroaches, rats, or mice in past year.	24	34	28

Note. Results exclude respondents who did not answer question or answered "not sure." Results are weighted. All column differences are statistically significant at .05 level or better.

Source. Harris Survey of a Cross-Section of California School Teachers, January 2002 (N= 1071).

learners (Table 5.2). Teachers in schools with high percentages of English learners were 50% more likely to report bathrooms that were not clean and open throughout the day and having seen evidence of cockroaches, rats, or mice.

More than one third of principals in schools with higher concentrations of English learners reported that their classrooms were never or often not adequate, compared to 8% of principals with low concentration of EL students (Table 5.3).[6] Such conditions not only make it more difficult to teach ELs, they also make it difficult to retain teachers since, as we showed earlier, a considerable body of research finds that teachers are more likely to leave schools with poor working conditions.

TABLE 5.3
Characteristics of California Elementary School Facilities by EL Concentration, Spring 1999

	25% or less	*More than 25%*	*Total*
Principal questionnaire responses:			
Classrooms never or often not adequate[7]	8	35	19

Note. Results are weighted (S2SAQW0).
Source. ECLS base year data for California public elementary schools ($N = 69$).

The see-sawing policies around legal and appropriate methods of instruction of English learners also exacerbates the difficulty of the job of teaching English learners, and provides a disincentive to enter and stay in the position (Maxwell-Jolly & Gándara, 2002). For example, teachers interviewed in a statewide study of the implementation of Proposition 227 noted feeling pressured by the precipitous changes in instructional policy, testing, and accountability, without sufficient time or training to prepare for them. Several of the teachers interviewed mentioned considering leaving the field (Gándara et al., 2001; Maxwell-Jolly, 2001).

Ironically, although we make the job of bilingual teachers unnecessarily difficult because of changing instructional policies and inadequate support, materials, and working conditions, the potential pool of teachers is large and could be tapped relatively easily. In California, approximately 40% of students in the public schools are language minorities—that is, these young people speak a language other than, or in addition to, English at home. Thus, a huge percentage of California's youth already have the

[6]It is interesting to note that 19 percent of all principals in California reported that their classrooms were never or often not adequate, compared to 9 percent of principals in the rest of the United States.

[7]This question did not require the respondent to specify in what way the classroom was inadequate.

linguistic background and cultural knowledge (as we have noted, the most difficult characteristics to "train" in a new teacher) and could be recruited and prepared for the teaching force. We also know that these same individuals are more likely to choose to work in the communities in which they live and are more likely to stay in these teaching positions than are teachers without this background (Murnane et al., 1991).

APPROPRIATE CONTENT AND STRUCTURE OF PROFESSIONAL DEVELOPMENT FOR EL TEACHERS

Although recruitment and preparation are important issues with respect to strengthening the teacher corps for English learners, the reality is that most teachers who will be teaching these students in the foreseeable future have already completed their training and are in the schools. For these teachers the key to strengthening their skills is professional development. A number of studies have demonstrated that good professional development increases teachers' sense of competence and provides them with tangible strategies for better meeting the needs of their students (Garcia, 1992; Herman & Aguirre-Muñoz, 2003; Herman, Goldschmidt, & Swigert, 2003). Given these findings, teacher professional development has been a cornerstone of many states' education reform plans. Yet, surprisingly little emphasis has been placed on the specialized needs of teachers of English learners.

We noted earlier that nationwide, teachers of ELs received only a median of 4.2 hours of professional development dedicated to instructional strategies for EL students in a 5-year period. The situation in California is not terribly different, although our data are for only 1 year. Data from California show that even where teachers are teaching a majority of ELs, they receive minimal professional development dedicated to helping them instruct these students. The percent of professional development time that teachers reported focusing on the instruction of English learners in 1999–2000 ranged from 3% to 10% with a mean of only 7%, or less than 3 hours on average (Stecher & Bohrnstedt, 2000). See Table 5.4.

These data are corroborated by several other recent studies. Hayes and Salazar (2001), in their study of 177 classrooms in the Los Angeles City Unified School District, noted that teachers discussed "the problematic lack of resources and training to assist them to provide quality services to ELs" (p. 23). A report on the results of a California Department of Education (California Department of Education, 1999) survey of every California school district found that professional development to help teachers with EL instruction was one of the most significant unmet needs in the aftermath of the passage of Proposition 227, which severely curtailed bilingual programs.

TABLE 5.4
Professional Development of Teachers in Grades 1 to 4 by Classroom Concentration of English Learners, 1999–2000

Percent English Learners in the Classroom	*Mean Number of Days*	*Mean Number of Hours*[a]	*Percent of Hours on Teaching ELs*
0	3.5	28	3
1–25	3.6	30	8
26–50	3.3	32	9
51–100	3.8	35	10
Total	3.6	31	7

[a]Number of hours estimated by recoding responses (8 hours or less = 4 hours; more than 8 = 12 hours).

Note. Results are weighted.

Source. 2000 Class Size Reduction Teacher Survey (N = 774).

The University of California provided professional development for the state's teachers through its Professional Development Institutes (CPDIs) for several years. This is not the only professional development activity in the state, in fact, many school districts sponsor extensive professional development programs, but it was the largest state-wide effort, with more than 45,000 teachers participating in CPDI workshops in 2000–2001. In that same year, a total of almost 51 million dollars was provided for this purpose. Of this amount, only a little more than 8 million was earmarked for professional development in the area of English Language Development (Office of the President, University of California, 2002). This constituted about 16% of the professional development budget, although ELs constituted fully 25% of the students in the state. A state study found that only 18% of the teachers in their sample had even heard of the professional development workshops aimed at English language development, and only 8% had attended one or more (Parrish et al., 2002, p. 40), suggesting that relatively little is done to disseminate information about resources that may be available to teachers of English learners.

Of course, one issue is the provision of professional development services, but another is the content of these services. There have been major debates over the structure and content of professional development for teachers of ELs. On the one hand, some experts argue that English should be learned through instruction in the content areas (e.g., math, science, reading) and that language will develop naturally in this context. Others argue that the acquisition of a second language constitutes "content" in itself, that there are features of language that must be taught explicitly and that are not simply "absorbed" in another context (Wong Fillmore & Snow, 2002). Many experts agree that teaching a second language through content instruction is appropriate much, if not all, of the time. But, this also requires knowledge of sophisticated techniques and strategies, and there is a dearth of professionals available with such skills.

SUMMARY AND RECOMMENDATIONS

The lack of any consistent policy for the education of English learners, and the constant shifting of programmatic goals, leaves administrators with little guidance for what kinds of teachers they should train and recruit. A goal of producing bilingual, biliterate students suggests one kind of teacher, whereas a goal of shifting students as rapidly as possible out of their native language and into English may suggest another. In either case, teachers need specialized knowledge and skills in order to adequately meet these students' needs—something that too few currently practicing teachers of ELs have. Moreover, the perception that all ELs are found in the early grades means that little attention is paid to training and recruiting teachers at the secondary level. One result is a corps of struggling and under-prepared teachers who need additional skills to work effectively with the students in their classrooms. Another, more pernicious result is that many secondary English learners struggle and drop out of school when they can find nothing in the middle and high schools that addresses either educational or personal needs (Gándara et al., 2003; Olsen et al., 1994).

Although considerable debate has ensued in recent years over the definition of a "highly qualified teacher," in large part spurred by *No Child Left Behind* legislation, little attention has been paid to the definition of such a teacher for ELs. Nonetheless, we think it is clear that specific, additional competencies are necessary in order for teachers to be effective with this population. These teachers must understand the challenges that EL students face in adapting to a new culture, learning a new language, and integrating both the linguistic and cognitive demands of schooling simultaneously. Teachers must also have the pedagogical skills and strategies to address these challenges. And because today so many ELs are mainstreamed into regular, English only classrooms, teachers must have the skill to organize their instruction in a way that meets the needs of both English learners and English speakers at the same time. This is a big job for the most highly qualified and experienced teachers; we find little reason to believe that it can be accomplished well by teachers with limited experience and virtually no training specific to these challenges.

The lack of a clear and articulated policy for the education of ELs also leads to weak commitment to recruitment. It is entirely within the capacity of most states to train all the teachers for English learners that they need. Yet, despite this capacity there is a chronic shortage of these teachers because no one has taken responsibility for making it a legislative priority to guarantee that every EL will have a qualified teacher. Without such teachers, the educational achievement gap is not likely to close for EL students, no matter how many times we chant the mantra of "no child left behind."

RECOMMENDATIONS

English Learner Policy

The involvement of the U.S. Department of Education in research on the instruction of English learners has principally been through the funding of studies to answer the question: Which kind of program most rapidly moves English learners into the academic mainstream? The question has never been asked, however, What should be our goals for the education of ELs from preschool to high school graduation, and what are the impediments that stand in the way of meeting those goals? The answers to this question would provide significant guidance to the field about the appropriate aims of local policies and the attendant role of support from the federal government. Certainly, one answer would be to provide all EL students with teachers who have sufficient knowledge and expertise to truly meet their educational needs. Providing incentives for the states to prepare and recruit these teachers would be an important policy response.

Preparation and Recruitment

In order to develop the EL teaching force, it makes sense to concentrate efforts where the target population is found in greatest numbers. For example, most Latino and other underrepresented linguistic minority high school graduates who enter postsecondary education attend community colleges. Currently, we lose most of these students before they complete a Bachelor's degree. Among the most prominent reasons for this loss are financial pressures, inadequate career counseling, and lack of a focused goal for their studies. Thus, we recommend state and federal policies that would foster:

- Teacher preparation programs that begin at the community colleges, with focused coursework and counseling, and forgivable loans for educational and other expenses of the student's education. Such an initiative could help stem the drop-out problem among students of color in the community colleges, and could ultimately add significant numbers to the teacher pool. As a part of this program, a specialized Associate degree awarded to these students at the completion of their community college coursework could prepare them to work as classroom aides, serving the objective of helping students to acquire needed experience and supplement their incomes while they continue their studies.

- Sign-up bonuses for well-qualified teachers of English learners. The armed services pay substantial sign-up bonuses, as well as funding the education of promising recruits in order to enhance their pool of candidates. Surely the need for qualified teachers is as great as our need for service people. Sign-up bonuses should be paid to qualified teacher candidates who have the skills, background, and experience that are needed to teach diverse students. Thus, individuals with multiple language competencies and experience living and working among culturally diverse populations should be eligible for a sign-up bonus large enough to attract these individuals who clearly have many other occupational options.
- Support of students who are already in the college pipeline, who have special knowledge of minority communities and languages, and who have demonstrated an interest in teaching. They should be eligible for forgivable loans sufficient to ensure that they complete their undergraduate degrees and credentials in a timely manner, and quickly enter the teaching force. This recommendation is a matter of degree not innovation. Forgivable loan opportunities already exist but it is our suggestion that to be maximally efficient such programs should provide students enough support through these loans to allow them to forgo other work and focus solely on their teacher preparation studies.

Preservice Content and Professional Development

The literature is clear and consistent that effective practices for preparing teachers to teach diverse students must be infused into the entire preparation program, and possibly prior to that, through the undergraduate program. Nonetheless, the literature is equally clear that although there are some admirable examples of programs that incorporate this infusion approach, the majority do not, and many pay only cursory attention to issues of linguistic and cultural diversity. This neglect in preservice programs makes the need to focus on the skills and knowledge to better prepare teachers to work effectively with these students essential.

Furthermore, these skills and knowledge should be an integral part of the planning of all professional development rather than an add-on or afterthought. Therefore we recommend that:

- Professional development should focus specifically and to an adequate degree on the instructional strategies, skills, and knowledge shown in the literature to be present in successful programs for English learners including an infusion of content related to issues of teaching culturally and linguistically diverse students into all aspects of the program.

A Federal Guarantee of a Highly Qualified Teacher for Every English Learner

English learners should be provided with the same guarantee of a qualified teacher that all other students receive. This will require explicit guidance from the U.S. Department of Education about the kinds of qualifications such teachers should possess, and should make explicit how these competencies are additional to the regular competencies of a "highly qualified" teacher.

RECOMMENDED RESEARCH

Although there is a growing body of research on effective strategies for increasing the quantity and quality of teachers for EL students, there is much we still need to know. For example:

1. Why do we lose 40% to 60% of those who earn credentials from the field before they ever take a teaching job? To what extent is this related to the feelings expressed by some teacher education students that they did not feel prepared by their programs to be effective teachers for culturally and linguistically diverse students?
2. How successful in preparing teachers who are effective with ELs are the alternative routes to teacher credentials, including internships and district credentialing programs? How successful are these programs at increasing the diversity of the teacher corps?
3. What are the sources of the high rates of attrition from the ranks of teachers, particularly among those working with EL students?
4. How can we most effectively increase the status of the teaching profession in order to attract more qualified candidates particularly from linguistic minority communities?

REFERENCES

Blanton, L. L. (1999). Classroom instruction and language minority students: On teaching to "smarter" readers and writers. In L. Harklau, K. M. Losey, & M. Siegal (Eds.), *Generation 1.5 meets college composition: Issues in the teaching of writing to US educated learners of ESL* (pp. 119–142). Mahwah, NJ: Lawrence Erlbaum Associates.

Bohrnstedt, G. W., & Stecher, B. M. (2002). *Class size reduction in California: Findings from 1999–00 and 2000–01.* Sacramento: California Department of Education.

Cahnmann, M. S., & Hornberger, N. (2000). Understanding what counts: Issues of language, culture, and power in mathematics instruction and assessment. *Educators for Urban Minorities, 1,* 39–52.

California Department of Education. (1999). Education Demographics Office, *Spring 1999 Language Census.* Available online at http://www.cde.ca.gov

California Department of Education. (2003). *Language Census, 2003.* Available online at http://www.cde.ca.gov

Crawford, J. (1998). Language politics in the United States: The paradox of bilingual education. In C. Ovando & P. McLaren (Eds.), *The politics of multiculturalism and bilingual education: Students and teachers caught in the cross-fire.* New York: McGraw-Hill.

Crawford, J. (1999). *Bilingual education: History, politics, theory, & practice.* Los Angeles, CA: Bilingual Educational Services.

Darling-Hammond, L. (2002). *Access to quality teaching: An analysis of inequality in California's public schools.* UCLA Institute for Democracy, Education, & Access. Available online at http://www.ucla-idea.org

Economist. Available online at http://economist.com/cities/displaystory.efm?story_id=2609395

Educational Testing Service, ETS. (2003). The no child left behind act: A special report. Available online at http://www.ets.org/aboutets/child/index.html

Gándara, P., Maxwell-Jolly, J., Garcia, E., Asato, J., Gutierrez, K., Stritikus, T., & Curry, J. (2000). *The effects of Proposition 227 on the instruction of English learners: Year one implementation.* University of California, Santa Barbara: Linguistic Minority Research Institute.

Gándara, P., Rumberger, R., Maxwell-Jolly, J., & Callahan, R. (2003). The inequitable treatment of English learners in California's public schools, *Educational Policy Analysis Archives, 16,* Available online at http://www.asu.edu/epaa

Garcia, E. E. (1992). *Teachers for language minority students: Evaluating professional standards. Focus on evaluation and measurement. Vols. 1 and 2.* Proceedings of the National Research Symposium on Limited English Proficient Student Issues (Washington, DC, September 4–6, 1991).

Garcia, E. E. (1996). Preparing instructional professionals for linguistically and culturally diverse students. In J. Sikula (Ed.), *Handbook of research on teacher education* (pp. 802–813). New York: Simon & Schuster.

Haberman, M. (1996). Selecting and preparing culturally competent teachers for urban schools. In J. Sikula (Ed.), *Handbook of research on teacher education* (pp. 747–760). New York: Simon & Schuster.

Hanushek, E. A., Kain, J. F., & Rivkin, S. G. (2001). *Why public schools lose teachers.* Working paper 8559. Cambridge, MA: National Bureau of Economic Research.

Harvey, W. (2002). *Minorities in higher education, 2001–2002, 19th Annual Status Report.* Washington, DC: American Council on Education.

Haycock, K. (1998). Good teaching matters: How well qualified teachers can close the gap, *Thinking K–16, 3*(2), 1–8.

Hayes, K., & Salazar, J. J. (2001). *Evaluation of the structured English immersion program. Final Report: Year 1.* Program Evaluation Branch, Los Angeles City Schools.

Hayes, K., Salazar, J., & Vukovic, E. (2002). *Evaluation of the structured English immersion program. Final Report: Year 2.* Program Evaluation Branch, Los Angeles City Schools.

Herman, J., Aguirre-Muñoz, Z. (2003). *Preparing teachers to teach English learners in California: CPDI year 2 evaluation report.* CRESST, University of California, Los Angeles.

Herman, J., Goldschmidt, P., & Swigert, S. (2003). *Evaluation of the primary and secondary English language arts California professional development institutes survey responses to teacher practices and institute evaluation.* CRESST, University of California, Los Angeles.

Huddy, L., & Sears, D. (1990). Qualified public support for bilingual education: Some policy implications. *Annals of the American Academy of Political and Social Science, 508,* 119–134.

Krashen, S. (1996). Surveys of opinions on bilingual education: Some current issues. *Bilingual Research Journal, 20,* 411–431.

Loeb, S., & Page, M. E. (2000). Examining the link between teacher wages and student outcomes: The importance of alternative labor market opportunities and non-pecuniary variation. *Review of Economics and Statistics, 82,* 393–408.

Maxwell-Jolly, J. (2001). *Exit, voice and loyalty: Bilingual teacher response to mandated reform.* Unpublished doctoral dissertation, University of California, Davis.

Maxwell-Jolly, J., & Gándara, P. (2002). A quest for quality: Providing qualified teachers for California's English learners. In Z. Beycont (Ed.), *The power of culture: Teaching across language difference.* Cambridge, MA: Harvard Education Publishing Group.

Milk, R., Mercado, C., & Sapiens, A. (1992). Rethinking the education of teachers of language minority children: Developing reflective teachers for changing schools. *NCBE Focus: Occasional papers in bilingual education.* Number 6, Summer, 1992. (online serial). http://www.ncbe.gwu.edu

Murnane, R., Singer, J., Willett, J., Kemple, J., & Olsen, R. (1991). *Who will teach? Policies that matter.* Cambridge, MA: Harvard University Press.

Office of the President University of California. (2002). *Evaluation of California Professional Development Institutes.* Oakland, CA: UCOP.

Olsen, L. (1998). The Unz/Tuchman "English for Children" initiative: A new attack on immigrant children and the schools. *Multicultural Education, 5*(3), 11–13.

Olsen, L., Chang, H., De la Rosa Salazar, D., Leong, C., McCall-Perez, Z., McClain, G., & Raffel, L. (1994). *The unfinished journey: Restructuring schools in a diverse society,* Oakland, CA: California Tomorrow.

Parrish, T. B., Linquanti, R., Merickel, A., Quick, H. E., Laird, J., & Esra, P. (2002). *Effects of the implementation of Proposition 227 on the education of English learners, K–12. Year two report.* Palo Alto, CA: American Institutes for Research.

Ruiz, R. (1984). Orientations in language planning. *Journal of the National Association of Bilingual Education, 2,* 15–34.

Ruiz de Velasco, J., & Fix, M. (2000). *Overlooked and underserved: Immigrant students in US secondary schools.* Washington DC: The Urban Institute.

Rumberger, R. W., & Gándara, P. (2000). The schooling of English learners. In E. Burr, G. Hayward, & M. Kirst (Eds.), *Crucial issues in California education* (pp. 23–44). Berkeley, CA: Policy Analysis for California Education.

Sanders, W. L., & Horn, S. P. (1995). The Tennessee Value-Added assessment system (TVAAS): Mixed model methodology in educational assessment. In A. J. Shinkfield & D. Stufflebeam (Eds.), *Teacher evaluation: Guide to effective practice.* Boston: Kluwer.

Sanders, W. L., & Rivers, J. C. (1996). *Cumulative and residual effects of teachers on future student academic achievement.* University of Tennessee Value-Added Research and Assessment Center.

Shields, P. M., Marsh, J. M., & Powell, J. P. (1998). *An inventory of the status of teacher development in California.* Menlo Park, CA: SRI International.

Solano-Flores, G., Trumball, E., & Nelson-Barber, S. (2002). Concurrent development of dual language assessments: An alternative to translating tests for linguistic minorities. *International Journal of Testing, 2*(2), 107–129.

Solis, A. (1998). In Bilingual education. IDRA Focus. Intercultural Development Research Association, San Antonio, TX, *IDRA Newsletter, 25,* No. 1.

Tikunoff, W. J. (1983). *An emerging description of successful bilingual instruction: Part I, SBIF study.* San Francisco, CA: Far West Laboratory for Educational Research and Development.

Villarreal, A., & Solis, A. (1998). In Bilingual Education. IDRA Focus. Intercultural Development Research Association, San Antonio, TX. *IDRA Newsletter, 25*, No. 1.

Wong Fillmore, L., & Snow, C. E. (2002). *What teachers need to know about language. Center for Applied Linguistics.* Available online at www.ncbe.gwu.edu

Zehler, A. M., Fleischman, H. L., Hopstock, P. J., Stephenson, T. G., Pendzick, M. L., & Sapru, S. (2003). *Descriptive study of services to LEP students and LEP students with disabilities, Volume I.* Washington, DC: U.S. Department of Education, Office of English Language Acquisition, Language Enhancement, and Academic Achievement of Limited English Proficient Students (OELA).

Zeichner, K. (1996). Educating teachers for cultural diversity. In K. Zeichner, S. Melnick, & M. L. Gomez (Eds.), *Currents of reform in preservice teacher education* (pp. 133–175). New York: Teachers College Press.

Chapter 6

Quality Instruction in Reading for English Language Learners

Margarita Calderón
Johns Hopkins University

SUCCESSFUL STUDENTS REQUIRE SUCCESSFUL TEACHERS

No Child Left Behind (NCLB) calls for reform and accountability in all U.S. schools. It is a well-known fact that America's schools need to improve and need help toward that goal. If schools want to improve student performance it means that they must begin by improving the performance of all teachers, since all teachers have to work with English Language Learners.

Based on the most recent survey results from state education agencies in the United States, it is estimated that 4,584,946 English language learner (ELL) students were enrolled in public schools (Pre-K through Grade 12) for the 2000–2001 school year. This number represents approximately 9.6% of total public school student enrollment, and a 32.1% increase over the reported 1997–1998 public school ELL enrollment.

According to State Education Indicators with a Focus on Title I (U.S. Department of Education, 2002),[1] the reading/language arts outcomes for language-minority students (LMSs) at the secondary level are very discouraging. According to dropout rates calculated by the National Center for Education Statistics (NCES), 11% of 16- to 24-year-olds were out of school

[1]There are virtually no state or national data on the educational outcomes of language-minority students or English language learners with the exception of the State Education Indicators with a Focus on Title I (U.S. Department of Education, 2002) cited in the text.

without a high-school credential in 2001. Each year between 1972 and 2001, dropout rates were lowest for Whites and highest for Hispanics. During this time frame, the rates dropped for White and Black young adults, but remained stable for Hispanics. Moreover, it is the high dropout rate for Hispanic immigrants that partly accounts for greater dropout rates for Hispanics. Among Hispanic 16- to 24-year-olds who were born outside the 50 states and the District of Columbia, the dropout rate of 43% in 2001 was more than double the rate for first- or later-generation Hispanic young adults born in the United States (15% and 14%, respectively). Dropouts from high school are more likely to be unemployed and earn less when they are employed than those who complete high school (NCES 2002-14). In addition, high-school dropouts are more likely to receive public assistance than high-school graduates that do not attend college (NCES 98-103, Indicator 34).

The limited English language skills and low academic performance of Hispanic and other language-minority students pose a major problem in middle and high-school settings. All language-minority students must be prepared to participate in a rigorous academic program and the time for this preparation is limited, often allowing for only the basic social language skills. This is not up to par with the literacy levels and academics demanded by secondary school curriculum (August & Hakuta, 1997). Consequently, most middle- and high-school language-minority students fail to develop to their fullest potential and become disaffected, drop out of school, and must settle for low-paying jobs without benefit of higher education (Slavin & Calderón, 2001; Snow, 2002).

Yet, upon entering the workforce, most teachers are unprepared to teach language-minority students, and have limited opportunities to update their knowledge and skills in an ongoing basis throughout their careers (Calderón & Minaya-Rowe, 2003). This is a serious problem because the opportunities for at-risk students to succeed academically depend on teachers' knowledge and applications of effective teaching in the classroom. According to NCES (2002),[2] in 1999–2000, 41.2% of teachers taught students with limited English proficiency. Only 12.5% of these teachers had 8 or more hours of training in the last 3 years on how to teach LEP students.[3]

To equip all teachers to work successfully with a growing at-risk population requires continuing renewal and extension of the skills, knowledge, and awareness needed to remain effective in a multicultural dynamic environ-

---

[2]Excerpted from U.S. Department of Educational Statistics (2002) Schools and Staffing Survey, 1999–2000: Overview of the Data for Public, Private, and Public Charter, and Bureau of Indian Affairs Elementary and Secondary Schools (NCES, 2002, p. 313). Washington, DC: Author. Table 1.19, pp. 43–44.

[3]According to the survey, the numbers include both full-time and part-time teachers in traditional public schools in the United States.

ment (Darling-Hammond & Sykes, 1999). NCLB calls for professional qualifications of teachers and profound knowledge among other topics: student academic achievement disaggregated by subgroups; comparison of students at basic, proficient, and advanced levels of language and literacy development; assessment processes, interpretation, implications for instructional improvement; and an ample instructional repertoire that reaches all students. However, teachers cannot possibly be fully prepared without quality preservice and quality ongoing professional development. Results-driven education and quality teaching requires teacher-focused quality professional development.

Potential and existing teachers need the type of professional development where they can explore their beliefs about their students and increase their repertoire of linguistic and culturally relevant pedagogy (Calderón, 1998, 2000). This also places teachers' needs within a larger context that includes institutional mission and goals, student performance data, and teacher support mechanisms. An institution's program (school district or university) must include measures for student performance and for measuring changes in educators' on-the-job performance. But, it must also apply those same measures to the institution preparing the teachers.

One area that needs dire attention and quality comprehensive professional development programs is reading. Although everyone in the nation is preoccupied with developing reading skills for all students, including ELLs, scarce attention is given to effective designs of professional programs to develop the teachers' skills, until now. As more researchers, practitioners, and educational institutions begin to dialogue and share ideas on the topic of quality teachers for ELLs, the field will hopefully begin to pay attention to teachers' needs within quality professional development designs.

A FRAMEWORK FOR THE PREPARATION OF TEACHERS OF ELLS TO TEACH READING

This chapter explores research-based literacy instruction for English language learners and possible ways to enhance professional development programs. It is the author's hope that this conceptual framework, and a review of relevant literature, will assist school districts in the design and implementation of quality professional development programs.

From the national data on ELL/LMS performance, it is evident that knowing how to teach reading to ELLs is critically important. Knowing how to prepare teachers to teach reading to ELLs becomes one of the most important goals of a school district. If every teacher in the schools today is expected to be a reading teacher, then everyone teaching in elementary and secondary schools with ELLs must also know how to teach reading, whether it is through social studies, science, math, or language arts domains.

WHY FOCUS ON QUALITY TEACHERS FOR READING?

The National Reading Panel (NRP, 2000) was highly concerned with teacher education for reading. The NRP found that preservice education focuses on changing teacher behavior without a concomitant focus on the outcomes of students who are eventually instructed by those teachers. This emphasis is also apparent in the field with the onslaught of "reading models" where the developers are quick to attribute student outcomes to their intervention and not the teachers. Although reading instruction involves four interacting factors: students, tasks, materials, and teachers, the NRP found that research has rarely focused on teachers, instead emphasizing students, materials, and tasks. Therefore, teacher education and its impact on the teachers' and their students' learning has been largely ignored.

The Learning First Alliance (2000) reported that teachers may be educated, licensed, and employed without knowledge of the most important tools for fighting illiteracy. Because so many textbooks and instructional programs have deemphasized some challenging aspects of beginning reading, including the explicit teaching of alphabetic skills, word attack, spelling, grammar, and vocabulary, gaps in teacher knowledge and skill may need to be remedied in these areas especially. They are pivotal for reading success and may deserve special emphasis. Teachers ideally would have the tools to teach the essentials of reading and language, as their children's needs were determined. Each dimension of reading acquisition is worthy of intensive focus in a professional program design. In addition, the study of any domain of reading and literacy development would be supported with readings, demonstrations, and peer practice that explain the psychological, linguistic, and educational reasons for the recommended practices.

Reading has also been approached as a matter of cognition, culture, socialization, instruction and language (Snow, Burns, & Griffin, 1998). The National Research Council committee headed by Snow agreed that reading is inextricably embedded in educational, social, historical, cultural, and biological realities. It is a cognitive and psycholinguistic activity because it requires the use of form to obtain meaning within the context of the reader's purpose (p. 33). Therefore, in planning and designing professional programs, the culture, language, literacy, and socialization patterns of ELLs in their school populations need to receive priority.

WHAT DOES THE RESEARCH SAY ABOUT TEACHING READING?

There is general scientific consensus among researchers and comprehensive research review panels that the following components are necessary for teaching basic reading skills (Learning First Alliance, 2000; National Reading Panel, 2000; Pacific Resources for Education and Learning, 2002; Slavin & Cheung, in press; Snow, Burns, & Griffin, 1998):

Knowledge Base for Early Reading

1. Phonemic awareness, letter knowledge, and concepts of print
2. The alphabetic code: Phonics and decoding
3. Fluent, automatic reading of text
4. Vocabulary
5. Text comprehension
6. Written expression
7. Spelling and handwriting
8. Screening and continuous assessment to inform instruction
9. Motivating children to read and developing their literacy horizons

In *Every Child Reading: A Professional Development Guide*, the Learning First Alliance (2000) synthesizes the scientific evidence relevant to these reading components into eight tables. The tables make recommendations for developing teacher knowledge and teacher skills as well as suggesting teacher professional development experiences. However, they also caution the reader that their recommendations are for mainstream student populations and that ELL issues are beyond the scope of their proposed guide.

WHAT DOES THE RESEARCH SAY ABOUT TEACHING READING TO ELLS?

Emerging studies on ELLs find that teaching to the basic principles is not sufficient to ensure success for ELLs (August & Hakuta, 1997; Calderón et al., in press; National Literacy Panel on Language Minority Children and Youth, in preparation; Slavin & Calderón, 2001). In an exhaustive review of the literature, Slavin and Cheung (in press) found only eight solid studies on ELL literacy. However, these few empirical studies concur that teachers of ELLs need to complement the 9 components listed above with an extensive teaching repertoire that includes

- second language acquisition (oracy, literacy, and subject matter integrated);
- bilingual instruction (when and how to teach in L1 and L2; literacy in both languages);
- contrastive linguistics, cognates/false cognates, and how to effectively employ this knowledge;

- teaching different tiers of vocabulary (basic for non-English speakers, high-frequency words to compete with mainstream students, domain vocabulary, and challenging levels);
- fast-track decoding in English if the student is literate in the first language;
- fast-track decoding and fluency skills for students in 4th–12th grades;
- reading comprehension for content mastery;
- other skills for students with limited formal schooling;
- written expression (e.g., bilingual or multicultural voice and mechanics—grammar, language conventions, spelling);
- screening and continuous assessment to inform instruction; and
- teaching love of reading and writing to some of the inexperienced students.

INTEGRATING READING AND ENGLISH LANGUAGE LEARNING FOR PROFESSIONAL DEVELOPMENT

Borrowing the concept of tables from the Alliance, but adding the elements that focus on English language learners, Tables 6.1 through 6.8 attempt to map out a framework for building concepts, skills, and teacher experiences (Calderón, in press). These frames were intended as a starting point for the project Preparing All Administrators, Counselors, and Teachers to Work with Linguistically and Culturally Diverse Students (PAACT) to share with university teacher education programs. The frames have been modified below to help school districts and schools conduct meetings with their teachers to identify needs and plan the designs of their comprehensive staff development programs. The following features of a staff development design are suggestions for initial planning.

Duration of Training

Each of the frames contains a set of activities that can be demonstrated and discussed at an initial 1-week workshop, to be followed by teacher practice in the classroom, simultaneously accompanied by weekly 30-minute discussions with teacher colleagues in Teachers Learning Communities (TLCs). In addition to the collegial learning at the school site, two or three additional days of inservice will be needed as refreshers and for building additional concepts, skills, and creative application.

Training Cohorts

The professional development activities can be adapted to K–12 instructional levels. However, the way secondary school teachers apply a domain such as phonemic awareness will be very different from a K–1 teacher application. Therefore, cohorts of teachers should be grouped at minimum: K–2, 3–5, 6–8, and 9–12. There will be occasions when kindergarten teachers need to work together on subcomponents that are relevant only to them; fifth-grade teachers may have to plan their students' transition into middle school; ninth-grade teachers may need to develop lessons for their incoming students, and so on. Some teachers need to observe a strategy 5 or 6 times before they feel comfortable applying it; others need 20 observations. A one-size workshop does not fit all. If we are to individualize student learning, we must begin by individualizing teacher learning.

Process of the Training

The process for professional development itself must be based on research. Making sense of experience and transforming professional knowledge into teaching habits requires time and a variety of professional activities (Learning First Alliance, 2000). Recognizing the link between professional development and successful educational change (Darling-Hammond & McLaughlin, 1995; Lieberman, 1995), and results-driven education (Sparks & Hirsh, 1997), quality teacher training has to be offered to teachers of ELLs. For teachers to learn a new behavior and effectively transfer it to the classroom, several steps need to be included in the design.

Teachers need theory, research, modeling or demonstrations of instructional methods, coaching during practice, and feedback in order to integrate instructional practices into their active teaching repertoire (Joyce & Showers, 1988). For example, teachers would need presentations on cutting-edge theory and research on reading/literacy; experts to model effective strategies for building word knowledge, comprehension, and writing for teaching English language learners; and time to practice and exchange ideas with peers after each segment or activity of the presentation (Calderón, Minaya-Rowe, & Duran, 2005; Calderón et al., 2005). Adult learners need to inquire, reflect, and respond to new ideas if they are to embrace them. Therefore, a teacher-oriented program would provide low-risk practice sessions in a workshop setting where teachers can practice teaching strategies in small teams. It is also important to use simple language to distill research on a given topic into a dozen or so principles (August, 2003). Workshop presenters could provide opportunities for reading and teacher reflection through cooperative learning activities. Presenters should also include as part of their workshop explanations and demonstrations of peer coaching practices that promote transfer of new teaching skills into the classroom (Calderón, 1994, 1998; Joyce & Showers, 1988).

According to Guskey (1998), Joyce and Showers (1988), and others, collegial activity is key for continuous learning on the job. Even after an inservice training, seasoned teachers need time to reflect and adapt new learnings into their teaching. Without collegial activity, teachers will begin to feel uncomfortable with an innovation after 4 weeks, and usually stop using the new instructional behaviors shortly thereafter. For this reason, it is critically important to build collegial skills and the mindset of continuous learning with peers before the inservice ends.

Weekly Collegial Study

As part of the inservice on reading, teachers need to learn how to set up and run their own TLCs. The studies of TLCs in schools have documented collegial activities of teachers as follows: to model new strategies for each other; solve problems of student adaptation: share their creativity through concrete products (lessons, curriculum, tests, etc.); analyze and evaluate student work regularly; provide ongoing peer support, responsiveness, and assistance to all teachers; share and discuss issues of classroom implementation, transfer from training, impact of teacher on student behavior and learning; share ideas for new lessons or next steps; and schedule peer observations and coaching (Calderón, 1994, 1999, 2000; Calderón & Minaya-Rowe, 2003).

When well implemented, TLCs can be places and spaces where teachers collaboratively examine profoundly, question, develop, experiment, implement, evaluate, and create exciting change. TLCs are opportunities for teachers to coconstruct meaning to their craft and do whatever necessary to help each other implement an innovation with fidelity. When studies are being conducted in their classrooms, teachers become coresearchers and eagerly contribute to the research and development of new programs. Their creative talents emerge as a new type of professional environment is established where they are respected for their expertise.

However, the studies have also documented the need to provide teachers with theory and practice on how to work in collegial teams. Because collegiality is difficult for many adults, the concept of collegiality needs to be established and practiced during all inservice workshops.

It is also important to recognize that teachers add analytical, creative, and practical learning to their teaching and assessment methods. This additive learning can also take place in brief 30-minute weekly TLC sessions at the school. These brief but productive moments serve to empower teachers to introduce new concepts, share instructional techniques, or revisit those that are more complicated or troublesome for some or all teachers. As teachers explore ways of integrating all the reading components into their instructional repertoires, their application becomes more meaningful to them and their students, when they become engaged in collegial learning. Perhaps the most exciting side effect of TLCs is the TLC teachers receive from one another.

Summer Curriculum Institutes

A well-skilled worker is nothing without his or her proper tools. Teachers need carefully crafted lesson plans and yearlong curricula to accomplish their tasks. As part of a comprehensive staff development, teachers will need 2 to 4 weeks in the summer to integrate new reading strategies into their lessons, curriculum standards, and assessments. It is foolish to require teachers to do all this during the year as they are teaching and attempting to learn something new such as the reading strategies described in the frames. Thus, the summer institutes are part of a serious design.

Training for Teacher Support

Principals, curriculum coordinators, mentors, and other support personnel need to be well equipped to assist teachers in this difficult phase. They need to be required to attend the workshops, and to attend one where "teacher support mechanisms" is the topic. The other topic might be "helping teachers recognize and capitalize on their strengths." Forming a successful teacher development program will require building communities of practice where teachers, administrators, and students are learning all the time. As additional research on reading continues to emerge, pedagogy must adapt and re-adapt. As teachers are better prepared to teach reading, particularly to ELLs, children's chances for learning to read will significantly increase.

Content of the Training

The following tables contain a few selected samples from a longer publication (Calderón, in press) and are being tested in two larger studies (Calderón et al., in press; Calderón, in preparation). The framework is being tested with elementary and secondary mainstream, bilingual, and ESL teachers. The secondary mainstream teachers are teachers of science, social studies, and language arts classes, and have anywhere from 5% to 50% ELLs. Tables 6.1 through 6.9 contain examples for instruction in either the students' primary language (L1) or for English as the students' second language (L2).

Phonemic Awareness, Decoding. Many studies have confirmed that there is a close relationship between phonemic awareness and reading ability, not just in the early grades (Ehri, 1998; Perfetti & Harat, 2001; Snow, Burns, & Griffin, 1998) but also throughout the school years (Shankweiler et al., 1995). Newcomer students entering the schools at the upper elementary, middle, and high-school grades need to be assessed to gauge the level of immediate interventions that can address the newcomers' phonemic and pho-

TABLE 6.1
Phonemic Awareness, Letter Knowledge, and Concepts of Print

Teacher Knowledge K–12	*Teacher Skills K–12*	*Professional Development Activities*
Know the speech sounds in English (consonants and vowels) and the pronunciation of phonemes for instruction.	Select and use a range of activities representing a developmental progression of phonological skill (rhyming; word identification; syllable counting; onset-rime segmentation and blending; phoneme identification, segmentation, and blending).	Practice phoneme matching, identification, segmentation, blending, substitution, and deletion. Order phonological awareness activities by difficulty level and developmental sequence in English and contrast with Spanish sounds.
Understand the casual links between early decoding, spelling, word knowledge, and phoneme awareness.	Plan lessons in which phoneme awareness, letter knowledge, and invented spelling activities are complementary.	Observe and critique live or videotaped student–teacher interactions during phonological awareness and alphabet instruction.
Understand how critical the foundation skills are for later reading success.	Have ability to monitor every child's progress and identify those who are falling behind.	Discuss children's progress, using informal assessments, to obtain early help for those in need of it.
Understand how phonemic awareness, word knowledge, and concepts of print compare and contrast across two languages.	Have ability to teach differences between English and the students' primary language, when teaching in bilingual programs.	Develop one lesson in English (L2) and one in the students' primary language (L1), highlighting differences.

TABLE 6.2
Phonics, Phonological and Morphological Awareness and Decoding

Teacher Knowledge K–12	*Teacher Skills K–12*	*Professional Development Activities*
Understand speech-to-print correspondence at the sound, syllable pattern, and morphological levels.	Choose examples of words that illustrate sound–symbol, syllable, and morpheme patterns.	Practice teaching various active techniques including sound blending, structural word analysis, word building, and word sorting in English and in the students' L1.
Identify and describe the developmental progression in which orthographic knowledge is generally acquired.	Select and deliver appropriate lessons according to students' levels of spelling, phonics, and word identification skills.	From classroom videos of ELLs in different grade levels, identify, on the basis of student reading and writing, the appropriate level at which to instruct.
Recognize the differences among approaches to teaching word attack (implicit, explicit, analytic, synthetic, etc.).	Teach active exploration of word structure with a variety of techniques.	Search a text for examples of words that exemplify an orthographic concept in L1 and L2; lead discussions about words. Use a science, math, or social studies text to teach word attack.
Know and anticipate differences between Spanish and English orthographies.	Enable students to use cognates and false cognates.	Review Spanish and English contrasting features, and cognates and false cognates. Make charts for each to share with peers.

nological gaps. Whatever the grade level, teachers with ELLs will eventually have students who need instruction in these basic skills before they can comprehend a text.

Fluency. Developing fluency in reading entails developing rapid and automatic word identification processes (LaBerge & Samuels, 1974). Although an exact definition of fluency has yet to be agreed upon, there seems to be a consensus regarding its primary components: (a) accuracy in decoding, (b) automaticity in word recognition, and (c) the appropriate use of prosodic features such as stress, pitch, and juncture (Kuhn & Stahl, 2000), which becomes commonly known as reading with expression. Samuels (2002) defined fluent reading as the ability to perform two difficult tasks simultaneously—the ability to identify words and comprehend a text at the same time.

TABLE 6.3
Fluent, Automatic Reading of Text

Teacher Knowledge K–12	*Teacher Skills K–12*	*Professional Development Activities*
Understand how word recognition, reading fluency, and comprehension are related to one another.	Determine reasonable expectations for reading fluency at various stages of reading development, using research-based guidelines and appropriate state and local standards and benchmarks.	Practice assessing and recording text-reading fluency of ELLs at different stages of English proficiency and different levels of decoding skills.
Understand who in the class should receive extra practice with fluency development and why.	Use techniques for increasing speed of word recognition.	Use informal assessment results to identify who needs to work on fluency. Devise a system for recording ELL and non-ELL progress toward reasonable goals. Compare results.
Learn a variety of strategies and techniques for helping ELLs.	Use techniques for repeated readings of passages such as alternate oral reading with a partner, reading with a tape, or rereading the same passage up to three times, choral reading, readers' theater, chants, and songs.	Conduct fluency-building activities with a peer teacher such as read alouds, listening comprehension, shadow reading, echo reading, and other techniques.
Recognize the differences between English and Spanish contrastive features that hinder or enhance fluency.	Use techniques to assess students' use of first and second language strategies.	Record a student reading in Spanish, then in English. Analyze with peers those features that transfer from one language to the other.

Vocabulary. Vocabulary correlates with reading comprehension. For ELLs, the greater the amount of attention extended to decoding, the less there is available for teaching new words and for building comprehension. Without word knowledge, there is little chance they can read with expression, and even less chance to comprehend what they just finished reading. If ELLs do not recognize words automatically (decoding and meaning), too much time will be devoted to figure out what the words say, and going back and forth looking for context clues (Calderón et al., 2005). Fluency is also increased by domain knowledge, which allows the reader to make rapid connections between new and previously learned content; this both eases and deepens comprehension (Hirsch et al., 2003). All this means that ELLs must have ample direct instruction in vocabulary and domain knowledge, along with fluency practice, in order to become good readers.

If ELLs don't know the words, they won't be able to construct a meaningful mental picture of what they are saying as they read aloud or what they are reading silently. Research on vocabulary emphasizes that for mainstream students, four encounters with a word did not reliably improve reading comprehension, while 12 encounters did (Stahl, 2003). That means that nonmainstream English as a second language students are more likely to need more than 12 encounters with words. Words need to be deliberately taught through a variety of fun activities (Beck, McKeown, & Kucan, 2002). Knowledge of words involves not only understanding the core meaning of a word, but also how it changes in different contexts. This involves exposure to the word in multiple contexts from different perspectives. Anderson and Nagy (1991) argued that words are polysemous, containing multiple meanings, rather than a single fixed meaning. Some meanings resemble each other as in Nagy's example:

John gave Frank five dollars.
John gave Mary a kiss.
The doctor gave the child an injection.
The orchestra gave a stunning performance.

Thus, a simple English word such as *gave* can give ELLs quite a bit of trouble. In other instances words have meanings that may not be so related. For instance, the word *trunk* can be attached to an elephant, a human, a car, or a tree. It can also be different objects used for various purposes. Unless ELLs are taught multiple meanings, their limited background knowledge of a word might lead them further away from comprehension (Calderón et al., in press).

Depth and breadth of vocabulary can be built through oral comprehension and background knowledge. Teacher read-alouds are generally phased out in second grade despite the fact that research has found that students benefit from read-alouds until eighth grade (Chall, 1996). Reading aloud to high school ELLs, particularly in different domains, in different subject areas, is proving to be an effective strategy (Calderón, Minaya-Rowe, & Duran, 2005) when teachers integrate vocabulary-building techniques in their read-alouds. Direct instruction on vocabulary, including the use of cognates, has been found to be one of the most effective tools in recent studies on ELL comprehension (August, Calderón, & Carlo, 2001; Calderón et al., 2005; Carlo et al., in press).

TABLE 6.4
Vocabulary

Teacher Knowledge K–12	*Teacher Skills K–12*	*Professional Development Activities*
Understand the role of vocabulary development and vocabulary knowledge in comprehension.	Select material for reading aloud that will expand students' vocabulary.	Collaborate with team to select best read-aloud books for ELLs and share rationales for those selections.
Have a rationale for selecting words for direct teaching before, during, and after reading.	Select words for instruction before a passage is read.	Select words from text for direct teaching and give rationale for the choice.
Understand the role and characteristics of direct and contextual methods of vocabulary instruction.	Teach word meanings directly through explanation of meanings and example uses, associations to known words, and word relationships.	Devise exercises to involve students in constructing meanings of words (Beck et al. or Calderón et al. strategies), in developing example uses of words, in understanding relationships among words, and in using and noticing uses of words beyond the classroom (Word Wizard; Homework Logs).
Know reasonable goals and expectations for learners at various stages of reading development; appreciate the wide differences in students' vocabularies.	Provide for repeated encounters with new words and multiple opportunities to use new words.	Categorize the words you select from a text into at least 3 tiers: Tier 1—ELL must-know words; Tier 2—high frequency words to learn content; Tier 3—low frequency words students will encounter but do not need to learn immediately.
Understand the concept of polysemy.	Teach how word meanings apply to various contexts by talking about words they encounter in reading.	Use a series of contexts to show how clues can accumulate, and how word meanings can vary.
How to use first and second languages effectively to build vocabulary skills.	Use English as a Second Language techniques to make English texts comprehensible; use appropriate first-language discourse; know when to use one or the other.	Have coaches record and give feedback on the language or languages used with the students, and the level of student comprehension and engagement with that discourse.
Understand if fluency difficulties stem from lack of vocabulary in English or other ELL-related factors.	Determine source of difficulty and help students develop those skills along with fluency.	Practice assessing first and second language oral and reading fluency with videotapes, then later in the classroom share results with peers.

Oral comprehension is the ceiling on reading comprehension (Biemiller, 1999). For many students, increasing reading comprehension will involve increasing oral language comprehension. Biemiller goes on to state that the gap between children with advanced language and children with restricted language grows wider during the elementary years, and current practices typically have little effect on oral language development. If instruction has had little effect in most children, this is definitely the case for ELLs. Schools spend entirely too much time teaching decoding and rapid reading to ELLs without giving much attention to oral language development and listening comprehension. Language can only grow through quality interaction with teachers and other students. For example, after teacher read-alouds, rich discussions directed by the teacher, with strategies for students to think, then pair with a partner to discuss an answer or an opinion, then to share with the whole class, gives ELLs opportunities to reflect on words, practice words with peers, add new words in the process of formulating responses, and then practice conveying meaning (Calderón, 1990, 1991; Calderón, Hertz-Lazarowitz, & Slavin, 1998).

Without domain knowledge, older students may be able to sound out the words in their textbooks but will not be able to extract adequate meaning from text. Walsh (2003) analyzed the most commonly used basal readers and found that they miss opportunities to build word and world knowledge because (a) they don't focus on systematically building essential knowledge and vocabulary; (b) they waste time by including many more lessons on formal reading comprehension skills than researchers have found are needed (the same skills are practiced year after year, e.g., sequencing); and (c) by offering mostly incoherent, banal themes, containing very ordinary vocabulary. When students experience problems with comprehending text, it is more likely due to the students' lack of knowledge of the subject matter. Older immigrant students coming into middle and high schools will never be able to catch up with domain knowledge if teachers rely solely on textbook learning/teaching.

Engaging students in text comprehension may occur before, during, and after reading a text. Using math, science, and social studies texts, teachers can build specific comprehension strategies when taught explicitly. Techniques that have been shown to enhance comprehension include self-monitoring for understanding, using semantic or graphic or conceptual organizers, answering questions and obtaining immediate feedback, formulating questions about the text and obtaining immediate feedback, becoming aware of the genre characteristics/text structure, and periodically summarizing key points, retelling the story or the process (National Reading Panel, 2000). Every opportunity should be taken to extend and enrich a student's metacognitive strategies, particularly with ELL students in the upper grades.

TABLE 6.5
Text Comprehension

Teacher Knowledge K–12	*Teacher Skills K–12*	*Professional Development Activities*
Know the cognitive processes involved in comprehension; know the techniques and strategies that are most effective, for what types of students, with what content.	Help students engage texts and consider ideas deeply.	Role-play and rehearse key research-supported strategies, such as questioning, summarizing, clarifying, and using graphic organizers.
Recognize the characteristics of "reader friendly" text.	Facilitate comprehension of academic language such as connecting words, figures of speech, idioms, humor, and embedded sentences.	Observe an ELL student work and record reading behavior (written responses, oral summaries, retellings, cloze tasks, recorded discussions) to determine where miscomprehension occurred and plan how to repair it.
Identify phrase, sentence, paragraph, and text characteristics of "book language" that students may misinterpret.	Facilitate comprehension by pre-teaching concepts and key vocabulary.	Plan a lesson around a literature selection; then, using the same strategies plan a lesson using a science and a social studies selection.
Understand the similarities and differences between written composition and text comprehension.	Help students use written responses and discussion to process meaning more fully.	Practice leading, scaffolding, and observing discussions in which students collaborate to form joint interpretations of text.
Understand the role of background knowledge in text comprehension.	Preview text and identify the background experiences and concepts that are important for comprehension of that text and that help students call on or acquire knowledge.	Discuss and plan to teach ways of helping students call on or acquire relevant knowledge through defining concepts, presenting examples, and eliciting students' reactions to the concepts in ways that assess their understanding.
Understand the importance of student–student interaction for building comprehension.	Use a variety of cooperative learning strategies and techniques to ensure ample opportunities for student interaction with peers and text.	Practice using a variety of cooperative learning strategies with fellow peers, demonstrating how comprehension of a given text is built into each.

One cannot separate reading from writing. Both are intertwined, and both need to be taught simultaneously. For decades, it was believed that learning English was a linear process that spanned throughout the school year: first teach listening, then oral production, then reading, and finally writing. Unfortunately, the more these four were separated, the harder it became to learn the language. ELLs benefit from writing from the start and writing daily. A variety of writing assignments can be integrated with the text they are reading. Story-related writing or text-related writing gives ELLs the vocabulary, syntactical structures, and familiar context to write about. ELLs, just as all students, need concomitant instruction on mechanics and composition. All these new skills can be practiced in the safety of small teams or partnerships. Drafting, sharing ideas, revisions, editing, proofreading, and publishing should start out with partners, until a student is ready for individual work. All teachers, particularly content teachers, need to model the writing process for different purposes: summaries, syntheses, analyses, storytelling, and even note taking.

Systematic instruction in sound segmentation, sound–symbol association, and awareness of spelling patterns leads to better spelling achievement (Bear, Invernizzi, Templeton, & Johnston, 1996; Learning First Alliance, 2000). ELL students benefit from direct instruction on prefixes, suffixes, and base words (Calderón et al., 2005; Calderón, Minaya-Rowe, & Duran, 2005; Carlo et al., in press). Story-related spelling or spelling related to the content text provides context and meaning to spelling activities. It is

TABLE 6.6
Written Expression

Teacher Knowledge K–12	*Teacher Skills K–12*	*Professional Development Activities*
Understand that composition is a recursive process of planning, drafting, and revising.	Organize writing program to support planning, drafting, and revising stages before publication.	Examine student work at various stages of the writing process and identify strengths and weaknesses.
Know different genre for writing.	Teach differences between narrative and expository writing and other writing variations.	Practice developing writing prompts and frames for different writing genre.
Understand the role of grammar, sentence composition, and paragraphing in building composition skill.	Teach sentence and paragraph awareness, construction, and manipulation as a tool for fluent communication of ideas.	Practice approaches such as sentence combining, analysis, elaboration, and coherent linking of sentences in paragraphs.
Know benchmarks and standards for students at various stages of growth.	Generate and use rubrics to guide and evaluate student work.	Work with a team to achieve reliability in evaluating student work.

TABLE 6.7
Spelling and Handwriting

Teacher Knowledge K–12	*Teacher Skills K–12*	*Professional Development Activities*
Describe and identify the progression in which spelling knowledge is gained.	Tailor instruction to students' developmental levels in spelling.	Give and analyze the results of a developmental spelling inventory.
Understand the similarities and differences between learning to read and learning to spell.	Coordinate the timing and sequence of spelling lessons to complement instruction in word recognition.	Develop time line, scope, and sequence for teaching spelling in relation to the reading program.
Understand the relationship between transcription skills and spelling and writing fluency.	Use techniques to build fluency, accuracy, and automaticity in transcription to support composition.	Practice teaching self-correction, dictation, think-aloud, proofreading, and other strategies.
Know/anticipate differences between Spanish and English orthography.	Review with students the English–Spanish contrasting features of affixes and root words.	Identify and practice using contrasting and similar spelling patterns. Identify and practice using prefixes and suffixes in English and Spanish.

not a matter of memorizing lists of words, but rather using them in sentences and hearing them in context. Teachers need to be prepared to teach basic spelling skills in an organized explicit manner.

"Instruction that targets the specific weaknesses most likely to cause reading difficulty often prevents later reading failure and facilitates the reading development of most children" (Learning First Alliance, 2000, p. 23). Upon entering a classroom, each student should be assessed, mainly so that information can be immediately used to plan instruction. However, because group and individual assessments are required to compare children with normative standards, teachers now need to know how to interpret standardized test results. Notwithstanding, the frequent use of informal assessments is also the responsibility of the teacher. Ongoing assessments such as running records and observations of students' reading behavior and writing products should be an integral part of daily instruction. Differentiated scales and rubrics to measure ELL progress, although not previously required of every teacher, are required now in every school. Thus, teacher education programs need to emphasize the latest valid, reliable assessment tools that have a strong theoretical and empirical support. As new assessments are developed to fill earlier gaps, the teacher education faculty must also learn their utility and application. Every component listed above will need to be assessed. In

TABLE 6.8
Assessment to Inform Instruction

Teacher Knowledge K–12	*Teacher Skills K–12*	*Professional Development Activities*
Understand that assessments are used for various purposes, including determining strengths and needs of ELL and non-ELL students in order to plan for instruction and flexible grouping; monitoring of progress in relation to stages of reading, spelling, and writing; assessing curriculum-specific learning; and using norm-referenced or diagnostic tests appropriately for program placement.	Use efficient, informal, validated strategies for assessing phoneme awareness, letter knowledge, sound–symbol knowledge, application of skills to fluent reading, passage reading accuracy and fluency, passage comprehension, level of spelling development, and written composition.	Participate in role-play of assessment after modeling and demonstration with ELL and non-ELL subjects. Receive feedback in role-play until skills of administration and scoring are reliable.
Select a program of assessment that includes validated tools for measuring important components of reading and writing.	Screen all children briefly; assess students with reading and language weaknesses at regular intervals.	Administer assessments and review results with team for purpose of instructional grouping.
Know the benchmarks and standards for performance.	Interpret results for the purpose of helping students achieve the standards.	Evaluate the outcomes of instruction and present as a team.
Understand importance of student self-assessment.	Communicate assessment results to parents and students.	Develop or select record-keeping tools for parents and students.
Recognize what students have learned and what they need to learn within the reading program being used.	Use efficient, informal, validated strategies for assessing phoneme awareness, letter knowledge, sound–symbol knowledge, application of skills to fluent reading, passage reading accuracy and fluency, passage comprehension, level of spelling development, and written composition.	Practice using, scoring, and/or interpreting tools for observations of students' reading behavior, writing products, and standardized test results.
Recognize if the reading program being used addresses the needs of ELLs.	Communicate assessment results to school officials.	Using score sheets from 3-month intervals, compare and contrast the progress of ELLs and non-ELLs.

TABLE 6.9
Love of Reading and Writing

Teacher Knowledge K–12	*Teacher Skills K–12*	*Professional Development Activities*
Know and understand the nuances of the students' cultural backgrounds.	Communicate effectively with students and their parents from diverse cultures.	Read about the students' cultural backgrounds with other teachers. Discuss in study groups how to approach and reach out to parents of different cultures.
Learn about literature from other cultures.	Use literature written by authors from diverse cultures.	In the study groups, read a text written by an author from one of your student's culture/country. Discuss how to approach this piece of literature with the students.
Model the joy of reading diverse genre and authentic literature from other countries.	Uses American literature to teach the American mind, and literature from other cultures to teach appreciation for diversity and to enrich the students' world view.	In the study groups, select an American text to highlight aspects of the American culture. Next, select a text from another country to highlight aspects of that culture.

some cases, assessments for each component of reading will need to be adapted to assess ELL needs, progress, and accomplishments.

Love of reading and writing stems from teacher modeling the love of reading and writing. Time (even 5 or 10 minutes) needs to be set aside daily, or at least a few days a week to just enjoy good books and poetry. Love of reading also comes when students read or listen to texts about their own culture and familiar things. Using American literatures helps students learn more about the American mind and traditions. Using authentic literature from other cultures helps students develop pride in their culture and appreciation for other cultures.

IMPLICATIONS FOR IMPLEMENTATION: ACCOUNTABILITY AND QUALITY

With poor ELL outcomes and more emphasis on accountability by state and national policymakers, transforming teaching practices has to go hand in hand with transforming professional development practices. Hard-nosed empirical studies and evaluation of staff development programs has to come to the surface each time a workshop, an inservice, or the implementation of a new program is being contemplated. We do not have a culture of rigorous professional development yet; much less an overabundance of evidence for what defines a high-quality teacher and what practices represent effective teaching for ELLs. As the National Literacy Panel for Language Minority Children and Youth concludes its findings, we can begin to make sure that all teacher training attempts be guided by evidence.

When Daniel Fallon from the Carnegie Corporation reviewed the literature for the American Council on Education, he only found, "a lot of touchy-feely stuff" and case studies about teaching. In my own searches, I find that most of the studies about teacher development are not scientifically rigorous enough to make generalizations. What is effective staff development? Effectiveness of teacher training interventions is not merely collecting anonymous evaluations after a workshop. Staff development must be linked to improving teaching practice and ELL achievement outcomes. Randomized assignment to training models, classroom implementation visits with valid protocols and instrumentation, pre–post assessments of teachers and their students, and ethnographic complementary data must become mandatory as part of any teacher training intervention.

As proponents of ELL excellence, we must become critical examiners of our own teacher training efforts and our research designs. The field of quality teaching for ELL success is very exciting. We have our living laboratories where all sorts of new questions can be asked and tested. As we invite teachers to become coresearchers of their and their students' learning, it becomes even more exciting. When teachers are highly engaged in research efforts, they themselves create a new professional environment that respects their expertise and creativity. With the support of teachers of ELLs, a comprehensive agenda for improving the quality of teaching can hopefully become a national priority. Access to quality education is every student's and teacher's right.

ACKNOWLEDGMENT

Paper prepared for the National Invitational Conference on *Improving Teacher Quality for English Language Learners*, sponsored by the U.S. Department of Education and the Laboratory for Student Success, the Mid-Atlantic Regional Educational Laboratory at Temple University, November 13–14, 2003, Arlington, VA.

REFERENCES

Anderson, R. C., & Nagy, W. E. (1991). Word meanings. In R. Barr, M. L. Kamil, P. Mosenthal, & P. D. Pearson (Eds.), *Handbook of reading research, Vol. 2.* White Plains, NY: Longman.

August, D. (2003). *Supporting the development of English literacy in English language learners: Key issues and promising practices.* Baltimore: Johns Hopkins University, Center for Research on the Education of Students Placed at Risk.

August, D., Calderón, M., & Carlo, M. (2001). Transfer of reading skills from Spanish to English: A study of young learners. *National Association for Bilingual Education Journal, 24*(4), 11–42.

August, D., & Hakuta, K. (1997). *Improving schooling for language-minority children: A research agenda.* Washington, DC: National Research Council.

Bear, D. Invernizzi, M., Templeton, S., & Johnston, F. (1996). *Words their way: Word study for phonics, vocabulary, and spelling.* Upper Saddle River, NJ: Merrill.

Beck, I. L., McKeown, M. G., & Kucan, L. (2002). *Bringing words to life.* New York: Guilford Press.

Biemiller, A. (1999). *Language and reading success. From reading research to practice: A series for teachers.* Cambridge, MA: Brookline Books.

Calderón, M. (1990). *Cooperative learning for limited English proficient students.* Austin, TX: Texas Education Agency, Distinguished Scholar Series Publication.

Calderón, M. (1991). Benefits of cooperative learning for Hispanic students. *Texas Researcher Journal, 2,* 39–57.

Calderón, M. (1994). Mentoring and coaching minority teachers. In De Villar & Cummins (Eds.), *Successful cultural diversity: Classroom practices for the 21st century.* New York: SUNY.

Calderón, M. (1998). *Staff development in multilingual multicultural schools. ERIC Digest.* New York: ERIC Clearinghouse on Urban Education.

Calderón, M. (1999). Teachers learning communities for cooperation in diverse settings. In M. Calderón & R. E. Slavin (Eds.), *Building community through cooperative learning. Special issue of Theory into Practice Journal.* Spring, *38*(2). Columbus, OH: Ohio State University.

Calderón, M. (November/December, 2000). Teachers' learning communities for highly diverse classrooms. *National Association for Bilingual Education Journal, 24*(2), 33–34.

Calderón, M. (in press). *No teacher left behind!* Washington, DC: National Clearinghouse for English Language Acquisition and Language Instruction Educational Programs.

Calderón, M. (in preparation). *Preparing content teachers in secondary schools to teach literacy skills and enhance the subject matter comprehension of English language learners.* Baltimore: Johns Hopkins University, Center for Research on the Education of Students Placed at Risk.

Calderón, M., August, D., Slavin, R. E., & Duran, D. (in press). *The evaluation of a bilingual transition program for Success for All* (Technical report). Baltimore, MD: CRESPAR/Johns Hopkins University.

Calderón, M., August, D., Slavin, R. E., Duran, D., Madden, N., & Cheung, A. (2005). Bringing words to life in classrooms with English language learners. In E. H. Hiebert & M. L. Kamil (Eds.), *Teaching and learning vocabulary: Bringing research to practice.* Mahwah, NJ: Lawrence Erlbaum Associates.

Calderón, M., Hertz-Lazarowitz, R., & Slavin. R. E. (1998). Effects of bilingual cooperative integrated reading and composition on students making the transition from Spanish to English reading. *Elementary School Journal, 99*(2), 153–165.

Calderón, M., & Minaya-Rowe, L. (2003). *Designing and implementing two-way bilingual programs: A step-by step guide for administrators, teachers, and parents.* Thousand Oaks, CA: Corwin Press.

Calderón, M., Minaya-Rowe, L., & Duran, D. (2005). *Expediting Comprehension to English Language Learners (ExC-ELL): Report to the Carnegie Foundation.* New York: The Carnegie New York Corporation.

Calderón, M., Slavin, R. E., Duran, D., Cheung, A., & August, D. (in press). *Evaluation of the success for all bilingual transition programs: A technical report.* Baltimore: Johns Hopkins University, Center for Research on the Education of Students Placed at Risk.

Carlo, M., August, D., McLaughlin, B., Snow, C., Dressler, C., Lippman, D., Lively, T., & White, C. (in press). Closing the gap: Addressing the vocabulary needs of English language learners in bilingual and mainstream classrooms. *Reading Research Quarterly.*

Chall, J. S. (1996). American reading achievement: Should we worry? *Research in the Teaching of English, 30,* 303–310.

Darling-Hammond, L., & McLaughlin, M. W. (1995). Policies that support professional development in an era of reform. *Phi Delta Kappan, 76*(8), 597–604.

Ehri, L. C. (1998). Grapheme-phoneme knowledge is essential for learning to read words in English. In L. Metsala & L. C. Erhi (Eds.), *Word recognition in beginning literacy* (pp. 3–40). Mahwah, NJ: Lawrence Erlbaum Associates.

Guskey, T. (1998). Follow-up is key, but it's often forgotten. *Journal of Staff Development, 19*(2), 7–8.

Hirsch, E. D., Hart, B., Risley, T. R., & Beck, I. L. (2003). The fourth grade plunge: The cause. The cure. *American Educator,* Spring. Washington, DC: American Federation of Teachers.

Joyce, B., & Showers, B. (1998). *Student achievement through staff development.* White Plains, NY: Longman.

Kuhn, M., & Stahl, S. (2000). *Fluency: A review of developmental and remedial practices* (Report No. 2-0008). Ann Arbor, MI: Center for the Improvement of Early Reading Achievement.

LaBerge, D., & Samuels, S. J. (1974). Toward a theory of automatic information processing in reading. *Cognitive Psychology, 6,* 293–323.

Learning First Alliance. (2000). *Every child reading: A professional development guide.* Baltimore: Association for Supervision and Curriculum Development.

Lieberman, A. (1995). Practices that support teacher development. *Phi Delta Kappan, 76*(8), 591–596.

National Center for Education Statistics. (2001). *Teacher preparation and professional development 2000.* Washington, DC: Author.

National Center for Education Statistics. (2002). *Student effort and educational progress: Elementary/secondary persistence and progress.* Washington, DC: Author.

National Literacy Panel. (in preparation). *Teaching language minority children and youth to read: An evidence-based assessment of the scientific research literature on reading and its implications for reading instruction.* Rockville, MD: National Institute of Child Health and Human Development.

National Reading Panel. (2000). *Teaching children to read: An evidence-based assessment of the scientific research literature on reading and its implications for reading instruction.* Rockville, MD: National Institute of Child Health and Human Development.

Pacific Resources for Education and Learning. (2002). *Readings on fluency for "A focus on fluency forum."* Honolulu, HI: Author.

Perfetti, C. A., & Harat, L. (2001). The lexical bases of comprehension skill. In D. Gortien (Ed.), *On the consequences of meaning selection* (pp. 67–86). Washington, DC: American Psychological Association.

Samuels, S. J. (2002). Reading fluency: Its development and assessment. In Pacific Resources for Education and Learning (2002), *Readings on fluency for "A focus on fluency forum."* Honolulu, HI: Author.

Shankweiler, D., Crain, S., Katz, L., Foweler, A., Liberman, A. M., Brady, S., Thornton, R., Lundquist, E., Dreyer, L., Fletcher, J., Steubing, K., Shaywitz, S. E., & Shaywitz, B. (1995). Cognitive profiles of reading-disabled children: Comparison of language skills in phonology, morphology and syntax. *Psychological Science, 6,* 149–156.

Slavin, R. E., & Calderón, M. (Eds.). (2001). *Effective programs for Latino students.* Mahwah, NJ: Lawrence Erlbaum Associates.

Slavin, R. E., & Cheung, A. (in press). *Effective reading approaches for English language learners: Language of instruction and replicable programs. A technical report.* Baltimore: CRESPAR, Johns Hopkins University.

Snow, C. (2002). *Reading for understanding: Toward a research and development program in reading comprehension.* Santa Monica: RAND Corporation.

Snow, C., Burns, S., & Griffin, P. (1998). *Preventing reading difficulties in young children.* Washington, DC: National Academy Press.

Sparks, D., & Hirsh, S. (1997). *A new vision for staff development.* Alexandria, VA: Association for Supervision and Curriculum Development.

Stahl, S. A. (1999). *Vocabulary development. From reading research to practice: A series for teachers.* Cambridge, MA: Brookline.

Stahl, S. A. (2003). How words are learned incrementally over multiple exposures. In E. D. Hirsch, B. Hart, T. R. Risley, & I. L. Beck (2003). The fourth grade plunge: The cause. The cure. *American Educator.* Spring. Washington, DC: American Federation of Teachers.

Walsh, K. (2003). The lost opportunity to build knowledge that propels comprehension. In E. D. Hirsch, B. Hart, T. R. Risley, & I. L. Beck (2003). The fourth grade plunge: The cause. The cure. *American Educator.* Spring. Washington, DC: American Federation of Teachers.

Chapter 7

Reculturing Principals as Leaders for Cultural and Linguistic Diversity

Augustina Reyes
University of Houston

Research shows the significance of the role of the principal, organizational management, and conditions of schools to improvements in instruction (Hallinger & Heck, 1997; Leithwood, Jantzi, & Steinbach, 1999; Newman & Wehlage, 1995; Purkey & Smith, 1983: Sergiovanni, 1996; Sheppard, 1995). School improvement research has shown that school leadership is the single most important factor to instructional improvement (Barth, 1986; Leithwood & Montgomery, 1982; NCSL, 2003). There is a strong link between the quality of school leadership and management, the key staff in a school and the quality of instruction (NCSL, 2003). The research on programs for English language learners (ELLs) show that the most successful programs are those programs with principal leadership, support, and knowledge of English language learners (Armendariz & Armendariz, 2000; Calderón & Carreon, 2000; Carter & Chatfield, 1986; Garcia, 2001; Gonzales, 1992; Montecel & Cortez, 2002; Sather, Katz, Henze, Walker, & Norte, 2001; Saville-Troike, 1984). School leadership and the role of the school principal are the most important variables associated with effective and successful schools, including those with successful programs for English language learning students (Lezotte, 2003). The purpose of this chapter is to examine the research on school leadership, the research on the effects of school leadership on successful programs for ELLs, the role of principal preparation, and to make recommendations on ways that principal preparation programs can prepare school leaders to be leaders for English language learners.

What is good leadership and how does good leadership affect the academic success of English Language Learners? According to Leithwood,

Jantzi, and Steinbach (1999), good leadership exhibits some basic skills; but outstanding leadership is exquisitely sensitive to the context in which it is exercised. Some define leadership as a process of social influence in which intentional influence is exerted by one person (or one group) over other people (or other groups of people) (Leithwood et al., 1999). Influence is synonymous with leadership (Leithwood et al., 1999). According to the research, leadership concepts include instructional leadership, leadership styles, transformation leadership, moral leadership, managerial leadership, and cultural leadership (Leithwood et al., 1999). Leadership models include instructional, transformational, moral, participative, managerial, and contingent (Leithwood et al., 1999). The instructional leader focuses on the behavior of teachers as they engage in activities directly affecting the growth of students (Leithwood et al., 1999). Moral leadership focuses on the values and ethics of leaders (Bolman & Deal, 1997). Participative leadership focuses on group and teacher leadership (Leithwood et al., 1999). Managerial leadership focuses on the basic skills of leadership, including functions, tasks, and behaviors (NPBEA, 1993). Contingent leadership focuses on the importance of how leaders respond to the unique organizational circumstances or problems that they face as a consequence, including the nature and preferences of workers and co-workers, conditions of the work and tasks to be completed (Leithwood et al., 1999). Context is important to contingency (Spillane, Halverson, & Diamond, 2001).

Research also shows that effective and successful school leadership is subject to organizational factors, like context, teacher culture, and teaming. We know that effective principals exhibit the skills to develop effective teaching and learning strategies while creating a supportive environment (Sergiovanni, 1987). Effective teaching and learning strategies are framed within the context of the school including, the quality of the staff, the school's current level of instruction, the school's reputation and image in the community, the location of the school and the community (SES, urban and rural), who the principal is (experience level, understanding of community, context). Leadership is contingent on context (Spillane, Halverson, & Diamond, 2002).

Teacher culture affects the principal's ability to develop effective teaching and learning strategies and has a direct effect on the school improvement process and student achievement (Fullan & Hargreaves, 1992). As schools progress in the school improvement process it is important to understand how teachers use their professional knowledge, expertise, and experience (Southworth, 1998). How do schools develop their internal capacity to grow and improve student learning? According to Southworth (2000), the capacity building process starts with faculty focusing on the quality of student learning and the progress that students are making while improving teaching using these analyses and evaluations.

The role of the school leader is to lead and create conditions for effective teaching and learning while focusing on the classroom (Southworth, 1998). The primary interest and focus on teacher classroom practices, teaching and student learning falls to the department chairs, grade level chairs, and lead teachers. To expect a long-term improvement on the quality of teaching requires that teachers relate to one another in particular ways or a strong teacher culture (Southworth, 1998). The quality of teacher culture appears to be affected by the relationship between staff development and the school's capacity to grow and improve, including a culture that supports strong professional ties between teachers (Southworth, 1998). Frequent, informal, and formal interaction and productive professional talk strengthened by openness, security, and trust nurture interpersonal relations and willingness to face and deal with professional differences (Southworth, 1998).

A strong teacher culture sets the environment for workplace learning constituted by teachers and staff sharing their talents, skills, and knowledge in a way that develops individuals and teams of individuals (Bolman & Deal, 1997; Southworth, 1998). Teams provide an opportunity for students to view teachers as they experience them during instruction (Southworth, 1998). Teams of teachers project a unity of instruction or a group working with agreed policies, principles of procedures, and classroom practices. Working teams provide opportunities for teachers to develop their pedagogy through rigorous and formalized practices, including principal and department chair classroom visits, monitoring activities, analyses of pupil learning data, pupils' and parents' input, best practices research (Brighouse & Woods, 1999).

A true culture of trust can provide the foundation to openly discuss evidence-based self-evaluations, identify weaknesses and strengths, and find ways to redesign, expand, or discontinue instructional and programmatic efforts (Argyris & Schon, 1974). Cultural leadership and professional learning provide an opportunity to create and disseminate new knowledge for the good of the order. The new knowledge created may be in identifying different strengths of teachers in the classrooms, new leaders in the school and sharing the new knowledge with colleagues. New knowledge creates teachers as leaders and leaders as learners.

THE CASE OF PROGRAMS FOR ENGLISH LANGUAGE LEARNERS

In many cases, the principal's attitude toward a program affects the program's level of success. The principal's attitude toward bilingual education and the concern expressed for language minority children affect the success of services provided for language minority children. Negative attitudes toward language minority children transfer to negative attitudes toward programs for language minority students. These children may be viewed as low scoring on the Texas Assessment of Academic Skills (TAAS), children who require social or economic support, children who have many special needs, and children who are time consuming. In some cases, deficit thinking drives leadership and instruction for linguistically and culturally diverse children (Valencia, 1997). Many principals assume that children who do not speak English or who speak English with an accent are of low intelligence. According to Halliday, McIntosh, and Stevens (1972), accents are identity symbols with a socioregional phonetic pattern. For example, when speaking with a person from East Texas, one may hear a distinct accent that may be different from the Queens English and make an unfounded value judgment; however, other than showing an identity with East Texas, the unique accent has no value in judging intelligence (Halliday et al., 1972).

Several studies were reviewed to identify the leadership practices of effective programs for English language learners (ELLs) (Armendariz & Armendariz, 2000; Calderón & Carreon, 2000; Carter & Chatfield, 1986; Garcia, 2001; Gonzales, 1992; Katz et al., 2000; Montecel & Cortez, 2002). These studies focused on what school principals do to increase achievement and learning for bilingual and ELLs (Armendariz & Armendariz, 2000; Calderón & Carreon, 2000; Carter & Chatfield, 1986; Garcia, 2001; Gonzales, 1992; Katz et al., 2000; Montecel & Cortez, 2002; Saville-Troike, 1983). The findings in these studies were very similar to the findings of other school leadership research. Principals have the power to influence the success of programs for ELL students (Garcia, 2001). Principals of schools with successful ELL programs integrated the ELL program into the school vision, mission, staffing, professional development, parental partnerships, instructional goals, instructional program, and assessment (Calderón & Carreon, 2000; Haberman, 1999; Montecel & Cortez, 2002). Principals supported and empowered ELL teachers to actively participate in school organizational and governance activities (Haberman, 1999). Principals discussed ELL program goals, implementation, progress, and assessment with ELL teachers (Montecel & Cortez, 2002). Principals provided ELL staff development for non-ELL teachers and staff. Principals valued the use of two languages and people who used different languages, including parents who only spoke their native language (Calderón & Carreon, 2000; Garcia, 2001). Principals were knowledgeable about the use and the research in second language learning (Montecel & Cortez, 2002). Principals were able to provide information about second language learning for parents (Haberman, 1999). Principals have the influence to hinder or support the ELL program.

Leadership and support of programs for ELLs and their teachers have produced increased achievement. According to Garcia (2001), in order to have effective schools for ELLs, principals must have the integrity or exhibit moral leadership to fairly allocate the time and resources needed by teachers, parents, and students. Most importantly, they need to listen to the teaching staff. Often, bilingual teachers are powerless in getting the support they need from principals. In Garcia's (1991) study, effective principals looked to teaching colleagues for program support. Principals need to exhibit basic managerial skills in leadership to be competent communicators and collaborators with other administrators, teachers, students, and parents. Principals as moral leaders need to be advocates for ELL students. In Garcia's (2001) study, principals rejected any notion that their students or community were disadvantaged. Their schools were run like families (Garcia, 2001). The principals of successful ELL programs were community builders.

In a study of bilingual programs in the United States, Montecel and Cortez (2002) identified characteristics that contributed to student high academic performance. The work of principals in the Montecel and Cortez study was more like missionary work than school management. Principals were described not just as committed to improving achievement for ELL students but being "actively committed" (Montecel & Cortez, 2002). The study showed that principals focused on improving student achievement, integrating bilingual programs into the school, communicating frequently with faculty and staff including bilingual faculty and staff, and involving the school faculty, staff, and community with the bilingual program. The principals were knowledgeable about the bilingual program and provided access to current research and best practices while providing all teachers with information about bilingual education, ESL strategies, students' cultural characteristics, and students' linguistic characteristics (Montecel & Cortez, 2002). Principals welcomed and involved bilingual parents as partners (Montecel & Cortez, 2002). The principals were instructional leaders who exhibited basic management skills and who were community builders.

In a study conducted by Haberman (1999), it was reported that in a school with 85% Hispanic students, primarily families from Mexico, the role of the principal and the practices of the principal were an important indicator of the school's success. Haberman (1999) described a transformational leader who nurtures a campus culture that values high-poverty students as exhibited in instructional practices and relationships in building the school community. More than half the faculty, including the principal at Buffalo Creek, was bilingual creating a bilingual program that actually goes on all day in informal ways as well as in formal classes (Haberman, 1999). The principal at Buffalo Creek created teaming efforts that enabled bilingual and ESL teachers to use bilingual methods throughout the day in all subject matters and activities (Haberman, 1999). Haberman concludes that the success at Buffalo Creek can be attributed to the faculty and staff who share a common ideology (vision) of why the school exists, what is supposed to happen to the children, and their role as teachers and principal to make it happen. Haberman concludes that in order for high-poverty students to be successful, teachers must be gifted at relationship skills—the teachers' desire and ability to want to live with the children all day, everyday, is a prerequisite to their learning. Finally, children in poverty must have teachers who can connect with them (Haberman, 1999).

Calderón and Carreon (2000) described two different leadership models. In one model the principal is an instructional leader with the moral values to move the organization beyond issues of diversity, differences, ethnicity, equity, and other biases. In the second model the principal is a manager who is there every day to open the school. They report how the commitment and leadership of one principal contributed to the success of a two-way bilingual program in one school while the laissez-faire behavior of another principal resulted in lower student achievement and dismantling of the two-way bilingual program. Calderón and Carreon conclude that without the support of school leaders comprehensive, well-planned and well-staffed programs for ELLs will fail. Calderón and Carreon (2000) recommended the following:

1. Programs for ELLs need to be an integral part of the whole-school reform initiatives with the involvement of all teachers, administrators, parents, and students.
2. Principals must maintain a supportive school-wide climate and be willing to learn with other faculty while providing the supervision and motivation to ensure successful implementation of programs for ELL students.
3. Principals must have the political skills and moral guidance to move the organization beyond small political mines.
4. Principals must have political, culture-building, and moral values to lead the organization beyond issues of diversity, differences, ethnicity, equity, biases, and power wars associated with changing times and changing populations.

In a related study, Henze (2000) investigated how school leaders mediate issues of race and ethnicity that are often equated with ELLs. The study made the following findings:

1. School leaders have the power to influence race relations in a positive direction.
2. Each school leader enters into a different learning context that may hinder or support the development of positive race relations.

3. Proactive school leaders attend to underlying as well as overt conflicts.
4. School leaders, other than the principal, can lead efforts to improve interethnic relations.
5. Proactive leaders used school organizing themes as a means to reflect the school's vision on intergroup relations.
6. School leaders used a multitude of approaches to increase racial harmony, no single measure was available to assess change.

Change is measurable in other indicators such as school climate, student achievement, and more collaboration among faculty (Henze, 2000).

In 1993, Ruiz suggested that bilingual education be a dimension of curriculum as an approach to the development of curriculum. Ruiz pointed out that while the major research in school reform recognizes diversity or multicultural issues, it does not include bilingual education. There exits a general lack of attention to Limited English Proficient (LEP) students in the comprehensive school reform movement. Ruiz suggests that given the quality of research in English language learning, the ELL research should inform education in general. For example, the structure of the school and its relationship to the community and how the school incorporates community language and culture can empower or marginalize parents in a school community (Cummins, 1989). Although there are several regional and national accreditation bodies like the National Council for the Accreditation of Teacher Education (NCATE) that recognize multicultural education, few are informed by the vast resources found in bilingual education research in the National Clearinghouse for Bilingual Education, the National Center for Research in Cultural Diversity and Second Language Learning, and the National Association for Bilingual Education (Ruiz, 1993). Whereas the dissonance between home and school account for much of the school failure of minority students, the research of scholars like Henry Trueba (1999) is excluded from the school reform movement. Research that shows that low-income children come to school with valuable cultural knowledge upon which teachers can build is disregarded as the culture of poverty (Ruiz, 1993). Ruiz (1993) suggested that research resources created by scholars in ELL should be at the center of developing effective organizations.

In a study conducted to examine the implementation and outcomes of comprehensive school reform (CSR) models and to identify the practices that improve education for culturally and linguistically diverse students, some schools implemented reform and bilingual education programs in mutually supportive ways; others had difficulty adapting reforms to suit the needs of Limited English Proficient (LEP) students (Datnow, Borman,

Stringfield, Overman, & Castellano, 2003). Although the reforms helped educators meet goals for multicultural education, in many cases educators' beliefs about student ability, race, and language served as constraints to reform (Datnow et al., 2003). The study found that conflicting policies in teacher certification policy and high-stakes testing policies also served as constraints to adapting reforms to LEP students (Datnow et al., 2003).

Research on the effects of school leadership on effective ELL programs supports the need for changing leadership for changing times (Leithwood et al., 1999). "Around the world, schools, and the societies of which they are a part, are confronting the most profound changes, the like of which have not been seen since the last great, global movement of economic and educational restructuring more than a century age" (Leithwood et al., 1999, p. vii). The role of the principal has changed. The traditional role of the school principal was based on a hierarchical system that gave the principal the sole responsibility and authority for setting the pace for the organization, controlling the budget, and determining school priorities. The new role of the principal reconceptualizes leadership as a participatory process that includes teachers, staff, parents, and members of the community. Societal changes like a more racially diverse student population, increasing numbers of second language learners, and demands for better educated graduates have challenged school leaders and principal preparation programs to change.

STANDARDS FOR PRINCIPALS

In response to the need for changing leaders for changing times, professional associations have provided guidelines for the reform of educational leadership preparation programs (National Association of Secondary School Principals (NAESP), 1990; National Policy Board for Educational Administration (NPBEA), 1989; UCEA, 1989). A major problem identified with principal preparation programs is the absence of field experiences that help to bridge the theory with the practice and produce preservice principal preparation programs that are not programs but a series of discrete courses (Milstein, 1993).

Several professional associations for school administration, including the National Policy Board for Educational Administration (NPBEA), University Council of Educational Administration (UCEA), Education Leadership Constituent Council (ELCC), American Association for School Administration (AASA), Interstate School Leaders Licensure Consortium (ISLLC), and National Council for the Accreditation of Teacher Education (NCATE) have worked together to identify the skills and knowledge school administrators need to improve schools and student achievement. The National Association of Elementary School Principals, National Association of Secondary School Principals, and American Association of School Administrators are represented in the NPBEA. These groups worked in a collaborative with the ELCC and developed a set of guidelines used by NCATE for the accreditation of university preservice programs in educational administration.

Although the standards developed by the professional associations do not specifically address the issues of ELLs, they are implied in all of the standards. The foundation of the Educational Leadership Constituent Council (ELCC) standards is that "A school administrator is an educational leader who promotes the success of all students by . . ." (Wilmore, 2002). "All students" includes more than 5 million English learning students in the United States (NCELA, 2003). It includes all children who speak Spanish, Vietnamese, Hmong, Haitian Creole, Korean, Cantonese, Arabic, Russian, Navajo, Tagalog, Cambodian, Chinese, Mandarin, Portuguese, Armenian, Serbo-Croatian, and other languages (NCELA, 2003). It the next 5 years it will include the projected 25% Hispanic enrollment in U.S. schools. Enrollments in U.S. public schools in Grades K–12 already consist of 35% in the South and 44% in the West (U.S. Census, 2002).

The following is a listing of the ELCC standards that could apply to linguistically and culturally diverse students, families, and their teachers:

1. Facilitate the development, articulation, implementation, and stewardship of a school or district vision of learning that is shared and support by the school community.
2. Advocating, nurturing, and sustaining a school culture and instructional program conducive to student learning and staff professional growth.
3. Ensuring management of the organization, operations, and resources for a safe, efficient, and effective learning environment.
4. Collaborating with families and community members, responding to diverse community resources.
5. Acting with integrity, fairness, and in an ethical manner.
6. Understanding, responding to, and influencing the larger political, social, economic, legal, and cultural context.
7. Substantial, sustained, standards-based experiences in real settings that are planned and guided cooperatively by university and school district personnel for graduate credit. (Wilmore, 2002)

Each of the standards affects the success of ELL students. For example, how can a principal facilitate the development of a school vision without consulting with the parents and the teachers of English learning students?

In the case of secondary schools, ELL students would also be included and consulted in the vision building process. Every school administrator in the United States is guided by the ELCC professional standards. The vision and the mission of every school principal are to promote the success of ELL students.

According to the Texas Administrative Code State Board for Educator Certification Standards,

> A principal is an educational leader who promotes the success of all students by implementing a staff evaluation and development system to improve the performance of all staff members, selects and implements appropriate models for supervision and staff development . . . an educational leader who promotes the success of all students by collaborating with families and community members, responding to diverse community interests and need, and mobilizing community resources . . . an educational leader who promotes the success of all students through leadership and management of the organization, operations, and resources . . . is an educational leader who promotes the success of all students by facilitating the design and implementation of curricula and strategic plans that enhance teaching and learning . . . is able to implement special campus programs to ensure that all students are provided quality, flexible instructional programs and services to meet individual student needs, . . . (TAC, 1999)

The Texas State Board for Educator Certification standards for principals are aligned with national professional standards association standards. At a minimum preservice principal preparation programs must show how coursework is accountable for the state standards. While the professional associations and others support the alignment of principal preparation with current practices and changing times, including preparing more minorities and women, there is evidence of resistance from the preparation programs to include minorities in school leadership programs (Milstein, 1993).

Standards provide the framework for a leadership preparation curriculum that prepares school leaders to provide the culture, the climate, and the environment for effective ELL programs; however professors of higher education and professional associations need to provide opportunities for more discourse on how to become leaders for ELL students. As the numbers of ELL students, teachers, and parents continue to increase there have to be opportunities for professors of educational leadership programs to better understand how to prepare school leaders of ELL schools. ELL students cannot continue to be the group of students that is excluded from school reform initiatives, not when 20% of the 5- to 21-year-old students in the United States speak a second language and 12% are enrolled in ELL programs (Ruiz, 1993; NCELA, 2003). In the Dallas-Fort Worth area, one third of the 31,000 students in the suburban district of Irving are classified by the state as LEP. The population has grown 200% in the last 10 years (Rian, March 10, 2004).

According to the research, principals with knowledge about culturally and linguistically diverse student populations provided more effective programs. Garcia (1991) reported bilingual teachers who were powerless without their principal's support. Montecel and Cortez (2002) described principals who are focused on improving student achievement, integrating bilingual programs into the school, including bilingual faculty and staff in school communication, and involving the school faculty, staff, and community with the bilingual program. Principals were knowledgeable about the bilingual program and provided access to current research and best practices while providing all teachers with information about bilingual education, ESL strategies, students' cultural characteristics, and students' linguistic characteristics (Montecel & Cortez, 2002). The principal provides the instructional leadership to integrate the bilingual/ESL program into the school.

RECULTURING PRINCIPAL PREPARATION PROGRAMS

As we consider principal preparation, there are questions about the focus of preparedness. The research is clear on the development and the maintenance of school improvement practices, including creating incentives and opportunities for improving teachers' practices, shared visions about instruction, norms of collaboration, collective responsibility for students' academic success, and an ongoing reflective dialogue among staff about practice (Spillane et al., 2002). Although principals are essential to the development and maintenance of school improvement practices, they may not be prepared to provide instruction for ELL students (Calderón & Carreon, 2000).

In reviewing the research literature on effective programs for ELLs which mirrors the research on poor, low-income, urban, minority, and other diverse learners, the major metaphors that describe the characteristics of leaders of successful programs for ELL are moral, ethical, and community builders (Garcia, 2001; Montecel & Cortez, 2002; Thomas & Collier, 2002). Garcia (2001) concluded that principals of successful programs for ELL students have to be competent managers with the integrity and moral leadership to fairly administer programs for ELL students while building schools like families. Montecel and Cortez (2002) described principals of successful programs for ELL students using the language of ministering, "principals who are actively involved" and "the work of the principal was more like a missionary." The research offered no new theories, knowledge base, role definitions, standards, or professional standards. However, the research discusses the significance of a belief system that is grounded in the values, ethics, and moral behavior to build a school community like a family (Murphy, 2002). Reculturing educational leadership to adapt culturally diverse and linguistic contexts is not about developing new leadership theories, models, or standards. It is about breaking the barriers of leadership morals, ethics, and justice. Leadership theories, models, and standards are filtered through a school leader's belief system. How will the profession promote moral stewards, educators, and community builders as school leaders?

The research on how principal leadership affects successful programs for ELL programs describes leaders who are moral stewards, educators, and community builders (Murphy, 2002). Murphy discusses the need to reculture educational leadership by using three new metaphors to sketch a portrait of leadership: moral steward, educator, and community builder. Murphy describes moral leadership as a process that acknowledges that values and value judgments are the central elements in the selection, extension, and day-to-day realization of educational purpose (Harlow, 1963, p. 67, cited in Murphy, 2002). As in the Montecel and Cortez study (2002), the moral steward is not only committed to improving achievement but "actively" involved in purpose defining activities, reflective analyses, and interventions. Murphy discusses reculturing the profession from management to education. In describing the educator, school leaders are at the forefront of instruction and curriculum leadership (Murphy, 2002). In describing school leaders as community builders, Murphy refers to reculturing school leaders as community builders with parental and student validation, community builders of professional learning communities, and community builders of personalized student learning environments. Community builders influence through moral imperatives rather than line authority, while enabling others to lead distributing leadership across the organization (Murphy, 2002; Spillane, Diamond, & Jita, 2003). Haberman (1999) described leaders of successful programs for ELL students as a transformational leader who nurtures a campus culture that values high-poverty students as exhibited in instructional practices and relationships in building the school community. Calderón and Carreon (2000) described the principal as an instructional leader with the moral values to move the organization beyond issues of diversity, differences, ethnicity, equity, and other biases. School leaders have the power to influence race relations in a positive way (Henze, 2000). Ruiz (1993) discussed the general lack of attention to cultural and linguistic diversity in the school reform movement. He shows how school reform leaders choose not to use a vast research reserve in cultural and linguistic diversity. In a study conducted in 13 elementary high ESL enrollment schools involved in comprehensive school reform, Datnow et al. (2003) showed that while the reforms helped educators meet goals for multicultural education, in many cases educators' beliefs about student ability, race, and language served as constraints to reform. The challenge in reculturing school leadership to meet the needs of culturally and linguistically diverse students is to understand the leaders' beliefs. Principal preparation is in need of a reculturation that fosters leaders who are moral stewards, educators, and community builders for learning environments that include culturally and linguistically diverse populations (Murphy, 2002).

According to Murphy, there is no need for new leadership theories, models, or standards. There is only a need to reculture the profession of educational leadership with the foundations for moral stewards, educators, and community builders. Murphy asserts that the profession of educational leadership has evolved to a profession with mental discipline, administrator roles, functions, tasks, and with a knowledge base and methods. There is a need to reculture the profession using the metaphors of moral steward, educator, and community builder. According to Murphy (2002), "leadership as moral stewardship means seeing the moral or the ethical and justice implications of the thousand daily decisions made by each school administrator" (p. 9). School leaders wishing to impact society must be directed by beliefs and values anchored by issues such as justice, community, and schools that function for all children, including culturally and linguistically diverse populations (Murphy, 2002). Like Montecel and Cortez (2002), Murphy believes that school leaders must view their task more as a mission than as a job. Imagine a school where the principal makes decisions about instruction, discipline, parent inclusion, and teacher development based on what is morally right with full justice for culturally and linguistically diverse students, their families, and their teachers rather than finding reasons why these students should have a lower tier education.

Imagine a school leader who, as an educator, is also the head learner (Murphy, 2002). Imagine a school leader who actually reads the most current research in bilingual education and second language acquisition. This same leader insists that the research on bilingual education and second language acquisition be used in school reform efforts. What effect will smaller learner communities have on immigrant students, on ESL students, and other culturally and linguistically diverse students? How do Annenberg reform efforts propose to affect culturally and linguistically diverse students or will they be silent voices in school reform (Ruiz, 1993)? Imagine a school leader who attends the National Association of Bilingual Education Conference and subscribes to *Bilingual Research Journal.* Imagine a school leader who read and understands *Deficit Thinking* (Valencia, 1997).

Murphy would recommend that the profession of school leadership be recultured to define community leaders as community builders. Community builders are in charge and not in control based on authority of position. They are in charge based on professional expertise and moral imperative and lead with as much heart as head (Murphy, 2002). A community builder is a leader who honors parents, building a community with parents and members of the school environment using access and voices as a foundation (Murphy, 2002). Imagine a school leader who honors extended families by inviting mothers, fathers, sisters, brothers, uncles, aunts, and cousins to school to familiarize families with the school community. Imagine the chatter of different languages in the hallways and the gatherings in the school environment. Image the relief of a linguistically diverse parent who feels that their voice and their language will be understood in the front office without having to keep an older child out of school to act as interpreter. Imagine a school leader who nurtures a campus culture that values linguistically and culturally diverse students as exhibited in instructional practices and relationships in building the school community (Haberman, 1999). Murphy's case for a new foundation and reculturing the profession of school leadership provides moral integrity, the intellect, and the voice that is often missing from the education of linguistically and culturally diverse students (Garcia, 2001). These are also the parameters often missing from preparation programs.

Principal Preparation in Texas

In Texas, principal preparation is driven by state policy. Chapter 241 of the Texas Administrative Code requires that principal preparation and certification candidates show that they have taken courses that cover the following standards:

1. Structured, field-based experiences in diverse types of campuses (internship);
2. Learner-centered values and ethics of leadership (School leadership, law, organizational management);
3. Learner-centered leadership and campus culture (school leadership, human resources, organizational management);
4. Learner-centered human resources leadership and management (human resources, school leadership, and organizational management);
5. Learner-centered communications and community relations (Communications, Human Relations, Community Relations);
6. Learner-centered organizational leadership and management (Leadership, organizational management, school finance, law);
7. Learner-centered curriculum planning and development (curriculum).

In revising the preservice principal preparation curriculum, no new theories, models, or standards are needed. With a focus on moral steward, educator, and community builder, existing courses need only to incorporate existing research and best practices for culturally and linguistically diverse populations. For example, the curriculum, instruction, supervision, and professional development course includes the theoretical frameworks and practice issues principals must know to be effective instructional leaders. Issues related to bilingual/ESL teacher supervision, development and curriculum are incorporated using research on culturally and linguistically diverse students.

The University of Houston Urban Principals Program

In fall 2000, the University of Houston developed a principal preservice preparation program focusing on the needs of ELLs. The goal of the grant program was to revise the principal preparation curriculum with educational administration content knowledge about ELLs, Teachers of ELLs, Parents and communities of ELLs, and curriculum for ELLs. The principal preservice preparation program investigated the purpose, foundation, and standards for principal preparation in the United States and explored the development of a preservice principal preparation program that would foster the success of language-minority students. The program's short-term goal was to certify elementary and secondary school principals and superintendents who have a background in ELL programs. Participants earned a graduate degree and/or state certification for principals and superintendents. The long-term goal was to improve the preservice preparation of urban/suburban principals and assistant principals by infusing all principal certification courses with a leadership context for second language learning students, including instructional leadership, moral leadership, and management skills.

Recruitment methods evolved with the program. Three student cohorts were recruited for the program. The original cohort used a self-selection method. The second cohort used a modified selection method. The final cohort used a school district/university collaboration model.

The program selection process used a collaborative four-step model. All students were required to meet the University of Houston, College of Education, and Department of Educational Leadership and Cultural Studies admission requirements. Students were brought in to participate in a leadership group activity to assess interpersonal skills. The third step in the process required that students complete an on-site administered writing sample. The final step was a panel interview. Department faculty, university administrators, school district administrators, and doctoral students, who were also school administrators, administered the admission process. Selections were made based on activity scores and committee members' recommendations.

Participant survey data were collected during the admissions process. The survey provided data on participant demographics, participant leadership experiences, participant reasons for seeking promotion from teacher to principal, participant satisfaction with their teaching positions, and student support systems. Participants were also asked to provide mentor information.

Curriculum rebuilding and staff development were the focus of the program. Curriculum rebuilding included the development of an interdisciplinary principal preparation curriculum. Preservice principals in the program had to take preparation classes in the Bauer College of Business, the College of Liberal Arts and Social Sciences, and the College of Education. Program administration required close coordination for the development of each course with the collaborating professor to assure that the curriculum was aligned with state principal preparation standards and the appropriate needs of second language learners. Although the interdisciplinary nature of the program was nationally unique, the college and department wars over course control were not. The pilot provided the opportunity to investigate the principal preparation curriculum and make recommendations to infuse principal preparation with instructional, moral, and management skills for changing times and changing populations.

Program Participants

This program targeted bilingual/ESL teachers for principal preparation. A group of 28 participants was selected. There were 6 (21.4%) males and 22 (78.6%) females. The ethnic makeup of the group consisted of 19 (67.9%) Hispanic or Latino and 9 (32.1%) Anglos. The overwhelming majority of individuals (71.4%) were born in the United States; however, the second 50% of participants who were from the United States were from Texas. The 28 students were seeking doctoral degrees, master's degrees, and/or principal certification.

The selection process identified participant preconditions, including demographic data, prior educational experiences, experience in leadership positions, and motivation for leadership. Personal demographic data included gender, ethnicity, birth place, and the stage of their graduate program. Prior academic information included GRE scores, MAT scores, and grade point average. Prior educational experiences included colleges attended, degrees completed, the individual's teaching experience, other work experience, goals, and languages spoken. Years of experience in leadership positions included professional honors, military and international experiences, publications, professional organization experiences, and research interests. Motivation for leadership included reasons for attending graduate school. Potential for leadership included items identifying the respondent's support network, including mentors and questions concerning support from the supervising principal.

Analysis

Seven of the respondents reported GRE scores with the mean of the GRE Verbal scores being 491.4, the mean of the GRE Quantitative scores being 494.3, and the mean of the analytical scores being 500.0 for the group. Twenty-three of the respondents reported MAT scores with the mean being 44 for the group.

The average graduate level GPA for the group was 3.58 on a 4-point scale. Eleven (39.3%) members of the group received academic honors and 17 members received professional honors. Only one member of the group served in the military, but six members had some type of international experience other then the military. Seven (25%) members had published articles in journals or been part of a team that developed a published curriculum. Eight (28.6%) members of the group held or were holding offices in professional organizations. Research interests of this group included: retention and dropout rates, second language acquisition, bilingual education, literacy, biliteracy, teacher retention, technology education, parental involvement, and research concerning the differences between traditional and alternatively certified teachers.

Fourteen of the participants held bachelor of sciences degrees and 14 held bachelor of arts degrees. Three of the participants held master of arts degrees, three held master's of education degrees and one held a master's of business administration degree. Twenty two (78.6%) members of the group belong to one or more professional organizations. These professional organizations include: NEA, ASCD, TEPSA, HSA, NABE, TABE, HABE, TASC, LUSO, NASSP, TABT, TASSP, TASB, TCTA, and IAL.

The reasons for attending graduate school ranged from personal improvement to the desire to advance their career by becoming an administrator with the school district. Twenty seven of the members (96.4%) listed members of their family as being an integral part of their support system. Twenty six of the members (92.9%) listed their friends as being members of their support team. Twenty three members (82.1%) listed their professional contacts as members of their support network. Twenty two members (78.6%) of the group had a mentor. The majority of the mentors were principals or assistant principals. Twenty one members (75%) felt their principal was committed to their success. Twenty two members (78.6%) felt their principals would be very receptive to letting them become involved in the everyday workings of the principalship. Fifteen of the members were fluent in Spanish, 12 were fluent in French, and 1 was fluent in Portuguese. Only one member did not speak a second language.

The members of the group listed five short-term goals. The short-term goals of the members were to complete certification following: principalship, superintendency, assistant principalship, central office, and to complete the degree. There were also five long-term career goals listed. These included the following: principalship, assistant principalship, superintendency, faculty position, and central office. The main focuses listed by the majority of these individuals was technology education, bilingual education, and leadership.

Surveys were distributed to students to measure the level of implementation of state standards in the preparation curriculum. Survey results showed that state standards for principal preparation were fully implemented. Student interviews were conducted with graduates. The participants highly rated the preparation component of the program; however, they wanted more exposure to issues of poverty, urban schools, cultural relevance, and school safety. "I only had one minority professor." "Issues of drugs, fights, weapons, and gangs were not discussed." Participants wanted exposure to developing rapport with students—using student rapport/student relationships to make schools safe.

Completion data for the first cohort of students showed a 90% first-time pass rate for the state principal certification exam. As of June 2004, 80% of the graduates were employed as principals, assistant principals, regional service center directors, instructional specialists, and consultants. Of the total, more than 50% were principals or assistant principals. As of May 2004, 20% were in teacher positions. These numbers are expected to change after they graduate from the program.

Challenges to Changing Principal Preparation Programs

A major challenge to preparing principals to successfully influence success for ELL programs is that some educational administration professors acknowledge that they have no knowledge about bilingual/ELS curriculum or how bilingual/ESL teachers are supervised. The question then is "Does the professor have the time, the will or the moral integrity to expand their research and teaching repertoire to include the issues of ELL and other diverse student populations?"

Classes like information management and evaluation have been more adaptable. Educational research is easily adaptable to research and studies on bilingual education. In an area like financial management and resource allocation, there are some simple issues like equity and bilingual/ESL finance formulae; however, there is also the need to explore campus-based resource allocation for ELL students and planning for the needs of ELL students and establishing the educational needs of ELL students as a school priority. Garcia (1991) talks about principals having the moral integrity to fairly allocate time and resources for bilingual/ESL programs.

Student personnel services like student advisement, counseling, and guidance services as they affect ELLs are general core course requirements for the degree. Student and family issues affecting ELL students are easily addressed in communications with faculty, staff, and community.

Issues of creating a school culture, climate, and learning environment for successful programs for linguistically and culturally diverse students are included in organizational management and exposure to organizational theories, system perspectives, and management. This course considers ethics, morals, justice, and the integration of curriculum and other programs for culturally and linguistically diverse students, ELL teachers, and ELL parents. Preservice principal preparation programs can enrich the principal certification process and masters program by providing on-going special seminars for linguistically and culturally diverse students.

The challenge in changing the preservice principal preparation curriculum is not content; it is the will of professors of educational administration and the will of departments and professional associations to provide appropriate development and research opportunities. For example, organizations like University Council of Educational Administration or the National Policy Board of Professors of Educational Administration might focus presentations on linguistically and culturally diverse student populations.

Changing the practices of principal preparation programs presents many challenges but the call to action by leaders of the profession to reculture the profession provide a foundation and plan for real change. Murphy's (2002) challenge to reculture the profession using metaphors like moral stewards, educators, and community builders holds promises for linguistically and culturally diverse principals.

REFERENCES

Armendariz, A. L., & Armendariz, E. J. (2000). An administrative perspective of a two-way bilingual immersion program. *Bilingual Research Journal, 26*(1), 169–179.

Argyris, C., & Schon, D. (1974). *Theory in practice: Increasing professional effectiveness.* San Francisco, CA: Jossey-Bass.

Barth, R. (1986). Principal centered professional development. *Theory into Practice, 25*(3), 156–160.

Bolman, L. G., & Deal, T. E. (1997). *Reframing organizations: Artistry, choice, and leadership.* San Francisco, CA: Jossey-Bass.

Brighouse, T., & Woods, D. (1999). *How to improve your school.* London, England: Routledge.

Calderón, M., & Carreon, A. (2000). *A two-way bilingual program: Promise, practice, and precautions* (Report No. R-117-D40005). Baltimore, MD: Center for Research on the Education of Students Placed At Risk. (ERIC Document Reproduction Service No. ED 447 706)

Carter, T. P., & Chatfield, M. L. (1986). Effective bilingual schools: Implications for policy and practice. *American Journal of Education, 95*, 200–232.

Cummins, J. (1989). Institutionalized racism and assessment of minority children: A comparison of policies and programs in the United States and Canada. In R. J. Samuda, S. L. Kong, J. Cummins, J. Lewis, & J. Pascal-Leone (Eds.), *Assessment and placement of minority students.* Toronto, CA: C. J. Hofgrefe/ISSP.

Datnow, A., Borman, G., Stringfield, S., Overman, L., & Castellano, M. (2003). Comprehensive school reform in culturally and linguistically diverse contexts: Implementation and outcomes from a four-year study. *Educational Evaluation and Policy Analysis, 25*(2), 143–170.

Fullan, M., & Hargreaves, A. (1992). *What's worth fighting for in your school.* Buckingham, England: Open University Press.

Garcia, E. (1991). *The education of linguistically and culturally diverse students: Effective instructional practices.* National Center for Research on Cultural Diversity and Second Language Learning. Education Practice Report 1. Santa Cruz: University of California.

Garcia, E. (2001). *Hispanic education in the United States.* New York: Rowman & Littlefield.

Gonzales, P. C. (1992). *The English-as-a-Second Language/Bilingual Framework. Washington State Office of Superintendent of Public Instruction.* Retrieved August 1, 2003, from http://www.ed.gov/about/offices/list/ocr/ell/otherreserouces.html

Haberman, M. (1999). Victory at Buffalo Creek: What makes a school serving low-income Hispanic children successful? *Instructional Leadership, 12*(2), 6–10.

Halliday, M., McIntosh, A., & Stevens, P. (1972). The users and uses of language. In J. Fishman (Ed.), *Reading in the sociology of language.* The Hauge, Paris: Mouton.

Hallinger, P., & Heck, R. (1997). Exploring the principal's contribution to school effectiveness. *School Effectiveness and School Improvement, 8*(4), 1–35.

Henze, R. C. (2000). *Leading for diversity: How school leaders achieve racial and ethnic diversity.* Oakland, CA: ARC Associates.

Leithwood, K., Jantzi, D., & Steinbach, R. (1999). *Changing leadership for changing times.* Buckingham, England: Open University Press.

Leithwood, K., & Montgomery, D. (1982). The role of the elementary school principal in program improvement. *Review of Educational Research, 52*(3), 157–168. Washington, DC: American Educational Researchers Association.

Lezotte, L. (2003). *Correlates of effective schools: The first and second generation.* Okemos, MI: Effective Schools Products, Ltd. Available from World Wide Web: Retrieved August 1, 2003, from http://www.effectiveschools.com/Correlates.pdf

Milstein, M. M. (1993). *Changing the way we prepare educational leaders.* Newbury Park, CA: Corwin Press.

Montecel, M. R., & Cortez, J. D. (2002). Successful bilingual education programs: Development and the dissemination of criteria to identify promising and exemplary practices in bilingual education at the national level. *Bilingual Research Journal, 26*(1), 1–21. Washington, DC: National Association for Bilingual Education.

Murphy, J. (Ed.). (2002). *The educational leadership conference: Redefining leadership for the 21st century.* National Society for the Study of Education Yearbook, 101A. Chicago: University of Chicago Press.

National Clearinghouse for English Language Acquisition & Language Instruction for Educational Programs (NCELA). (2003). *The growing numbers of limited English proficient students, 1991/92–2001/02.* Washington, DC: National Clearinghouse for English Language.

National College for School Leadership. (2003). Leadership and management: What inspection tells us. Retrieved February 1, 2003, from http://stage.ncsl.org.uk/index.cfm?pageID=ncsl-index-page-022003

National Policy Board for Educational Administration (NPBEA). (1993). *Principals for our changing schools.* Fairfax, VA: National Policy Board for Educational Administration.

Newman, F., & Wehlage, G. (1995). *Successful school restructuring.* Alexandria, VA: ASCD.

Purkey, S. C., & Smith, M. S. (1983). Effective schools: A review. *Elementary School Journal, 83*(4), 427–452.

Rian, R. (2004, March 10). Ensuring their future is bright. *Dallas Morning Times.* Retrieved March 17, 2004, from http://www.dallasnews.com/s/dws/news/localnews/stories/031104dnmeteslimpact.6a71b.html

Ruiz, R. (1993). *Critical issues in bilingual secondary education.* In proceedings of the Third National Research Symposium on Limited English Proficient Student Issues: Focus on middle and high school issues, *2,* 691–705.

Sather, S., Katz, A., Henze, R., Walker, E., & Norte, E. (2001). *Leading for diversity: How school leaders promote positive interethnic relations.* Thousand Oaks, CA: Sage.

Saville-Troike, M. (1984). What really matters in second language learning for academic achievement? *TESOL Quarterly, 17,* 199–219.

Sergiovanni, T. J. (1987). *The principalship: A reflective practice perspective.* Newton, MA: Allyn & Bacon.

Sergiovanni, T. J. (1996). *Moral leadership: Getting to the heart of school improvement.* San Francisco: Jossey-Bass.

Sheppard, K. (1995). *Content-ESL across the USA. Volume 1: A technical report. A descriptive study of content-ESL practices* (Report No. T291004001). Washington, DC: Center for Applied Linguistics place. (ERIC Document Reproduction Service No. ED 386 925)

Southworth, G. (1998). *Leading improving primary school: The works of heads and deputies.* Philadelphia: RoutledgeFalmer.

Spillanc, J., Halverson, R., & Diamond, J. (2001). A distributed perspective. *Educational Researcher, 32*(7), 23–28.

Spillane, J., Halverson, R., & Diamond, J. B. (2002). *Towards a theory of school leadership practice: Implications of a distributed perspective.* Retrieved March 2, 2004, from http:www.letus.org/PDF/DLS_ipr_paper.doc

Spillane, J., Diamond, J., & Jita, L. (2003). Leading instruction: The distribution of leadership for instruction. *Journal of Curriculum Studies, 35*(5). Retrieved October 1, 2003, from http://faculty.ed.uiuc.edu/westbury/JCS/Vol35/SPILLANE.HTM

Thomas, W. P., & Collier, V. P. (2002). *A national study of school effectiveness for language minority students' long-term academic achievement final report.* Project 1.1. Retrieved March 14, 2004, from http://www.crede.ucsc.edu/research/llaa/1.1_final.html

Trueba, E. (1999). *Latinos unidos: From cultural diversity to the politics of solidarity.* Lanham: Rowman & Littlefield.

U.S. Census Bureau Annual Demographic Supplement, March 2002.

Valencia, R. (1997). *Evolution of deficit thinking: Educational thought and practice.* Philadelphia: Taylor & Francis.

Wilmore, E. (2002). *Principal leadership: Applying the new educational leadership constituent council standards.* Newbury Park, CA: Corwin Press.

Chapter **8**

Successful School Leadership for English Language Learners

Elsy Fierro Suttmiller
Maria Luisa González
New Mexico State University

This chapter combines findings from field studies and the literature that address the issues of school leadership and its impact on the successful schooling of English language learners (ELLs). Additionally, the chapter presents leadership in terms of a supportive model, which provides a framework that enables schools to create successful schooling experiences for all students. The model is further clarified through a profile of a school situated along the Mexico-U.S. border that exemplifies the model's components and their application to practice.

School Leadership and English Language Learners

Schools and school districts are challenged through the No Child Left Behind Act (NCLB), to show through test data that all students are achieving "adequate yearly progress" in English (NCLB, H.R. 1, 107th Congress 1st Session, Sec. 3122 (b) (1) 2001). No longer can schools ignore the achievement gaps among the diverse student groups, specifically in the case of ELLs whose numbers increased by 105% percent as compared to 12% growth for the general school-age population (NCELA, 2002). Such large percentages of test takers can clearly impact the profile of schools and their districts by providing data that reflect whether this group of students is being taught successfully or not.

As school districts across the United States are held accountable for the academic success of all students, school principals must quickly learn how this goal can be attainable. In school districts where the ELL population may have once been waived from test taking (and in reality also excused from learning) administrators may now find themselves scrambling to gain knowledge about the instructional needs of this distinct student population. The following comment from a principal exemplifies the urgency felt by those administrators who may have once ignored ELL student needs. "We have to learn how to teach these bilingual kids or they're going to bring our test scores down" (9/25/03 Principal Interview).

While schools across the nation are grappling with the issue of how to best instruct ELLs another aspect of this dilemma lies in the testing of recent immigrant students. The NCLB requirement that recent immigrant students also be tested after their third year of enrollment is contrary to research from the field of language acquisition and bilingual education. Studies clearly point to the fact that students need 5 to 7 years to develop academic language proficiency (Collier, 1995; Cummins, 1996; Ovando, Collier, & Combs, 2002; Ramírez, Yuen, Ramey, & Pasta, 1991; Salinas, 1993). Yet, this well-established research-based fact is known to few school administrators. Thus, not only does the NCLB Act necessitate the need for school leaders to become informed about the instructional needs of ELLs but it also requires, in many cases, the reorientation of the current educational program that has failed to meet the needs of ELLs.

The difficulty surrounding this type of reorientation is that few school districts have the leadership or the instructional capacity to understand the needs of ELLs. The education of ELLs appears to have been isolated and designated to a few educators. As Griego-Jones (1995) explained: "those not directly involved in the delivery of bilingual instruction or administration of programs have not usually taken responsibility for implementing them. The implementation of bilingual programs in most districts has generally been regarded as the business of designated bilingual personnel, primarily teachers and programs directors" (p. 2).

If the school reorientation that is necessary for all students to meet the requirements of the NCLB Act is to take place, educational leaders must ensure that the education of ELLs is part of the overall school and district effort. This means that all school educators and leaders need to become well versed in the theoretical and research foundations of language acquisition and bilingual education. They must take into careful consideration issues related to language, culture, and the school context in order to provide a reframing of the fundamental organization of the school. Consequently, they would be creating a long-term systemic and systematic school reorientation that does more than fine tune the traditional structure (Cummins, 1996; González, 1998; Miramontes, Nadeau, & Commins, 1997; Montecel & Cortez, 2002; Stringfield, Datnow, & Ross, 1998; Torres-Guzmán, Abbate, Brisk, & Minaya-Rowe, 2002).

Villarreal (1999) suggested the use of a framework by school administrators, teachers, and parents that integrates research findings of successful schools serving ELLs. This framework provides a theoretical base for reframing schools as well as a base that highlights the practices of successful schools in serving ELLs. Two contextual dimensions are identified by Villarreal (1999). These dimensions include: "(1) support for the program at all levels of the school hierarchy, and (2) level of knowledge of bilingual education as evidenced through the curriculum and instructional activities" (p. 24).

The work of Cummins (1996), González (1992), and Miramontes, Nadeau, and Commins (1997), further contributes to the development of such a framework. Their research found corresponding components in their review of educational structures of successful schools serving ELLs. The researchers described the following components and educational structures: school context, parent involvement, language development, and assessment. The degree to which school leaders address these educational structures appears to determine the academic success of ELLs (Cummins, 1996; González, 1992; Myers, 2002; Reyes, 2002; Romo, 1999). Expanding on this research and attempting to illustrate what is involved in providing the optimal schooling for ELLs resulted in a leadership model developed by the authors of this chapter. This model is predicated on the belief that school personnel in most schools can successfully address the needs of ELLs if they understand that certain elements need to be in place (Cummins, 1996; Feinberg, 1999; González, 1992; Stringfield et al., 1998; Tharp, 1997; Torres-Guzman et al., 2002; Valverde & Armendariz, 1999).

SUCCESSFUL SCHOOL LEADERSHIP MODEL

The Successful School Leadership Model (Fig. 8.1) is a graphic representation of the key elements that must guide a school in meeting the needs of ELLs. The role of the principal in this model is to understand and implement these key elements into the general program of instruction for all students.

The model consists of two concentric circles centering on the school's priority: the student. The model's center, the student, is surrounded by the academic, sociocultural, and linguistic domains that must be taken into account by the principal and staff. These domains have been identified by various authors as essential in providing the type of instruction that will result in high student achievement for students who are ELLs (Cummins, 1996; Garcia, 1985, 2002; Miramontes et al., 1997; Tharp, 1997).

The principal's understanding of these domains will guide the reorientation of schooling for ELLs. The model also contains leadership components that involve a principal's ability to appreciate and attend to the (a)

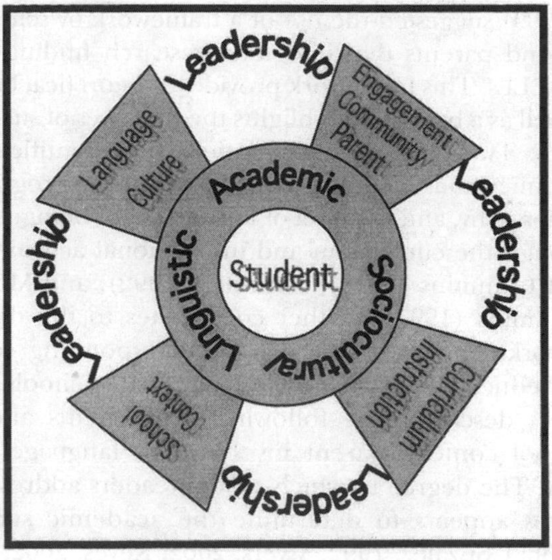

FIG. 8.1. Successful school leadership model.

school context, (b) curriculum and instruction as it relates to second language learners, the population's diverse (c) language and culture, as well as (d) parental and community engagement that is relevant and meaningful. Each of these four components is represented by a "fan blade" that is held together by the concentric circles that are connected by leadership. Each part of the model relies on the knowledge and coordination provided by the principal as the main school leader. Moreover, in this model district level leadership also plays a role in providing the support that the school needs to focus on the optimal learning climate for ELLs. Thus, the Successful School Leadership Model has a focal point that is learner centered, an awareness of the various domains, and the inclusion of the four components. All aspects of the model are held secure by leadership provided at the school level by the principal, staff, and parents, and at the district level by central office personnel.

Explanation of each of the model's components follows. Discussion will begin with a brief description of the three domains: academic, sociocultural, and linguistic related to the successful schooling of ELLs.

ACADEMIC DOMAIN

An effective instructional program for ELLs responds to the following questions affirmatively. Are the students learning? Are the students learning English? How this is accomplished depends largely on the academic program offered to students. Research by Cummins (1996), Miramontes et al. (1997), Thomas and Collier (2001), identified key features of classrooms that promote learning for ELLs. Some of these features include (a) opportunities for students to interact with both languages in written and/or oral form, (b) context-embedded activities that are meaningful and relate to the students' experiences, (c) thematic units that help students build concepts across the curriculum, and (d) cooperative learning activities that encourage reflection and vocabulary development.

SOCIOCULTURAL DOMAIN

The sociocultural domain addresses the hidden messages students receive through social interaction in their home, community, and school. This also includes exposure to the various types of media (i.e., books, newspaper, television, radio) that carry implicit and explicit messages about the individual's language and culture. Vygotsky (1978) posited that it is the interaction between the child and the external social world that actually shapes and defines the child's perception of self. In the case of ELLs, successful participation and learning in school depends largely on the attitudes and hidden messages the child receives regarding his or her language, socioeconomic status (SES), culture, race, or ethnicity. If the messages are debilitating, limiting the child's use of his or her language to make meaning or failing to value or acknowledge the child's culture, then the child's ability to successfully participate and learn will be restricted. Therefore school personnel need to become aware of and minimize the hidden messages, values, attitudes, school policies, curriculum, and methodologies that either value or devalue a specific language, SES, culture, race, or ethnicity (Garcia & McLaughlin, 1995; Miramontes et al., 1997).

The sociocultural domain also addresses the type of instruction that is needed for students. Vygotsky's (1978) sociocultural theory highlights the use of social (language mediated) activities that enhance a child's ability to process and construct knowledge. Therefore, activities that promote social interaction of students and provide the meaningful construction of knowledge are the most beneficial for all students, especially for ELLs, given that this type of instruction can scaffold the learning for students in the absence of native language instruction.

LINGUISTIC DOMAIN

The linguistic domain addresses the need for students to use and further develop their native language as well as the appropriate instruction that fosters the acquisition of English (Collier, 1995; Cummins, 1996; Ovando et al.,

2002; Ramírez et al., 1991). These researchers have found that the development of academic skills in English is largely dependent on the conceptual foundation the child has built in his or her native language. According to these researchers, the more time spent in developing a conceptual foundation in the native language of the child, the easier it will be for the child to acquire English. Therefore, instructional programs that teach children in their native languages are the most beneficial for students learning English.

LEADERSHIP COMPONENTS OF SUCCESSFUL SCHOOLS

The leadership components of the model are developed from a working knowledge of the domains previously discussed in this chapter. In this model principals are required to have an understanding of the school's distinct context, appreciation of language and culture, development of parent/community engagement and curriculum together with a proper instructional program that includes appropriate assessment practices. The extent to which these four components are understood and implemented in the school through the principal's leadership contributes to the academic success of ELLs.

Cedar Park Elementary[1] will guide our discussion by providing examples of how the components are applied into practice. Cedar Park Elementary is located less than a mile away from the U.S.–Mexico border. The principal, Ms. Thomas, has been at Cedar Park Elementary for 5 years. Ms. Thomas was assigned to Cedar Park Elementary when it was designated by the state as low performing and was categorized as "probationary." In spite of a highly mobile population, the percentage of ELLs, and the high-poverty statistics, Ms. Thomas was able to show improvement in student test scores within a 1-year period and the school was redesignated as "meeting state standards."

SCHOOL CONTEXT

School context refers to the social, cultural, political, and economic setting in which a school is situated. Understanding the school context of a school is crucial in order for a principal to address the learning needs of students and families. This understanding is part of what Pedroza (1993) referred to

[1]Pseudonyms have been used for people and schools to protect the confidentiality of information shared.

as cultural competence in leaders. A culturally competent administrator is defined by Pedroza as:

> A culturally competent administrator is a school leader who has clarified his/her own value and thinking regarding cultural incorporation, who has taken steps toward understanding the community culture, who has examined the relationships between his/her own cultural identity and that of the community, and who is willing to acknowledge that conflict can arise from a misalignment of perceptions or miscommunication or misunderstanding of cultural norms. Recognizing the richness of diversity and a willingness to act as a culture broker between the school and the community defines the culturally competent administrator. (p. 13)

Culturally competent principals do not adhere to the fact that the only thing that they have responsibility over lies within the walls of their school building. Although they can aptly articulate the needs of their students and their families they anticipate future needs and make provisions for services that eventually impact the community as a whole. They know the needs of their school and its population and find innovative ways to meet these needs.

How Ms. Thomas demonstrates this cultural competence is apparent: throughout all daily activities; in the support programs offered; and through the instruction and curriculum implemented in the school. Following is a description of the various ways Ms. Thomas addresses the cultural, social, political, and economic context of Cedar Park Elementary and exemplifies Pedroza's (1993) definition of a culturally competent administrator.

Cultural Context

The school serves a majority–minority student population of 98% Latino students and 51% of them are ELLs. The principal ensures that all curriculum decisions are made with the cultural context in mind; this includes careful selection of textbooks, library books, and trade books for teaching their reading instruction. Furthermore, the principal acknowledges and values the cultural differences among Latino groups attending her school. She ensures that reading materials and family support services respect the numerous cultural dynamics of all the Latino groups. The reading materials and library books are representative of the various dialects of Spanish from Mexico as well as other Spanish-speaking countries.

Her work with parents, described later in this chapter, also addresses her understanding of the differences within and among the Latino culture. There are noted differences among (a) the group of recent immigrant students, (b) those who are second and third generation Latinos residing in the United States, and (c) those whose family have lived in the community for nearly 200 years.

Social Context

Ms. Thomas uses student demographic data to further her understanding of the social context of her school. Through home language surveys and multiple language proficiency tests that are administered yearly, Ms. Thomas is aware that the majority of her students come with a language other than English as their first language and realizes that her students' parents do not always speak or understand English. Furthermore, she recognizes that her fluctuating monthly enrollment is due to the fact that 30% of her students are mobile depending on their parents' ability to pay the rent and 10% are newly arrived immigrants. She also keeps in mind that the majority of her students are second and third generation children of immigrants born in the United States.

Ms. Thomas utilizes the information surrounding the school's social context in addressing student mobility and absenteeism. She often makes home visits with the parent liaison and discusses mitigating circumstances causing absences with guardians, parents, or the children themselves. When addressing student mobility, the principal and assistant principal greet each incoming student and their family (or parent) and review the student's enrollment paperwork. The number of schools the child has attended is considered. If the number of schools is more than one for a given school year, the home liaison pays periodic home visits. The home liaison keeps in contact with the parents to provide any needed referral services to social service agencies. Ms. Thomas depends on the home liaison to establish a relationship of trust, "confianza" (Moll, 2001), with the child's family in order to support the feeling that parents are valued members of the school community. This practice encourages parents to curtail moving their children from one school to the other by convincing them that mobility is detrimental to the learning process of their children (González et al., 1998). Moreover, because she understands the reasons as to why parents often move outside the school attendance area, she is able to help families find solutions to keep their children at Cedar Park Elementary. When the situation is complicated and the problem cannot be resolved, Ms. Thomas ensures that the transfer school receives the child's cumulative folder with clear and accurate information concerning the child's academic success and progress. She then has a staff member confirm that the child's cumulative folder has indeed been received and answers any questions concerning the child's progress.

Ms. Thomas expands on her knowledge of the social context in various ways, in the forming of advisory committees, in the planning of any school activity, and in her daily interactions with parents and other community members. In the case of forming an advisory committee to discuss the school's remodeling, the principal ensured that the committee was representative of the different parent groups (including newly arrived immigrant parents and non-immigrant parents). The times of the meetings are scheduled taking into account the different work schedules of parents (Antunez, 2000).

Political Context

The political context of Cedar Park Elementary revolves around the issues of language and immigration encompassing documented and undocumented students. The difficulties surrounding these political issues rely on the principal's ability to understand that all children in her school are her responsibility and that the school is not an agent of immigration but rather an agent of change. She realizes that change takes place through appropriate instruction, monitoring learning gains, and ensuring equitable treatment of all the children regardless of their citizenship.

Latino immigrant groups often grapple with questions of maintaining their language versus ensuring that their children learn English (Ayoungman, 1995; DiCerbo, 2000; MacGregor-Mendoza, 2000; Trueba, 1989; Trueba, Jacobs, & Kirton, 1990; Valverde & Armendariz, 1999). Parents who are recent immigrants fear that their children may never learn English if they are enrolled in bilingual education (Brunn, 1999; Crawford, 1997). As a result, some often fill out the home language survey stating that their children only speak "Inglich."

The parents of second and third generation children also struggle with the issues of language recovery (Spanish) but usually want their children to speak Spanish (Cline & Necochea, 2001). However, their childhood memories related to schooling may not have been positive. Many were often denied the right to speak Spanish and punished for doing so. These memories may still haunt them and they fear that learning in Spanish might keep their children from academic success.

In these two instances, the role of the principal is imperative. The principal becomes the cultural broker at the school, not relying solely on faculty or staff to articulate the instructional needs of the children to the parents. Ms. Thomas explains that her role is one of advocacy that entails explaining the benefits of bilingual education and conveying that the two main goals of bilingual education are for students to learn and for students to learn English.

The political divide among recent immigrants and second and third generation immigrants is also something the principal recognizes. According to Ms. Thomas, some of her staff members have stated that this divide has existed for generations and for reasons that few of these individuals can articulate. Ms. Thomas states that sometimes one group feels that the other group is acting or feeling superior due to language or economic reasons. For example, some of the new immigrant families feel that the second or third generation families feel they are superior to them because they speak English and may have better paying jobs. While the second and third generation families feel that the newly arrived immigrants feel superior because they are able to speak Spanish fluently and they often arrive with a higher level of schooling.

As a result, it is not uncommon for these groups to find it difficult to work together in committees and create a common vision for their children. Ms. Thomas has found that she must go beyond the traditional structure of PTA and PTO meetings. She arranges for individual meetings and house meetings to begin a conversation among parents that fosters a common understanding of schooling (Brillant, 2001; Henze, 2000; Kyle & McIntyre, 2000; Sosa, 1997).

In the 5 years the principal has been at Cedar Park Elementary, she has held more than 300 individual meetings with parents and teachers, where she listens and holds a conversation with them about their understanding of schools and their purpose. She begins the initial first meeting with a question that asks, "Tell me about your experiences with schools." This open-ended question begins the conversation in developing a clearer understanding of the individual's perceptions about schooling and their expectations for their children.

In addition to individual meetings Ms. Thomas also brings parents, community members, and teachers together to small house meetings of no more than 10 people to discuss questions such as, "Tell us about one memorable experience you had in a school setting." After this initial meeting this group of people schedule another time to meet and begin discussing pertinent issues related to the school. Sometimes the meeting agenda is unique to the particular group and other times it is a common issue and the various house meeting groups may decide to meet as one larger body to decide on a plan of action. The use of individual and house meetings improves the relationships among the various Latino groups in the Cedar Park Elementary community and encourages these groups to interact for a common purpose and create needed changes inside and outside of the school (Giles, 1988; Jacobsen, 2001).

Economic Context

According to the demographic census data, Cedar Park Elementary is located within the zip code area with the second highest percentage of families living in poverty in the state. Ms. Thomas recognizes the effects that poverty may have on student health, school attendance, and student readiness to learn. Therefore, Cedar Park Elementary offers a variety of social services and instructional support for students and their families including after school tutoring, advocating for early childhood programs, and collaborating with community resources to support students and their parents.

Two years ago the principal began a partnership with the local YWCA to begin a tutoring program for Cedar Park Elementary students. The YWCA provided funding for materials and hired college student as mentors to assist teachers. She was also able to gain financial support from school district's Title I director to hire teachers to tutor for 2 hours, 3 days a week. The tutoring program is an enrichment program where students are taught through meaningful activities that engage their mind and creativity. The principal insists that the instructional programs extend the students' knowledge and experiences and not merely remediate basic skills. Therefore, after-school activities revolve around the premise that students should be challenged and uses an instructional format that is often found in programs for the "gifted students."

In this national climate of high-stakes testing it is important that principals review and evaluate the impact of other learning activities that take place beyond the classroom. Thus, Ms Thomas ensures that the tutoring program, offered after school, has a positive impact on student achievement. The principal analyzed 6-week report card grades and found that overall; the students attending tutoring sessions had higher 6-week grades.

Another example of how Ms. Thomas leads efforts that positively address the economic context of the school is evident through her advocacy of early childhood programs that not only affect her school but impact the city as a whole. According to Ms. Thomas, the majority of students entering kindergarten come with a vocabulary level in their native language, either English or Spanish, equivalent to that of a 3-year-old child. This information became apparent after the principal conducted a careful evaluation of the language proficiency testing administered to incoming kindergarten students. As a former kindergarten teacher Ms. Thomas believes that the answer to improving student vocabulary and school readiness lies in establishing a citywide early childhood program. Through Ms. Thomas' leadership, a community group was started to prepare a proposal to fund an early childhood education program for the city. The foresight of Ms. Thomas led her to ensure that the committee was comprised of individuals who would be instrumental in the success of this effort. The committee included the mayor of Cedar Park, a school board member who also served as a city council member, a state legislator, teachers, parents, and business representatives. She even reached into a neighboring state to seek guidance from the director of a well-respected early childhood program. Ms. Thomas believes that it is her responsibility to go past her school's walls to seek support for efforts that will ensure the academic success of her students and other children as well.

Ms. Thomas also collaborates with various community groups to support the economic context of her students and their families. She states that her goal is for the school to provide a setting where students feel they are cared for and supported. She has joined forces with several organizations to provide clothing drives for school uniforms, seasonal food baskets, and after-school care for children whose parents work late into the evening.

CURRICULUM AND INSTRUCTION

The next leadership component in the model of Successful School Leadership for ELLs is the teaching and learning process. A student's success in school is ultimately dependent on the quality of instruction offered (Cummins, 1996; Thomas & Collier, 2001). Building on the earlier research, Ms. Thomas has insisted that the content of instruction for all students be aligned, taking into account several elements that research has found to support student learning aligned with state benchmarks and standards, (a) extend across different grade levels, (b) address various learning styles and multiple intelligences, (c) acknowledge students' prior experiences and family's funds of knowledge, (d) incorporates instructional technologies, and (e) includes the teaching of higher order thinking skills (Cummins, 1996; González et al., 1998; Miramontes et al., 1997; Moll, 2001; Montecel & Cortez, 2002; Stringfield et al., 1998; Torres-Guzman et al., 2002).

Ms. Thomas works alongside her teachers to ensure that instruction offered at the school is relevant and reaching the students. Subsequently, Ms. Thomas recognizes that teachers need time during the work-week to reflect and reorganize their curriculum and instruction. To this end Ms. Thomas and the assistant principal created a unique schedule for the school, in which all special classes (i.e., music, P.E., art, library, and computer lab) are blocked for each grade level. This type of scheduling affords the grade levels time to meet for a 3-hour period every 2 weeks. Teachers then have the opportunity to discuss current concerns, revisit instructional issues, work on curriculum alignment, and receive a minimum of a 1-hour staff development session conducted by the designated Title I Staff Development Specialist.

A professional learning community is evident in the role that the principal and teachers play in attempting to develop a culturally responsive curriculum and instruction for the students at Cedar Park Elementary (Eaker, DuFour, & DuFour, 2002). The principal participates in every meeting as a partner with teachers in the learning processes as they seek answers to the following three questions: "What are our students expected to learn at each grade level?" "What strategies can we use to accomplish our learning goals?" and "What materials should we use?" During the bi-monthly meetings grade level teachers and the principal review the on-going curriculum alignment documents. In their discussion of samples of student work, they clarify the intent of an objective or goal.

As an instructional leader, Ms. Thomas believes that teachers need to revisit instructional questions continuously to gain ownership of pedagogical revisions that take place. This establishes a system of continuous renewal that evaluates student learning goals and objectives as well as the instructional approaches and student work (Cummins, 1996; González et al., 1998; Miramontes et al., 1997; Moll, 2001; Montecel & Cortez, 2002; Stringfield et al., 1998; Torres-Guzman et al., 2002).

Another important aspect of leadership in curriculum and instruction is the attention given to student assessment. According to the Cedar Park Elementary principal, student assessment takes into account the data obtained from state mandated standardized testing and alternative assessments (i.e., portfolios and projects) designed by the teachers during the grade-level meetings. The Cedar Park Elementary principal sees the state mandated tests as a requirement that is less than informative for evaluating student learning and improving curricular content (Cummins, 1996; González et al., 1998; Miramontes et al., 1997; Moll, 2001; Montecel & Cortez, 2002; Stringfield et al., 1998; Torres-Guzman et al., 2002).

According to the Cedar Park Elementary principal, in order for student assessment to be informative in evaluating student learning and improving curricular content, it must assess what students are taught, be relevant to students' cultural and linguistic needs, and provide accurate and reliable data to assure that all students are learning. The assessment must go beyond highlighting students' deficits but must take into account students' strengths as well. In this way, the assessment informs curricular modifications and focuses on closing achievement gaps among all students (Garcia, 2002; Montecel & Cortez, 2002; Torres-Guzman et al., 2002).

Ms. Thomas further explains that at one time the biggest challenge in assessing ELLs involved some teachers' perceptions that the students could not be held to the same standard or content mastery as the non-ELLs. She cites an example of a teacher who insisted that because ELLs did not understand English, they could not be expected to learn the same content and skills in Spanish and English. Ms. Thomas exposed the teacher and her colleagues to a series of staff development sessions on language acquisition and effective instructional strategies for teaching ELLs.

The principal continues to inform her staff on the need for one curriculum with a variety of staff development on instructional strategies that accommodate students' differing learning styles, multiple intelligences, and cultural and linguistic diversity. She regularly challenges teachers to hold high expectations for all students, including ELLs. An outcome of her participation in all professional development activities can be seen in how the teachers have gained ownership and developed expertise in working with the students. This in turn has allowed for the school to provide a continuous mentoring process for new teachers and has led to the establishment of a permanent professional learning community at Cedar Park Elementary.

Another curricular aspect of the schooling offered at Cedar Park Elementary that safeguards the academic success of all students living in poverty is the focus on schoolwork versus homework. Teachers are encouraged to assign homework but it carries less weight than schoolwork. This is an accommodation for those students unable to study outside the school who might otherwise be penalized for circumstances surrounding their home environment. In this particular border community some of the children are living in one room with multiple relatives; others are latch key children who must baby-sit younger siblings until parents return late at night; others live with guardians because their parents live far from the school's attendance area.

The Cedar Park Elementary principal believes that the role of the principal in curriculum and instruction is one of advocacy for both students and teachers. She states that her role is to ensure students are assessed and placed properly in classrooms where teaching is learner centered to promote risk taking and active engagement in a language rich environment that challenges all students linguistically and intellectually.

ENGAGEMENT OF COMMUNITY AND PARENTS

Parent and community involvement at Cedar Park Elementary is one that redefines involvement as engagement. According to the Cedar Park Elementary principal, parents and community members are viewed as resources and not seen as scapegoats for justifying student failure. The principal strives to include parents in every aspect of the school's committees and creates opportunities to bring families together to celebrate student achievement and learn strategies to help their children at home.

As described earlier, the principal spends a large portion of her day holding individual meetings with parents and house meetings hearing about parents' expectations of the school and of their children. This form of parent and community engagement distinguishes between communication and conversation (Giles, 1988; Jacobsen, 2001). Schools have traditionally communicated with parents and community members in the form of instructions, mandates, rules, and the like. Holding a conversation with parents and community members is different. It involves listening and engaging these individuals on what they value the most, their children. These conversations build relationships of trust and mutual respect that may contribute to the increase in student achievement at Cedar Park Elementary.

Parents are further acknowledged through the Spanish translation of all documents and meetings. All meetings with parents and all documents sent home are in English and Spanish. PTA meetings are held in Spanish while providing simultaneous translation through headphones for parents who prefer English or only speak English. Meetings with parents are scheduled at various times during the day or evening in order to ensure easy access for parents working early or late shifts in the local canning factories. An additional noteworthy component is the community collaboration the Cedar Park Elementary principal has established with various social service agencies and businesses. For example, Cedar Park Elementary is one of two schools that receive funds from a golf tournament held at the local country club on their behalf. This relationship was established through the diligent networking of the principal to gain access to the area businesses for support. Area businesses have also financially supported the yearly student achievement celebration held at an exclusive hotel to honor students with high grade point averages. This form of community collaboration establishes a supportive and caring environment for students to learn and achieve.

LANGUAGE AND CULTURE

The principal's role is essential in ensuring that the issues of language and culture are incorporated in operationalizing the components of the leadership model. As discussed previously, the Cedar Park Elementary principal addresses issues of language and culture in understanding the school context, in securing appropriate curriculum and instruction, and in engaging community members and parents. Languages and cultures are valued at Cedar Park Elementary. This is apparent in the content of the Literature Book Room that contains books in both English and Spanish. Other examples are found throughout the curriculum and in classroom practices where students are provided opportunities to read and write in either English or Spanish. Furthermore, teachers are encouraged to use instructional strategies and activities that acknowledge the students' prior experiences and interweave them into their teaching and instructional content.

The most meaningful example of how the students' languages and cultures are valued is through the consistent implementation across grade levels of the bilingual education program. At Cedar Park Elementary, the principal has secured a strong research-based bilingual education program in the school, including implementing clear guidelines and criteria for exiting students from the program after sixth grade. Out of the four classrooms at each grade level, three classrooms are bilingual education classrooms. The fourth classroom is an English-only classroom to accommodate students whose first language is English and the few students whose parents have chosen to not enroll them in bilingual education. The bilingual education model used at Cedar Park Elementary is a 90/10 transitional bilingual education model. Students begin in kindergarten with 90% of their instruction in Spanish and 10% of their instruction in English. As students progress through the grade levels, the percentages change incrementally up to sixth grade where they receive 90% of their instruction in English and 10% of their instruction in Spanish. Students are not eligible to be exited from the bilingual education program until they reach the sixth grade and they must also demonstrate academic proficiency in English on the state standardized tests, a language proficiency test, and the alternative assessment instruments designated by the sixth grade level teachers. These criteria ensure that the students master the academic content in both languages and become fluent in English in order to continue their learning in the middle school grades.

DISTRICT LEADERSHIP

A principal like Ms. Thomas does not exist in a vacuum. Though her school is unique in addressing ELL student and family needs, her ability to follow through with her initiatives can be attributed to her relationship with district level leadership. Ms. Thomas describes that district level leadership is supportive of her initiatives partly due to her ability to approach them proactively (district level administrators) "with not just problems but with a plan for a solution." Ms. Thomas believes that her greatest strength in working collaboratively with district level administrators lies in developing clear concise plans developed in conjunction with her staff and parents on identified areas of need that are aligned with district level academic goals. She believes that this demonstrates to district level administrators that the proposed initiatives are truly collaborative decisions and are based on a need identified by all Cedar Park Elementary stakeholders.

The successful schooling of ELLs cannot be left to the principal, teachers, and school staff alone. The district must become a partner in strengthening this effort as well. The same type of knowledge and understanding evident at the school level must be present at the district level, resulting in practices and policies that safeguard the educational attainment of ELLs. In the Successful School Leadership Model for ELLs, district leaders are expected to pay close attention and attend to the needs of these students and their families. They do this by taking into account the context of the district stakeholders, the adopted curriculum and instruction, as well as the type of parental and community engagement that is taking place, and their distinct language and culture.

Just as a principal must understand the school context, so must district level leadership understand the multiple contexts of the various schools in the district. District leaders, those individuals who are located at a central office and who make decisions that impact the schools directly, must be cognizant of the demographics in each school and the implications in serving this population. For example, one district along the U.S.–Mexico border is requiring its entire central office personnel to spend a day at different schools every week. Central office personnel experience the school context on a first-hand basis, thus becoming familiar with the demographics of schools that serve ELLs. The information that they obtain through their observations and involvement with the schools can assist the schools in creating the advocacy for much needed resources that might only be possible through the support of central office staff. District level leaders learn to appreciate the work of teachers, parents, and principals as they spend time in the school understanding the context of the student population and its impact on instructional programs.

The component of curriculum and instruction also applies to district level leadership. Leaders at the district level need to become informed about the rationale for bilingual education and work to integrate the program structure as part of every district-wide initiative and instructional program. When adopting certain programs and curricula, implementation often fails because district level leaders disregard or are oblivious to the ramifications on the learning of ELLs.

In hiring for district level positions, district leaders need to ensure that all individuals either have or are willing to learn about the instructional needs of ELLs. Districts must avoid leaving the impression that the only educators who are responsible for the education of ELLs are those associated with the bilingual program. One district that is making great strides in reorienting their hiring practices is committed to hiring principals for a targeted area who were raised in this particular part of town that continues to the have highest percentage of ELL and immigrant students. The district expects these principals to have a better understanding of the school context and the ensuing curricular demands.

In turn, when addressing the staff development needs of the district, district level leaders need to ensure that all teachers and administrators build an understanding of the curricular and instructional needs of ELL students. Staff development in most districts is devoid of any application of cultural and linguistic diversity. Therefore it does not take into account the learning needs of ELLs, let alone the staff development needs of teachers and principals that work with this population. An example from a local school district is the use of a nationally popular consultant that addresses issues of poverty as they relate to the instructional program but fails to address issues of race, class, ethnicity, and language.

Leadership for district level administrators in engaging parents and community members is dependent on creating a climate of welcome at the central office. This entails the hiring of staff and administrators that are culturally and linguistically competent to address parent and community members' input and concerns. Other elements necessary for district level leaders to provide a climate conducive for appropriate instruction and successful schooling for ELLs are found in the 1987 research by the National Coalition of Advocates for Students (NCAS). One recommendation is the need to provide: "comprehensible information about the schools to immigrant parents. Information should be disseminated through print and electronic media, including native language publications and radio and television programs that regularly reach immigrant communities" (First, 1988, p. 209).

Districts should demonstrate their respect for students' language and culture by developing mission statements that "express strong commitment to the success of immigrant students" (First, 1988, p. 209) and other ELLs as well. In addition, districts with large numbers of ELL students should provide language courses that cover the culture of its student population. Educators and other frontline personnel should be expected to communicate in Spanish. If they value biculturalism and bilingualism then they need to become role models for the students and their families at the central office as well.

Districts are responsible for providing the type of leadership addressed in the Successful School Leadership Model. Each component within the school building will function more effectively and efficiently when district level leadership is attuned to the needs of ELLs. More importantly, district level leaders need to understand that they are full-fledged partners in supporting the education of this rapidly growing number of students instead of relinquishing their roles and responsibilities to solely one department—the one housing bilingual education. Segregating the needs of ELLs to a small group of bilingual educators does not serve a district or its students well. There must be active and full engagement by the top leaders in a district who understand that in every activity related to the success of schools the needs of ELLs must be taken into account and that the educators specialized in bilingual education must be integrated into the various elements that comprise the schooling process. Districts cannot continue to expect the schools to work in a vacuum and set policy and make curricular decisions that could hinder the learning of the ELL population. In this current period of high stakes testing and accountability schools require the advocacy, support, and resources to meet the demands of changing student enrollments that districts should be ready to provide.

SUMMARY

In this chapter, we have attempted to provide a model for understanding the key leadership components found in schools serving ELLs. Our contention is that school leaders who understand and implement these components will ultimately create a school in which ELL students succeed beyond the current expectations. The key to implementing these components is through the principal's understanding. A large part of our discussion has focused on the work of a school principal who exemplified the components found in this model and demonstrated a deeper level of understanding. Principals play a critical role in the successful practices at a school. This role appears to be magnified in contexts where there is a majority of ELLs. Clearly Ms. Thomas exemplifies the benefits of school leaders becoming informed about the instructional needs of ELLs and points to the need to reorient the current educational programs that have failed ELLs.

As the Successful School Leadership Model implies, the student is the priority in any school and the principal must be aware of the academic, linguistic, and sociocultural domains that must be addressed throughout the schooling experience. In addition, within these domains the language and culture of the students and their families must be respected, understood, and maintained by the school and its staff. Understanding the school context leads to the appropriate instructional practices and curriculum development that must take into account the needs of ELLs. It is the principal who must be a full participant throughout the instructional program and ensure that the education of ELLs is part of the overall school and district effort.

As we have seen in the example of Cedar Park Elementary, the implementation of the Successful School Leadership Model requires that the principal be an instructional leader, an advocate that understands and articulates a clear vision for the success of ELLs. The principal must know how to work with parents, not at a bureaucratic level, but at a level that fosters caring and mentoring relationships. This is an extension of understanding the school context where parents are engaged in instruction and decision making beyond the traditional models of PTO/PTA.

However, principals cannot serve their schools in isolation. Central office support is also needed. Many times central office administrators are not cognizant of a school's context, its linguistic and cultural differences, or the type of curriculum and instruction that is required within the particular contexts. They are often not aware of the type of parent engagement that is necessary. Therefore, in order to support the leadership of culturally competent principals, such as Ms. Thomas, central office staff needs to become fully immersed in the work of its schools. Where there are substantial numbers of ELLs in a district it is incumbent upon the district's leadership to go beyond looking upon the directors of bilingual programs as the sole support for schools in matters of instruction. Every individual serving the schools at central office should be fully apprised of the types of programs that are required to successfully address the needs of ELLs and their families.

Principals that operationalize the Successful School Leadership Model components break the mold of traditional administrators. Their involvement in leading the school extends beyond the school walls. There are no ceilings, walls, or barriers that impede them from serving children. They accept no excuses for student failure and negate the notion that children are victims. They do not permit the type of schooling that furthers this notion. In their world, there is no reason why the best cannot be offered to their students and they move everything in their power to this end.

REFERENCES

Antunez, B. (2000). *When everyone is involved: Parents and communities in school reform.* National Clearinghouse for Bilingual Education.

Ayoungman, V. (1995). Native language renewal: Dispelling the myths, planning for the future. *Bilingual Research Journal, 19*(1), 183–187.

Brilliant, G. C. (2001). Parental involvement in education: Attitudes and activities of Spanish speakers as affected by training. *Bilingual Research Journal, 25*(3).

Brunn, M. (1999). The absence of language policy and its effects on the education of Mexican migrant children. *Bilingual Research Journal, 23*(4).

Cline, Z., & Necochea, J. (2001). ¡Basta Ya! Latino parents fighting entrenched racism. *Bilingual Research Journal, 25*(1&2).

Collier, V. P. (1995). *Promoting academic success for ESL students: Understanding second language acquisition for school.* Woodside, NY: NJTESOL-BE, Inc.

Crawford, J. (1997). The campaign against proposition 227: A post mortem. *Bilingual Research Journal, 21*(1).

Cummins, J. (1996). *Negotiating identities: Education for empowerment in a diverse society.* Ontario, CA: California Association for Bilingual Education.

DiCerbo, P. A. (2000). *Common practices for uncommon learners: Addressing linguistic and cultural diversity.* National Clearinghouse for Bilingual Education.

Eaker, R., DuFour, R., & DuFour. R. (2002). *Getting started reculturing schools to become professional learning communities.* Bloomington, IN: National Education Service.

Feinberg, C. R. (1999). Administration of two-way bilingual elementary schools: Building on strength. *Bilingual Research Journal, 23*(1).

First, J. M. (1988). Immigrant students in U.S. public schools: Challenges with solutions. *Kappan, 70*(3), 205–211.

Garcia, E. (2002). *Student cultural diversity: Understanding and meeting the challenge.* Boston: Houghton Mifflin.

Garcia, E., & McLaughlin, B. (1995). *Meeting the challenge of linguistic and cultural diversity in early childhood education.* New York: Teachers College Press.

Giles, H. C. (1988). *Parent engagement as a school reform strategy.* ERIC Clearinghouse on Urban Education, New York. (No. ED491031)

González, M. L. (1992). Educational climate for the homeless. In J. H. Stronge (Ed.), *Educating homeless children and adolescents: Evaluating policy and practice* (pp. 194–211). Thousand Oaks, CA: Sage.

González, M. L., Huerta-Macias, A., & Tinajero, V. J. (Eds.). (1998). *Educating latino students: A guide to successful practice.* Lancaster, PA: Technomic Publishing Co.

Griego-Jones, T. (1995). Implementing bilingual programs is everybody's business. *NCBE Focus Occasional Papers in Bilingual Education,* 11.

Henze, R. C. (2000). *Leading for diversity: How school leaders achieve racial and ethnic harmony.* Santa Cruz, CA: Center for Research on Education, Diversity, & Excellence.

Jacobsen, D. A. (2001). *Doing justice: Congregations and community organizing.* Minneapolis, MN: Fortress Press.

Kyle, D., & McIntyre, E. (2000). *Family visits benefit teachers and families-and students most of all.* Santa Cruz, CA: Center for Research on Education, Diversity & Excellence.

MacGregor-Mendoza, P. (2000). Aqui no se habla español: Stories of linguistic representation in southwest schools. *Bilingual Research Journal, 24*(4).

Miramontes, O. B., Nadeau, A., & Commins, N. L. (1997). *Restructuring schools for linguistic diversity: Linking decision making to effective programs.* New York: Teachers College Press.

Moll, L. C. (2001). The diversity of schooling: A cultural-historical approach. In M. de la Luz Reyes & J. J. Halcón (Eds.), *The best for our children: Critical perspectives on literacy for Latino students* (pp. 13–28). New York: Teachers College Press.

Montecel, R. M., & Cortez, D. J. (2002). Successful bilingual education programs: Development and the dissemination of criteria to identify promising and exemplary practices in bilingual education at the national level. *Bilingual Research Journal, 26*(1).

Myers, L. M. (2002). In the spotlight. *NABE News.*

Ovando, J. C., Collier, V. P., & Combs, M. C. (2002). *Bilingual & ESL classrooms: Teaching in multicultural contexts* (3rd ed.). New York: McGraw-Hill.

Pedroza, A. (1993, October). *Ethnic and racial conflict in schools: Implications for school administration.* Paper presented at University Council for Educational Administration Annual Conference, Houston, TX.

Ramírez, J. D., Yuen, S., Ramey, D., & Pasta, D. (1991). Longitudinal study of structured English immersion strategy, early-exit and late-exit bilingual education programs for language minority children. (Final Reports, Vols. 1 & 2). San Mateo, CA: Aguirre International (ED 330 216).

Reyes, A. (2002). Preparing school leaders to promote the success of all students. *NABE News,* 15–18.

Romo, D. H. (1999). *Reaching out: Best practices for educating Mexican-origin children youth.* Huntington, WV: Clearinghouse on Rural Education and Small Schools.

Salinas, S. A. (1993). *Questions and answers about bilingual education.* San Antonio, TX: Intercultural Development Research Association.

Sosa, S. A. (1997). Involving Hispanic parents in educational activities through collaborative relationships. *Bilingual Research Journal, 21*(2&3).

Stringfield, S., Datnow, A., & Ross, S. M. (1998). *Scaling up school restructuring in multicultural, multilingual contexts: Early observations from Sunland County.* Santa Cruz, CA: Center for Research on Education, Diversity & Excellence.

Tharp, R. G. (1997). *From at-risk to excellence: Research, theory, and principles for practice.* Santa Cruz, CA: Center for Research on Education, Diversity & Excellence.

Thomas, W. P., & Collier, V. P. (2001). *A national study of school effectiveness for language minority students' long-term academic achievement.* Santa Cruz, CA: Center for Research on Education, Diversity & Excellence.

Torres-Guzmán, M. E., Abbate, J., Brisk, M. E., & Minaya-Rowe, L. (2002). Defining and documenting success for bilingual learners: A collective case study. *Bilingual Research Journal, 26*(1).

Trueba, T. H. (1989). *Raising silent voices: Educating the linguistic minorities for the 21st century.* New York: Newbury House.

Trueba, T. H., Jacobs, L., & Kirton, E. (1990). *Cultural conflict and adaptation: The case of hmong children in american society.* New York: Falmer Press.

Valverde, L. A., & Armendariz, G. J. (1999). Important administrative tasks resulting from understanding bilingual programs. *Bilingual Research Journal, 23*(1).

Villarreal, A. (1999). Rethinking the education of English language learners: Transitional bilingual education programs. *Bilingual Research Journal, 23*(1).

Vygotsky, L. S. (1978). *Mind in society; The development of higher mental processes.* (Eds. M. Cole, V. John-Steiner, S. Scribner, & E. Souberman). Cambridge, MA: Harvard University Press.

Chapter 9

Future Directions for Improving Teacher Quality for English Language Learners

Hersh C. Waxman
University of Houston

Kip Téllez
University of California, Santa Cruz

Herbert J. Walberg
University of Illinois at Chicago, Emeritus

A growing number of U.S. students are not native English speakers. With the increasing pressure placed on all students—and their teachers—to score well on standardized testing, an issue that has previously received little attention has been justly brought into the spotlight. What is the best way to help English language learners (ELL) achieve academic success? What are the most effective teaching methods one can use when teaching ELLs? And going to a different level, what kind of training are teachers receiving in order to ensure ELL students' success? What kind of preparation should they receive?

English Hispanic students constitute the largest group of ELLs, but they have the lowest levels of education and the highest dropout rate. Presently, about 56% of all public school teachers in the United States have at least one ELL student in their class, but less than 20% of the teachers who serve ELLs are certified ESL or bilingual teachers. Furthermore, in a recent profile of the quality of our nation's teachers, The National Center for Education Statistics found that most teachers who taught ELLs or other culturally diverse students did not feel that they were well prepared to meet the needs of their students. In another recent national survey of classroom teachers, 57% of all teachers responded that they either "very much needed" or "somewhat needed" more information on helping students with limited English proficiency achieve to high standards. In addition, nearly half of the teachers assigned to teach ELLs have not received any preparation in methods to teach ELLs. Furthermore, the number of teachers prepared to teach ELLs falls short of the tremendous need for teachers of ELLs. ELLs are three times as likely as other students to have an underqualified or uncredentialed teacher.

These are all questions that were discussed at a National Invitational Conference, Improving Teacher Quality for English Language Learners, sponsored by The Laboratory for Student Success (LSS), the Mid-Atlantic Regional Educational Laboratory, at Temple University Center for Research in Human Development and Education. The conference convened in Arlington, Virginia on November 13–14, 2003. Its purpose was to provide insights and research-based information on how to improve the quality of teachers for all ELLs.

In small work groups, conference participants explored issues raised in the general discussion. They generated next-step recommendations for improving the teaching of ELL and for improving the links between research and practice. Work-group discussion focused on the importance of effective training to teacher quality. The conferees achieved considerable consensus on the recommendations, although not all work-group participants agreed on all points. Recommendations can be organized in five broad areas: policy, preservice education, professional development, research, and dissemination.

POLICY

Participants proposed that policies affecting ELLs should broadly define teachers of ELLs as those with any ELLs in their classes. All teachers, not just English teachers, need policies supporting their work with ELLs. At the same time, policies should encourage more college students with skills in more than one language and knowledge of more than one culture to become teachers; participants maintained that the growing number of ELLs in American classrooms requires that teachers in all disciplines have the skills and knowledge to meet the needs of these students. Policies like the Dream Act, which helps undocumented student immigrants qualify for in-state tuition levels, can support the recruitment of qualified teachers for ELLs.

Federal policy that mandates a strict scientific basis for curricular interventions should be modified. Given the qualitative nature of much research on interventions for ELLs, such policy limits the number of programs that can be used and might hamper the quality of teaching for ELLs. Moreover, federal and state policies should be better aligned with research findings on ELLs. For example, the 3-year timeframe for district improvement under No Child Left Behind legislation could be better aligned with research showing that 5 to 7 years are needed for language acquisition. To further improve federal policy, some conferees suggested instituting a national test of language skills for ELLs, adapted to their linguistic and cultural needs. Some deemed such testing to be unnecessary or unfeasible. However, participants generally agreed that ELLs should be assessed in the language in which they can most ably perform.

At the state and local levels, administrators should ensure that professional development programs be recognized as part of a teacher's day instead of onerous after-school responsibilities. Sufficient funding and structural support for long-term inservice initiatives that can benefit teachers of ELLs, such as learning communities, should be provided. It was urged that advocates work with policymakers to promote staff development targeted at meeting the needs of ELLs. Further, state preservice and permanent certification requirements should include coursework in language development and acquisition as well as knowledge of social justice and advocacy for ELLs. Dual certification in ELL teaching and a content area may not be practical, but a hybrid certification including skills for teaching ELLs should be advocated for all teachers.

Moreover, state and local policies that may lead to deprofessionalization of teaching, such as some states' reduction of teaching requirements to a bachelor's degree and a teacher's exam, should be discouraged. At the same time, state and local policymakers should increase efforts to retain high-quality ELL teachers. Retention efforts should include provision of professional working conditions: adequate classroom space, preparation time, paraprofessional support, and democratic relations within school governance. Crucial to retention of novice teachers is that they not be given the most difficult students. Also important to retention can be multistate credentialing (such as that underway in the mid-Atlantic region) for portability, effective mentoring programs, and funding for conference attendance and other development opportunities.

There was much discussion of state and local policies focused on educating ELLs predominantly in English without consideration of their knowledge of their native languages. The research reviewed in the chapters suggests that the English-only instructional approach has not been proven effective for ELLs or their teachers. Thus, it was recommended that English-only curriculum programs that have not been proven effective should be critically evaluated before adoption by states and districts. Moreover, district and school policies that base high-school progress and graduation on passing a test in English should be reformed to take the needs of ELLs into account.

PRESERVICE EDUCATION

Considerable discussion focused on trends in preservice training of ELL teachers in colleges of education. Of concern were possible threats to teacher quality posed by alternatives to the use of teachers trained in colleges of education, such as the use of teachers with nonstandard certifications and the use of online programs instead of teachers in some charter schools. In this context, participants agreed that colleges of education must promote and follow the implications of research that shows the need for high-quality teacher preparation, such as that disseminated by the National Council for Accreditation of Teacher Education.

Specifically, colleges of education should identify training focused on ELLs as a major initiative. Preservice curriculum should contain comprehensive features that make it more relevant to improving the quality of ELL teaching. Preservice curriculum for ELL teachers should develop deep understanding of first and second language acquisition, strong content mastery, cross-cultural understanding, acknowledgment of differences, and collaborative skills. Coursework in literacy instruction, including second-language issues, should be required for both elementary and secondary preservice teachers. All preservice programs—both elementary and secondary—should include a greater ELL component in methods courses. Additionally, field experiences for preservice teachers should integrate work with ELL students. Such experiences need to occur in linguistically and culturally diverse settings, because educators must develop the skills needed to engage with and learn from diverse families and communities.

Preservice curriculum must also support greater understanding of ELLs. Teachers must learn to adapt instruction to the needs and realities and ELLs, maintaining compassion and high expectations for students while viewing them not just as language learners but as whole persons. Future teachers of ELLs must learn to value students' native languages, whether they speak them or not. To that end, training programs must help teachers examine their preexisting attitudes about linguistic differences. Moreover, both teacher and administrator preparation curriculum should include issues of language, race, poverty, privilege, and social justice. Preservice educators also need greater knowledge of political issues and of personal beliefs that influence teaching of ELLs.

PROFESSIONAL DEVELOPMENT

Professional development for ELL teachers must be comprehensive and systematic at all levels; fragmented, short-term inservice training is ineffective. Professional development should include demonstration of theories of language, sustained coaching, and evaluation programs measuring teacher implementation and impact. Integration of inservice programs with preservice curriculum for ELL teachers should be promoted. A holistic approach emphasizing teacher cooperation and ongoing analysis of what makes schools and teachers successful would be more useful in professional development than emphasizing specific teaching skills. Several of the chapters in this book specifically address this issue.

Professional development should begin with the needs of teachers, not administrators. Staff developers should carefully assess what ELL teachers and their students need and include classroom-based training with a focus on implementation of knowledge gained through professional development. Developers should also build on teacher competencies that already exist. Because teachers need to share knowledge of both language-learning strategies and individual student issues, inservice initiatives that team content teachers and ESL teachers, embedded within the workday, should be implemented

The needs of ELLs should also be a priority in professional development efforts. Schools should thus promote inservice training in language acquisition and in instructional strategies specific to ELLs. Teachers of ELLs should continually develop their understanding of the significant connection of language with learning, identity, and social and emotional well-being. Like preservice programs, inservice programs for ELL teachers need to incorporate outreach to parents, families, and communities in order to foster students' continued language development in the home, where parents are most likely ELLs themselves.

Teachers need to become educational leaders who bring critical thinking and advocacy to their work with ELLs. Inservice programs encourage teachers of ELLs to reflect on and assess their teaching and conduct action research that helps them change their attitudes and practices. As role models for teacher leadership, administrators must be active participants in the ongoing training of ELL teachers, setting expectations that all students will succeed and balancing other demands like state accountability with a focus on the needs of growing ELL populations.

RESEARCH

Much more research on teacher quality for ELLs at the national, state, and local levels is needed. A crucial goal of this research should be defining the skills that highly qualified ELL teachers should have and identifying appropriate credentialing requirements. In particular, more research on the knowledge, skills, and dispositions of teachers and administrators that are relevant to ELL student outcomes should be conducted. Further research should also focus on the impact of external policies such as standardized testing and alternative routes to certification on teacher quality and ELL student outcomes. Another desirable area for research is the relation of early childhood education to school success. Research-based models of culturally, linguistically, and developmentally appropriate instructional practices for different age groups should inform early childhood education training programs.

A national study of successful ELL teachers is needed in order to build the knowledge base on teacher quality for ELLs. The study should be as rigorous and extensive as possible, given the complex differences in ELL policy and teaching across the country. National, state, and local agencies should provide funding and resources for this study. Moreover, educational researchers should develop a comprehensive knowledge base on student outcomes relevant to ELL teaching, using data gathered from across the country. To improve their instruction, teachers need access to broad-based research that shows them what connections exist between specific practices and a range of academic and personal benefits.

DISSEMINATION

Organizations such as regional educational laboratories should play a larger role in disseminating research findings to teachers, administrators, and policymakers. In particular, disseminating organizations should gather and publish data on professional development for teachers of ELLs. Teachers need data that shows that successful instruction for ELLs requires not only good teaching practices but inservice training that specifically addresses the needs of ELLs. A national data bank on professional development for ELL teachers is needed to improve access to information on training programs and outcomes research. This data bank should include information on dealing with linguistic and cultural issues in the classroom.

Several suggestions in the chapters and from the conference were made for improving communication among educators, institutions, and other stakeholders in English language learning. For example, learning collaboratives among institutions serving ELLs should be established in order to foster professional interaction, build advocacy skills, and facilitate dissemination of knowledge about high-quality teaching for ELLs. Also, national organizations responsible for setting teaching standards should sponsor a conference focused on redefining ELL teacher quality in the context of the growing population of ELLs. Conference deliberations need to be communicated to policymakers at all levels. Local learning communities for teachers of ELLs and other stakeholders should be developed in support of broader dissemination initiatives.

CONCLUSION

The chapters and discussions from the conference all pointed to the conclusion that teaching informed by knowledge about language acquisition, cultural differences, and the social context of schooling can improve outcomes for English language learners and that increasing such knowledge among teachers, administrators, researchers, and policymakers is both necessary and achievable. Strengthening links between evidence-based research, thoughtful policy development, and improved classroom teaching can benefit the growing population of English language learners in American schools and those who share responsibility for educating them.

Author Index

A

B

C

D

E

F

G

H

I

J

K

O

P–Q

R

S

T

U

V

W

Y–Z

Subject Index

H

I

J–L

M

N

T

V

W

Z